LONG HARD TRAILS & SLED DOG TALES

MY ADVENTURES IN TRACKING DOGTEAMS ACROSS
ALASKA, AND WHAT I LEARNED ALONG THE WAY

~ Helen Hegener ~

NORTHERN LIGHT MEDIA

LONG HARD TRAILS & SLED DOGS TALES

My Adventures in Tracking Dogteams Across Alaska, and What I Learned Along the Way
by Helen Hegener

© 2014 by Helen Hegener, Northern Light Media. All rights reserved. No part of this book may be reproduced or transmitted in any form or by any means, electronic or mechanical, including photocopying, recording, or by any information storage and retrieval system, in whole or in part, without written permission from the author and publisher, except for the inclusion of brief quotations for the purposes of reviewing this book.

First printing 2014 by Northern Light Media.
Printed in the United States of America.

ISBN-10 0-9843977-7-9
ISBN-13 978-0-9843977-7-8

Northern Light Media
Post Office Box 298023
Wasilla, Alaska 99629

http://northernlightmedia.com
http://northernlightmedia.wordpress.com

Long Hard Trails and Sled Dog Tales

For my children, and my grandchildren,
who might someday ask what really happened.
And for my mom,
whose many questions
went unanswered.

LONG HARD TRAILS & SLED DOG TALES

~

My Adventures Tracking Dogteams Across Alaska, and What I Learned Along the Way

Trail Markers

Chapter One: **McCabe Creek, Yukon Territory** ~ 9

Chapter Two: **Bannon Creek, Washington** ~ 20

Chapter Three: **Dawson City, Yukon Territory** ~ 32

Chapter Four: **Pelly Crossing, Yukon Territory** ~ 49

Chapter Five: **Wauconda, Washington** ~ 53

Chapter Six: **Whitehorse, Yukon Territory** ~ 59

Chapter Seven: **Willow, Alaska** ~ 65

Chapter Eight: **Nome, Alaska** ~ 74

Chapter Nine: **Seward Peninsula, Alaska** ~ 84

Chapter Ten: **Nome, Alaska** ~ 95

Trail Markers continued

Chapter Eleven: **Wasilla, Alaska** ~ 102

Chapter twelve: **Circle, Alaska** ~ 112

Chapter thirteen: **Anchorage, Alaska** ~ 122

Chapter fourteen: **Wasilla, Alaska** ~ 130

Chapter fifteen: **Fairbanks, Alaska** ~ 140

Chapter sixteen: **Willow, Alaska** ~ 153

Chapter seventeen: **Wasilla, Alaska** ~ 165

Chapter eighteen: **The Haunted Forest, Land of Oz** ~ 184

Chapter nineteen: **Wasilla, Alaska** ~ 196

Chapter twenty: **Circle, Alaska** ~ 200

Chapter twenty-one: **Nenana, Alaska** ~ 206

Chapter twenty-two: **Willow, Alaska** ~211

Chapter twenty-tree: **Philadelphia, Pennsylvania** ~219

Chapter twenty-four: **Circle, Alaska** ~ 229

Chapter twenty-five: **Talkeetna, Alaska** ~ 240

Epilogue: **McClaren, Alaska** ~ 244

Long Hard Trails and Sled Dog Tales

PREFACE

Meadow Lakes, Alaska

There are several quotes and truisms which I've taken to heart over the years, and some of them helped me keep a good perspective when I was writing this book. My family and closest friends can tell you that my most often quoted phrase is simplicity itself, from my all-time favorite book, *Illusions: The Adventures of a Reluctant Messiah*, by Richard Bach:

Perspective. Use it or lose it.

I love that quote because it rings so true for me. There have been many times in the last few years when it would have been very easy to lose my perspective, and I credit these few words from my favorite author for helping me keep a steady course. When it seemed like the world was crashing down around me, I told myself things weren't as bad as they could be, that other things had happened which were much worse and I'd survived those so of course I would survive this too. It was all a matter of perspective.

Another inspiring quote which I often said to myself came from a computer science professor with a terminal disease and a rare gift for inspiring others. Randy Pausch's "Last Lecture," delivered a month after he learned that his cancer had advanced and he had less than a year to live, encouraged people to follow their dreams. The entire speech is quite magnificent and worth seeking out, but the part which I seized upon and wrote in my journals was this:

The key question to keep asking is are you spending your time on the right things, because time is all you have.

I still tell myself that almost every day, because time is finite, and fleeting, and no one has enough of it to spend on the wrong things.

There were many others: *Not all who wander are lost.* -J.R.R. Tolkien. *Get your facts first, then you can distort them as you please.* -Mark Twain. *A good traveler has no fixed plans, and is not intent on arriving.* -Lao Tzu.

I employed a good bit of Winnie-the-Pooh philosophy: *How lucky I am to have something that makes saying goodbye so hard;* and *I used to believe in forever, but forever's too good to be true.*

I've made my living as a writer and an editor for over 35 years, which means I work with words on almost a daily basis. I choose them carefully and I take them seriously. That made it even harder when a lawsuit was filed against me in 2010 for something I wrote in earnest, hoping to right a wrong. The lawsuit was eventually identified as being a SLAPP suit, defined as "a strategic lawsuit intended to censor, intimidate, and silence critics by burdening them with the cost of a legal defense until they abandon their criticism or opposition."

The end result of the lawsuit was to very effectively silence me, but this book is my breaking of that silence. It brings to mind another quote I've loved and lived by for decades:

We have to continually be jumping off cliffs and developing our wings on the way down. -Kurt Vonnegut

I've jumped. Now where are those damn wings...

Long Hard Trails and Sled Dog Tales

"It's a dog race and anything can happen..."

–Lance Mackey

Long Hard Trails and Sled Dog Tales

CHAPTER ONE

McCabe Creek, Yukon Territory

It's three AM in the middle of nowhere and Donna's determinedly nodding off in the driver's seat; it's my turn to watch for them. I scan the dark snowy landscape outside the car, note that all the black shadows are still in their proper places, and go back to watching the northern lights shimmer across the sky.

The colors are almost unreal: mauve, teal, an occasional flare of amber gold. People have said they make noise... I wonder if one could really hear them out here in this land where there's no sound. I slowly become aware that a few favorite lines of Service are echoing through my mind, and I smile, as they've always made me smile: *"With the northern lights a-runnin' wild..."*

No, waitaminute, that's not Service, silly. Horton. Johnny Horton, John Wayne, *North to Alaska* and all that...

I fret about something I read once, centuries old folklore which held that some ancient peoples of northern Europe cautioned against singing about the northern lights lest they become angry and attack the singer. But surely they wouldn't get upset about my silently thinking the lyrics to myself.

Besides, the northern lights in the song were dancing over some faraway country, "just a little southeast of Nome." We'll get there in a few weeks, but first we need to follow the Iditarod, and before that, this Yukon Quest...

It's getting cold in the car.
Where the hell *are* those guys?
C'mon, Lance...

Long Hard Trails and Sled Dog Tales

Donna and I were on the road to cover the Yukon Quest sled dog race. It had taken weeks of long nights on the computer, emails flying back and forth, researching website after website of trail maps, checkpoint listings, mileages and driving times between cities and villages and checkpoints, learning about the typical weather in February in the Yukon Territory, all to nail down a plan, an itinerary, to make the well-advised reservations for lodging in the only-guessed-at timeframes we'd been given.

Donna was heading into a land she'd never seen before, but I started with at least a bare-bones knowledge of the route, having traversed it a few summers previously with my daughter Jody, then 25. With no schedule to keep and with picture-perfect weather, Jody and I had taken our time, stopping to explore everything that caught our attention, to read the historical signs and to enjoy just being in that big, wide open land. We read Robert Service poems aloud and thrilled to be in the very country where he'd penned his best-loved lines.

I came to the marge of Lake Lebarge, and a derelict there lay; It was jammed in the ice but I saw in a trice, it was called the 'Alice May.'

I knew there wasn't much where we were going; I knew the Klondike Highway ran hundreds of miles through sparsely populated country; it would be wise to chart a cautious path, and to think twice before passing an open gas station in February.

The white land locked tight as a drum.

I knew Dawson City was going to be a highlight of the trip, a treasure trove for a couple of history buffs, a gold rush town still a little rough around the edges.

A bunch of the boys were whooping it up in the Malemute Saloon...

I knew the weather this far north could turn on a dime, and the temperature could easily drop to minus 50 and stay there.

On a Christmas day we were mushing our way over the Dawson trail. Talk of your cold! through the parka's fold it stabbed like a driven nail.

I knew I was going back to a country I'd loved for almost as long as I could remember, and I'd travelled the southern part of it, the Alaska

Long Hard Trails and Sled Dog Tales

Highway, since I was 15; the land of Sergeant Preston and Yukon King, Jack London and the Bard of the Yukon.

There's a land where the mountains are nameless, and the rivers all run God knows where...

No question about *those* being the lines of Robert Service.

We were about six months into the video production business when Mark and I decided maybe we'd gotten ahead of ourselves. We really didn't know anything about producing or selling videos, yet here we were with a little 45 minute video that was steadily getting good reviews but not exactly selling briskly. We felt confident we could edit all our good race footage and interviews into a powerful second video, but we needed more good footage of sled dogs actually racing, and we needed to figure out the distribution game a little better. Producing good videos was only half of the equation; we needed to be able to sell them if we wanted to stay in the game and create more videos about sled dog racing and Alaskan history.

Still, while we didn't know a lot about videos, we did have almost thirty years of publishing experience under our belts; we knew how to publish award-winning books, and how to sell them. We reasoned that videos couldn't be that much different. But the one recurring criticism of our first video was that there weren't enough dogs in it – we needed more film of dogs racing, resting, eating, being harnessed and unharnessed, loaded into dogtrucks, unloaded from dogtrucks, and running. The Yukon Quest, with many of the checkpoints accessible by road, was the perfect place to get the additional footage we needed.

A year previously we'd decided to write a book about the first Iditarod Trail Sled Dog Race, and I thought the experience of being out on the Quest trail might provide good perspective for that project as well. I knew a thing or two about the original running of the now world-famed Iditarod Trail Sled Dog Race, because 35 years before I'd been living in an old log cabin near Wasilla, and I'd dropped in on a few organizational meetings, which were often held in the back room of the Kashim restaurant.

Long Hard Trails and Sled Dog Tales

I knew a couple of the people involved with the preliminary efforts to get the Iditarod off the ground, and I did some legwork to help raise money and garner publicity for the race. I talked it up to a writer friend at the *Anchorage Times* newspaper, and finally one afternoon I dragged him out to Knik to meet my dad's friend, Joe Redington, who was happy to chew his ear off about how the plans were coming together.

My friend wrote a couple of good articles, which probably helped a bit, but unfortunately he couldn't see the true significance of it all, and not long after that we drifted off in separate directions. I sent a query letter to *National Geographic*, advising them that the Iditarod Trail Sled Dog Race was going to be a historic event and they should send writers and photographers to cover it. They thanked me but politely declined my hot tip, which I always figured was their loss. I kept their rejection slip for many years as my own weird little trophy of the initial race.

It's funny what comes back to you after three decades. Snippets of conversation, pieces of memory floating about like jigsaw puzzle pieces with no puzzle to fit into. I recall a meeting at the Kashim when the discussion was what the drivers should carry in their sleds for the trip. The looming question seemed to be whether or not they should be required to carry a gun. No one questioned whether or not it should be an option, only whether it should be mandatory gear. I don't recall the outcome, and I don't know what the rules are today regarding firearms on the trail, but I remember sitting there at that long table in the back room and listening to the earnest conversation of those trail-hardened men.

In early December of 2006 the sled dog racing world lost a giant of a musher when Herbie Nayokpuk, known as "The Shishmaref Cannonball," passed away. Herbie had run the first Iditarod Trail Sled Dog Race in 1973, coming into a very respectable fifth place finish behind Dick Wilmarth, Dan Seavey, Bobby Vent, and George Attla; and just ahead of Issac Okleasik, Dick Mackey and the rest of an illustrious field of mushing pioneers. Iditarod Hall of Fame nomination committee member

Long Hard Trails and Sled Dog Tales

John Larson said, "If I had to chose one heart, it would be Herbie's. If I could only meet one Iditarod musher ever -- Herbie again. This Eskimo from Shishmaref was everything that was good about the Iditarod: tough, strong, savvy, kind. No one was more respected on the trail, and his team was a thing of beauty to see."

Herbie Nayokpuk's passing reminded many of us that the original mushers were becoming lost and forgotten in the escalating glamour and glitz of the now world-class race, and that loss was underscored the following spring when jazz musician-turned-musher Barry MacAlpine, another of the original 1973 mushers who started for Nome, perished when his cabin burned to the ground. That was in June, 2007 in Chugiak, just north of the Anchorage suburb of Eagle River. Barry MacAlpine didn't finish that first Iditarod, being one of the 14 mushers who scratched that year, but ten years later, in 1983, one of his sons, Norman MacAlpine, completed his run in 21 days, becoming the first black man to successfully finish the Last Great Race.

As I read the many glowing tributes to Herbie, and then read about Barry's sad passing, I found myself remembering two other people who were no longer around to talk about the first race, Joe and Vi Redington. My parents were casual friends with the Redingtons, seeing them around Wasilla occasionally, but always sharing some time when they bumped into each other, which usually meant mom and Vi rifling through the local Salvation Army store for nifty treasures while dad and Joe swapped tales as they waited outside.

Joe didn't run his big race that first year because he was too busy orchestrating the event and trying to secure funding for the finisher's purse. His son Raymie was tasked with taking Joe's team from Anchorage to Knik as a kind of Redington presence in the race, and he was expected to drop out at that point, but he didn't. Brian Patrick O'Donoghue later explained what happened: *Raymie Redington, the race-organizer's son, was only supposed to drive his father's team as far as Knik. But the 28-year-old musher couldn't bring himself to quietly bow out of the historic event.*

'I started with nine dogs and they was running so good I decided to keep going,' Raymie Redington recalls. 'But I wasn't packed or anything, I didn't have nothing.'

Raymie and Joe's team did eventually scratch that first year, but the following year, 1974, saw Raymie place seventh, and he ran the race another ten times after that. His brother Joee, a world champion sprint musher, took ninth place in 1974, and third place in 1975. Joe Redington Sr. ran his own team in the 1974 race, and in the next 18 years he only missed one Iditarod. He placed in the Top Ten seven times, placing fifth four times, and in 1979 Joe and his friend Susan Butcher made an unprecedented trek, taking their dogteams to the top of Mt. McKinley.

And then there was Vi. My mom always said Violet Redington reminded her of her sister Phyllis, having the same quiet, almost shy demeanor, while under the surface roiled a feisty, perky personality. The obituary for Vi in the *Frontiersman* newspaper, April 2, 2006, noted her importance to the race:

'A dog race to Nome is impossible' seemed to be the general consensus of everyone around. But a few hardy (many would say foolhardy) souls, led and inspired by Joe Redington Sr. and supported all the way by Vi, made it happen. Though not officially known as the 'mother' of the Iditarod, few would argue that Vi was the matriarch of the event - hosting, sometimes tolerating, musher after musher in her never-locked home in Knik and in various cabins, including a much-loved place in the Petersville Hills.

For one who'd been there when it all got started, it seemed like a good idea to me to start collecting the stories from the mushers who wanted to tell them, so Mark and I began searching for any 1973 Iditarod mushers still living, and of the original 38 who started, we located over a dozen. It didn't seem like many, but it was a start.

When word got around that Mark and I were working on a book about the 1973 Iditarod, our friend Donna Quante said she was interested in developing a companion film, and we entered a loose partnership to produce a book and DVD set on the first race to Nome. Donna had recently retired from broadcast television with three Emmy awards under her belt; and she had produced her first independent video, about the Iditarod musher Karen Ramstead, whose "Pretty Sled Dogs" all-Siberian Husky team was a crowd favorite. Donna lived just up the road from us, in Willow, and her easygoing attitude and experiences with her growing family of huskies made it fun to spend hours talking with her about mushing related ideas and projects.

Donna and I spent several months interviewing and videotaping mushers who had ridden their sleds up to the starting line of the first Iditarod: Alex Tatum, Ken Chase, Ford Reeves, Mike Schreiber, Bill Arpino, Dave Olson... Their riveting tales of the trail always left us wanting more – and wondering how we would ever fit everything we wanted to include into a single book and video. Each musher we talked with was delighted to answer my questions and share his memories, sometimes talking for several minutes without any prompting when he came to an especially interesting section of the trek.

Ken Chase, who lived in Anvik, met us at his brother's lakeside home north of Wasilla for a couple of hours. He told us about the kinds of runners used on the mushers' sleds and how they searched in vain for the trail, which had been marked by spray painting on the snow. The wind had covered the spray paint, so the mushers would brush the snow off until they located the telltale marks again, but eventually they lost the trail completely...

Donna and I drove to Denali Park's Glitter Gulch to interview Ford Reeves and Mike Schreiber, who had teamed up as one of three two-musher entrants in the first race to Nome. Ford, owner of a large gift shop and theater in the touristy Gulch district, laughed as he told of their heavily overburdened sled finally getting the best of them, and hiking 50 miles to notify race officials that they were scratching. While he was gone Mike stayed warm with a fire which melted down through the heavy snowfall until Ford returned to find his buddy several feet lower than when he'd left him!

Long Hard Trails and Sled Dog Tales

In his Anchorage office Alex Tatum - the first black man to sign up for the Iditarod - explained with a warm, infectious grin how he navigated the route across the Palmer Hayflats, and why he was disqualified when he arrived at the Knik checkpoint minus two of his dogs.

Dave Olson and his wife welcomed us into their Knik home and brought out photo albums and framed pictures. Over coffee Dave told us some of the most interesting 'tales of the trail,' and then graciously posed for photos with his granddaughter on the lawn.

We spent an entire day driving to Tok to interview Bill Arpino, who came in 11th in 1973 with a time of 24 days, 12 hours, and 12 minutes, to claim a purse worth $1,000. Bill brought out large envelopes of newspaper clippings, old flyers, his original bib (#13), and photos and tape recordings from the race. We sat in one of the log cabins at his Burnt Paw Lodge in Tok, Bill wearing a specially decorated leather vest reminiscent of his racing career, and he told story after story of running the first Iditarod to Nome. Then he took us on a tour of his collection of historic racing and freight sleds - and told us how he built sleds for many mushers over the years.

With a growing collection of delightful interviews, Mark and I and Donna were on a roll... And then, in midstream, we switched horses.

One of the mushers who was instrumental in organizing the first Iditarod was Dick Mackey, a trucker who'd moved to Alaska almost 20 years earlier, arriving, according to a 2007 article by Doug O'Harra in the *Anchorage Daily News*, "...in Mountain View with $14, his family – wife Joan, sons Rick and Bill, daughter Becky and the last truck from his fleet. Within a day he had a job."

After Dick and Joan got divorced a few years later, he married a bush pilot with a penchant for sled dog racing named Kathie, and they had two more sons, Lance and Jason. Dick Mackey loved sled dog racing, and along the way he met Joe Redington, who called him up one day and asked what he thought about running a race from Anchorage to Nome, one thousand miles through the roadless Alaskan wilderness.

According to reports, Dick's memorable response was "I'll be the second one to sign up!"

To which Joe asked what he meant, and Dick replied "You haven't signed up already?"

Iditarod lore includes many stories about Dick Mackey. He ran the 1973 race and came in seventh out of the thirty-eight mushers who started from Anchorage. As Mackey headed out on the trail to Nome his father in New Hampshire passed away, and his mother requested that he not be told until he'd finished the race, two weeks later.

Dick Mackey was a fixture in the Alaskan sled dog racing scene for decades, serving long after his competitive racing days had ended. But he started out running a team partly made up of pups he'd raised from the family pets: an old black Labrador and a purebred Siberian husky. Mackey ran the first five Iditarod races, placing in the top ten each time, and finally, in 1978, he won the race by one second over Rick Swenson, who had claimed the title the year before and still holds the record for the most wins (five), in the race's closest-ever and still most controversial Iditarod finish.

The classic telling of the tale was Doug O'Harra's 1989 article in *We Alaskans*, the former Sunday magazine of the *Anchorage Daily News*:

It was a moment that belonged on a poster. The two windburned mushers pausing, their beards crusted with ice, their bodies aching from 1,000 miles of trail. Both had reputations as tough mushers, ruthlessly competitive men capable of seizing any advantage. As they squinted through the predawn darkness, mutual distrust hung between them as thick as the blowing snow. And then, as he urged his dogs forward, Swenson shouted back at Mackey: "We've got first and second sewn up. Just stay right where you are!"

And Mackey thought to himself: "Like hell."

When Dick's son Lance won the 2007 Iditarod, after having just won the Yukon Quest two short weeks earlier, he made sled dog racing history in much the same way his father had before him. The *Anchorage Daily*

Long Hard Trails and Sled Dog Tales

News decorated their front page with Lance Mackey's nine Super Dogs – an unprecedented honor for the Alaska state sport.

Before Lance even made it to Nome the state's largest newspaper was crowing, *"The dog team of Fairbanks musher Lance Mackey was rolling toward Nome on Monday and a place in the history of Alaska sled-dog lore that could put the driver right up there with the likes of Leonhard Seppala, Scotty Allan and Iron Man Johnson."*

Lance won his place in Alaskan sled dog lore, and on a whim, having only talked with him briefly as friends and I snapped some photos at the 2007 Iditarod vet check, I sent him an email message shortly after he won, asking if he had a book planned yet. I never got a reply, which wasn't surprising in the midst of all the media craziness following his spectacular dual win.

In November of that year I sent another inquiry, this time suggesting a video documentary. I still didn't expect a response, but I've always functioned on the philosophy of nothing ventured, nothing gained, and I kept thinking that Lance, like his father before him, probably still had a few tricks up his sleeve. It helped that another of our newfound friends, Theresa Daily, was close friends with Lance and had indicated that he might be more interested in something video-based rather than involving a lot of writing and editing.

A month later Lance replied to my email, expressing interest in the idea of a video documentary and giving me his phone number with an invitation to call him. That phone call resulted in a lengthy interview at his home in Fairbanks. I was in Washington state at the time, so Mark and Donna made the trip to Fairbanks together and shot what became the primary footage for the documentary at Lance's home. A few weeks later they travelled back to Fairbanks to film Lance at the start of the 2008 Yukon Quest.

The 1,000 Mile Yukon Quest International Sled Dog Race follows historic 1890's Klondike gold rush trails, which later became regular mail delivery and travel routes for those living in the northern reaches of

Alaska and Canada's Yukon Territory. The race route begins and ends in Fairbanks, Alaska and Whitehorse, Yukon Territory, reversing direction every year. Named for the fabled Yukon River – the Highway of the North – the race follows the frozen lakes and rivers of the northland, crosses four mountain ranges reaching an elevation of almost 4,000', and travels through remote wilderness camps and villages. Ten race checkpoints allow for veterinarians to ensure the health and welfare of the dogs, and there are four specific dog drops, although dogs can be dropped at any point if needed.

Weather conditions on the Yukon Quest can be life-threatening, with temperatures often dropping as low as sixty degrees below zero, and winds blowing up the Yukon River at speeds of 100 miles an hour. Extremes can swing in the other direction as well, creating dangerous overflows and treacherously thin ice, open water and snow too soft for dogs to run in. The Yukon Quest is known as 'The toughest sled dog race in the world' for good reason.

Having finally resolved my business in Washington state, I flew back into Anchorage at 2:00 a.m. on the morning of February 11, 2008, and left for the Yukon Quest checkpoints of Whitehorse and Dawson City with Donna the next day, leaving Mark busy with editing the final production of our first DVD, *"Appetite and Attitude: A Conversation with Lance Mackey."*

While I was gone Mark had purchased a state-of-the-art Macintosh computer and a first-rate software program capable of handling the video production, a major investment of several thousand dollars. While in Washington I researched video cameras at length, and then with Donna's advice on the options I purchased a sweet little Canon HV20A video camera for shooting additional documentary footage, all of which was made possible by the increasing success of our education-based publishing business. But perhaps I should set the snowhook here and go into a little backstory on that...

CHAPTER TWO

Bannon Creek, Washington

    I was about seven years old the first time I remember skipping school. I think it was the second grade, in the small town of Healdsburg, California, about 75 miles north of San Francisco, where my parents had built a house for my grandmother many years before. I loved going to grandma's house, because there were cherry trees in her yard and a huge grape vineyard across the fence, many big apple trees on the back of her land and a tremendous old willow tree outside her kitchen window. She always had a yard full of wonderful flowers - especially roses - and there was a creek winding down from the nearby hills which was always fun to explore.

    Grandma, or Granny as most people called her, was a tiny birdlike no-nonsense woman who was always accompanied by her little copper-colored chihuahua, Penny, who would nip at you if you got too close to

Granny. Very possessive little dog. Granny would sit and watch television and roll Penny's hide between her fingers, picking the fleas off her for hours at a time. I don't know how Granny felt about the task, but Penny quite obviously relished the procedure: her eyes would narrow, then close, and she'd doze off, but get too close to Granny's rocker and somehow she would know you were there and growl menacingly.

We lived with Granny for a time when I was small, and every morning she would fix oatmeal and toast, and she would plop a big dollop of homemade jam onto the oatmeal. I still prefer mine that way. On Sundays I would put on my best dress and walk to the Fitch Mountain Baptist Church with her, where I learned to love time-worn hymns like "The Old Rugged Cross" and "Amazing Grace."

My dad's brother and his wife lived in the house next door to Granny, which supplied me with a ready-made playmate in my cousin Barbara. We spent hours building tree forts in the apple trees out back, but when Barbara and her two older brothers decided to build in the high branches of one of the giant oak trees I decided that wasn't my cup of tea.

Every morning Barbara and I walked about a mile to the Fitch Street Elementary School. We'd skip along and sing songs and pick flowers on the way. We'd always stop to pet the beautiful collie who slept on the front porch of a little house owned by Barbara's aunt. The big friendly dog looked just like "Lassie," and we loved her. She would always follow us a little ways toward the school, then turn around and go home. But one morning she didn't turn around; she kept following us, closer and closer to the school. Barbara and I tried to shoo her toward home, but she'd just wag her tail at us and give us a toothy doggie-grin.

We knew we couldn't take her to school, and we knew that if we took time to take her home we'd be late to class and be scolded, so we turned off the sidewalk out into a orchard and headed for the creek we knew ran along the far side. We spent the whole day romping with the big collie, picking flowers and grapes and wild onions and making mudpies and catching tadpoles and just laying in the tall grass, happy to be free from schoolish concerns. School had been out for hours when we finally headed for home. The collie bounded toward her house and Barbara and I wandered on toward our homes, tired and dirty from our adventures. It had been a grand day and, as young as I was at the time, I still remember it very fondly.

The overriding message to my young impressionable mind was that school was an expendable part of life, and there were betters ways to spend a lovely sunny afternoon than sitting in a classroom trying to figure out how to keep the teacher happy. I skipped many schooldays after that, and while my parents weren't happy about it, I never suffered any punishment for ditching school. I managed to keep my grades good enough, which seemed to be the only thing anyone was concerned about, but my attendance record was shot full of holes.

There was a definite family precedence for my increasingly bad habit. My mother used to tell us wonderful tales of when she and her sister and brothers would skip school and go riding their horses or swimming in the river or treasure-hunting in the hills of northern California. She always made those adventures sound far more interesting and compelling than going to school, and she often said the stuff she learned by not going to school had always been far more useful to her than the things she'd been forced to sit through in the classroom. Whether that was true or not I had no way of knowing, but there was no doubt in my mind about Mom being one of the smartest people I've ever known.

So I missed a lot of school when I was growing up, but I still kept my grades good enough that one day I was called into the principal's office and informed that I was being moved into the next grade, skipping from the middle of fifth grade into the middle of sixth. The only thing I remember about it was being led into a roomful of strangers and introduced as the new kid. I'm not sure what happened after that, but the last grade I actually completed was the seventh (barely) and things went downhill from there. By high school I'd given up on the idea of school completely and dropped out, preferring to spend my time reading, writing, riding my horses, or just hanging out. Our home was always full of books and magazines, and we had multiple sets of the latest encyclopedias, and I was a voracious reader. Because of Dad's work as a computer systems analyst we travelled extensively, both in the U.S. and in Europe, spending three years in Germany and another three in France when I was at my most impressionable young ages: from five to eight and then from nine to eleven. Mom and Dad made sure we always checked out the historical sites, museums, zoos and other local places of interest. My brother and I were scrambling through Roman ruins and ancient cathedrals, learning street games from the local children, and exploring quaint little villages on our bicycles by day, then sitting around Gypsy campfires in the evening, trying to understand their melodic tales and join in their happy songs. Even without school my young life was full of opportunities for learning and filled with adventures!

Long before I had children of my own I was telling people that mine weren't ever going to school. People would smile condescendingly and explain why not sending my someday-kids to school would be a very bad idea. I listened, but I wasn't buying their arguments.

I didn't buy a lot of what was accepted as standard practice. My first two sons were born in the small community hospital in Palmer, Alaska, but their sister and my next two sons were all born at home, with only their father in attendance. We built our own home, grew our own food, and started our own business. But I'm getting ahead of my story again.

When our two oldest sons, John and Jim, reached school age, we were living a couple of miles northwest of Palmer, which, while not exactly out in the bush, wasn't exactly middle-American suburbia, either. Moose and bears frequented the neighborhood, and I decided my young sons didn't need to run into them on the mile-long walk to the school bus stop each morning. I didn't think it was very healthy for my children to be exposed to sub-zero temperatures on a regular basis either, so I asked around and discovered that the State of Alaska ran a correspondence program which was open to any Alaskan child who lived more than two miles from a school. We fit that description, so we signed the boys up for kindergarten and first grade.

We were assigned a teacher who explained the lesson plans and oversaw the teaching and learning process through monthly meetings in her office, but otherwise we were on our own. We received two oversized boxes of books, pens, papers, crayons, storytapes, arts and crafts materials - it was almost like Christmas!

The story and song tapes became great family favorites, and our kids still remember the lyrics to many of the catchy tunes. As a special project we helped John build a paper mache globe by pasting strips of newspaper around an inflated balloon and painting it to look like the planet Earth. His overseeing teacher was so impressed with the globe that she asked to hang it in her office - and John just beamed!

Both boys passed their respective grades with glowing reports, and we figured the next year we'd repeat the process, moving each up a grade. But life had other plans for our family. In late August of that year my dad suffered a debilitating heart attack and we suddenly found our young family moving to Washington state to help with my parent's ranch. In between worrying about the operations on Dad, we spent the rest of that summer learning about horses and cows and chickens and hauling hay and firewood - and when fall rolled around again I blithely headed down to the local school office and asked how I could enroll my boys in the Washington state correspondence course. They just gave me a blank look and said they didn't know what I was talking about.

By the time school opened John and Jim had made friends with some of the children on neighboring ranches who were about their own age. The boys decided that since everyone else from our little valley was going off to school in town, they wanted to go too.

Between helping to care for Dad, helping with chores, building our own place and expecting our fourth child in a few weeks, it didn't sound like a bad idea to me, so one brisk fall morning they walked down the road beside Bannon Creek, met up with their friends, and waited by the last gate in the valley for the local school bus to come rolling up the dusty mountain road. They were excited about their shiny new lunchboxes.

It took about a month for the novelty to wear off. We started hearing reports of lunches being stolen by other kids, jackets torn in playground bullying, one boy ridiculed because he was coloring a squirrel picture the wrong color, another was made to miss lunch because he went to the restroom without asking first. When a teacher rapped John's knuckles with a ruler because he was talking to a friend in class we decided the school experiment was a failure and the boys never went back.

A friend of my mother's had given her two thin copies of a recently created newsletter, *Growing Without Schooling*, which shared ways other families across the nation were taking or keeping their children out of school. Mom had already taken my youngest brother and sister, then ages 12 and 14, out of school permanently, and the newsletter, edited by the ex-teacher of a pricey and respected private school, was full of reasons why this route was a good idea for anyone willing to buck the system and take charge of their childrens' education: "We teachers - perhaps all human beings - are in the grip of an astonishing delusion. We think that we can take a picture, a structure, a working model of something, constructed in our minds out of long experience and familiarity, and by turning that model into a string of words, transplant it whole into the mind of someone else. Perhaps once in a thousand times, when the explanation is extraordinary good, and the listener extraordinary experienced and skillful at turning word strings into non-verbal reality, and when the explainer and listener share in common many of the experiences being talked about, the process may work, and some real meaning may be communicated. Most of the time, explaining does not increase understanding, and may even lessen it."

The newsletter's editor, John Holt, was featured in *The Mother Earth News* magazine's trendy Plowboy Interviews, and soon afterwards appeared on television's popular *Phil Donohue Show,* among others. He published a book based on his newsletter writings, and what he wrote made good sense to me: *We ask children to do for most of a day what few adults are able to do for even an hour. How many of us, attending, say, a lecture that doesn't interest us, can keep our minds from wandering? Hardly any.*

And this also rang true for me: *Of course, a child may not know what he may need to know in ten years (who does?), but he knows, and much better than anyone else, what he wants and needs to know right now, what his mind is ready and hungry for. If we help him, or just allow him, to learn that, he will remember it, use it, build on it. If we try to make him learn something else, that we think is more important, the chances are that he won't learn it, or will learn very little of it, that he will soon forget most of what he learned, and what is worst of all, will before long lose most of his appetite for learning anything.*

And one of my favorites: *I think children need much more than they have of opportunities to come into contact with adults who are seriously doing their adult thing, not just hanging around entertaining or instructing or being nice to children. They also need much more than they have of opportunities to get away from adults altogether, and live their lives free of other people's anxious attention.*

And so, with our determination redoubled, we ignored the multiplying and increasingly threatening letters from the local school superintendent. The last letter they sent us advised us that they had arranged a meeting we were mandated to attend, and that we were being charged $25 per day, per child, for every day the boys were absent from school. At $50 per day the bill was undoubtedly adding up pretty quickly, so we took evasive maneuvers and told them we were planning on returning to our home in Alaska.

That seemed to bring an end to their interest in our family, although we were pretty certain they knew we were still living in the area. We later decided that telling them we were leaving probably let them check off some little box on a form and file it, because we never heard from the school officials again.

Long Hard Trails and Sled Dog Tales

In the summer of 1983 I made a trip to Seattle, 300 miles away, to discuss raising calves with a friend who was already successful in that business. We'd been casting about for something we could develop into a livelihood, and had decided that perhaps we could make a living at raising calves, and perhaps pigs, and a large garden, of course. I decided that we needed a computer for whatever lay ahead. Mark was dubious, but I had grown up with computers; while Dad was doing his thing as a computer programmer and analyst for the big room-sized IBMs of the late fifties and early sixties, I'd been playing with punch cards and programming circuit boards, and I knew computers were powerful tools, capable of wondrous things. So when I found out I could buy a powerful little blue and gray machine called a Kaypro II for only $1,500, I didn't even hesitate.

For the first few weeks, with Dad's enthusiastic help, we studied our new machine and learned how it worked. I did some bookkeeping and letter writing, and the boys explored the drawing program, but we mostly just played games with our new computer. It came with a disk of classic standards like *Ladder*, *Aliens*, and a version of *Pac-Man*, and the entire family enjoyed these newfangled electronic diversions.

Then in the fall of 1983 I saw a short newspaper item about a homeschool conference in Spokane, Washington, 200 miles from where we lived. It advertised homeschool advocates and authors Dr. Raymond and Dorothy Moore as the featured speakers, and conference attendees would receive a free copy of their new book, *Home Grown Kids*.

Not having any idea what I was getting into, but excited about the prospect of meeting others interested in the concept of homeschooling, I drove the 200 miles and took my seat on a hard metal folding chair in the large and impressive Spokane Convention Center.

I don't recall much about the conference other than liking what the Moores had to say and how they said it. They'd had an article published in the *Reader's Digest* about late-reading children, and they seemed very knowledgeable about the potential of parents teaching their own children.

Long Hard Trails and Sled Dog Tales

They were warm, friendly, sincere and encouraging. They spent a long time answering individual questions afterwards, and they were kind and patient with everyone they spoke with. Little did I know that a few short years later these remarkable pioneering leaders would become dear friends and trusted allies.

At the conference I met and joined a small group of people who were drafting a bill to make homeschooling legal in Washington state. Mark and I drove back to Spokane two or three times a month for the next few weeks, attending meetings and drafting sessions and coffee klatches for local legislators.

We organized the first statewide gathering of homeschoolers in Washington and presented our bill draft, then we gained a strong sponsor for our bill in Senator Scott Barr and set about garnering more support. Kathleen McCurdy, a feisty, spirited mother of several homeschooled children and a newfound friend, had been responsible for organizing the conference, and now she became the bill's lobbyist. When she headed for the state capitol in Olympia to begin work in earnest I went along and stayed with her at Senator Barr's home while I learned first-hand what it takes to get a bill passed through the legislature.

That winter I started a little one-page newsletter to keep local homeschoolers and alternative schoolers informed about our progress with the bill. At some point that December I decided that what the homeschooling movement really needed was not just another newsletter, but a full-fledged magazine with articles, columns, photos, and artwork. John Holt was doing well in publishing *Growing Without Schooling* and the Moores were publishing another newsletter, *The Family Report*, but they were both just newsletters. I wanted to edit and produce a real magazine about homeschooling.

The first issue of *Home Education Magazine* was twenty pages long; ten double-sided sheets of paper stapled along the left-hand side. It featured an editorial, a couple of articles, an interview with a homeschooling family, reviews of several educational items, a book

Long Hard Trails and Sled Dog Tales

review, a report from the Washington Legislative Action Committee, a few good quotes and a short listing of helpful homeschooling resources.

That first issue sported a sharp graphic header designed by my artistic brother, Bill, and our son John provided a bit of artwork. I sketched a couple of small images to run with the quotes which related to learning, but that was it as far as graphical content. We didn't think photos would reproduce well on a print shop's printers.

We sent that first issue to everyone we thought would be even remotely interested in reading it. We sent copies to John Holt and to Dr. and Mrs. Moore, to friends we'd made around the state while working on the homeschooling bill, to legislators who had shown support, and to anyone with any connection to homeschooling who we could find a mailing address for. We were surprised when the first subscription arrived in our mailbox, but it was soon followed by another, and then one from out of state, and then another...

Somewhere in the middle of putting our third issue together we realized that we were really turning into magazine publishers, and then our homeschooling bill passed, and we started getting phone calls from the national news media, and we became featured speakers at conferences across the country, and the little magazine we started on our kitchen table and the books we began publishing as a part of the effort won prestigious national awards and life was never the same again.

As co-publisher and managing editor of *Home Education Magazine* I spent a lot of time thinking about what it means to learn. My contribution to every issue was an editorial which explored the concepts, the ideas, the realities and often the politics of learning. There were stretches when I felt like I didn't have anything to contribute on the topic, and readers would complain and eventually I'd find my muse again and write things like this introduction to 'Watercolor Children,' from the July-August, 2002 issue:

As a writer I work with the precise meanings of words. Control and mastery are important when one is trying to convey an idea, an emotion, or an experience. Realizing many years ago that writing was a very controlled activity, and seeking an alternative which might help me loosen up my thinking and perspective, I turned to watercolor painting. I've always loved the free and easy look of a good watercolor, the translucent hues and deep layers of color, and I've occasionally even wished I'd spent the last 40 years playing with paints instead of words. But taking heart in the knowledge that it's never to late to start doing something you love, I took up learning to paint with watercolors a few years ago.

Sometimes I would share stories about our family, as in this excerpt from 'Hold the Center,' January-February, 2002:

The house is uncommonly quiet. I miss my kids. I walk outside and sit on the porch step and three dogs run up hopefully, tails wagging, eyes asking if a walk through the falling snow is perhaps imminent. No? Okay. They settle for a scratch behind the ears. They miss the kids too.

Our youngest son, Michael, is off working with friends, earning money for this winter's snowboarding adventures. Michael is the rascal, the party dude, the one voted most likely to show up in a snowboarding commercial. He talks about the possibility of exploring new mountains this winter, traveling further afield in search of more challenging slopes. Oregon, Utah, maybe beyond. But he quickly adds that most of his snowboarding will still be done close to home, with his buddies, on the familiar terrain where he first learned to do impressive jumps and tricks.

Michael's older brother Jim, the electrician, has taken a job 250 miles south of here, and his wife Mary and their two little girls, Lilly and Jesse, went with him, leaving an empty house next door. At least once a day I find myself looking wistfully down the trail that winds around the cattail pond and past the huge cottonwood trees, anticipating two little smiling faces running over to Grandma's house...

Our other three kids are in Alaska: John, the oldest, also with a wife and two little girls, Nikki and Ally, and a baby due in June. Christopher, who just turned 22, is helping his brother build a log home this winter while enjoying snowboarding Alaska's steep terrains once again. And then there's Jody Ellen, our seeker of truths, our wayfaring wanderer who might be here one day, gone the next, calling to say hello from Seattle or Lahaina or Anchorage... wherever there's warm sunshine or good powder. She's seeing to it Chris actually gets out there on those Alaskan slopes...

The kids are all healthy and happy and getting on with their lives, as they should. I think about the things we did together, the time we spent when they were younger, and I miss the sweet seeming endlessness of it all. But I know that the years ahead will bring happy homecomings, still more proud new parent moments, laughing grandchildren discovering berry-picking, and long lazy days of sailing or riding our horses together, exploring and sharing and remembering when.

Mark and I had been publishing *Home Education Magazine* and a growing library of books on homeschooling for 24 years when we finally moved back to Alaska and bought five beautiful acres of land with a rushing creek through the middle of it. We'd maintained our connections with Alaska over the years, and coming north this time was coming home. We'd brought our four horses to Alaska several years before, but being born and bred in the high sagebrush deserts of eastern Washington they didn't appreciate Alaska's lengthy sub-zero winters, so we moved them back to their home range again. Over the next few years we developed our creek property, sold it and purchased a beautiful four bedroom log home, and then, when our sons went into business restoring classic and antique cars, we sold the log home and invested in a large shop for them with an apartment upstairs, on an acre of land in a prime location. That's where we were living when we decided to go into documentary film production.

We still owned two homes on twenty-six acres in Washington state, and we figured once we sold those we could once again invest in a home for ourselves. With our publishing business steadily grossing six figures we felt life was good, and our new venture would likewise prove successful and fun.

CHAPTER THREE

Dawson Creek, Yukon Territory

Several hours into our trip north to Whitehorse and Dawson Creek, Donna and I stopped in Tok and paid a visit to Bill Arpino, the 11th place finisher from the very first Iditarod in 1973, at his beautiful Burnt Paw Gift Shop and Cabins, where we'd stayed the summer before when we drove up to interview him. Bill and his wife Nancy had been gracious and spent hours talking with us about the history of sled dog racing, living in Tok, Alaskan politics and other topics, and Bill had given us a personal tour of his impressive collection of dogsleds. He still owned the original sled he ran the 1973 race with, and his knowledge of the history of sleds, sledges, and other modes of dog-related travel and freighting kept us fascinated for hours.

We had originally planned to spend the night at Bill and Nancy's place again, but we decided to push on through when we arrived there much earlier than we'd anticipated. We chatted with Bill for a while in his office, refilled our coffee cups, then refueled Donna's Blazer and headed for the Canadian border. We stopped for the night at a motel with cute little cabins in Beaver Creek, the first village across the border. By early the next evening we were in the Yukon Territorial capital of Whitehorse, wandering through the Canadian Wal-Mart as I searched for a trail-worthy thermos and some good winter boots. Boots were the one piece of cold weather gear I needed to replace, and I found some good Kamik knee-high boots which I thought would do nicely. I got a large men's size so I could wear a couple of layers of socks and maybe even add some chemical toe-warmers when the temperature really dropped, and we headed over to Canadian Tire to see about getting a spare fixed. That done, we got a bowl of soup and a roll at Tim Horton's, refilled our thermoses, and headed back up the Alaska Highway to the turnoff to Dawson City. Our goal was to make it to Dawson City before the first musher arrived the next afternoon, and we still had 350 miles to go.

I dozed and Donna drove through the night, and at one point I heard her say she could see the trail markers next to the road for a long stretch, and we should remember where that was for the trip back. We could shoot some teams traveling alongside the highway; we'd had good luck doing that on the Copper Basin 300 race the month before.

By the time we got to Pelly Crossing, a First Nations community on the river of the same name, we were too low on gas to continue. It was just after four in the morning, Valentine's Day, when we pulled into the Selkirk Service Centre and went to sleep. Around eight the owner arrived to meet an expected delivery, and while the station wasn't due to open yet, we explained the situation and he let us get fuel so we could get back on the road again.

Long Hard Trails and Sled Dog Tales

As part of our effort to document the Yukon Quest, Mark had created a weblog and had given our good friend Theresa Daily access to post updates and information about the race. Theresa had been tracking the progress of the teams and making regular posts, interviewing people involved with the event, reporting scratches, and uploading audio tracks of phone calls from out on the trail. One of her earliest posts had noted this was the 25th Yukon Quest, the Silver Anniversary, and Lance Mackey, having won the previous three times, was looking to make this his fourth consecutive win.

While Donna and I were cruising northward in warmth and comfort, the mushers on the Yukon Quest trail were making their way past Circle City, Slaven's Roadhouse, through Eagle, over Rosebud, Eagle and American summits, and up the frozen Yukon River to Dawson City, the halfway point where they would have a 36 hour layover. I found myself watching the icy landscape and wondering what it was like to be out there on the trail with a dogteam.

While in Washington settling our business affairs the previous month, I'd been reading John Balzar's book *Yukon Alone*, in which the award-winning journalist traced the 1998 Yukon Quest as the press corps liaison. He writes of musher Dave Dalton: *Behind him, a full moon hangs bloated over the horizon and showers light across the snow on the high hills ahead. In the sky opposite, the first flickers of northern lights emerge in faint, smoky streaks of green. As the celestial voltage rises, the green intensifies into neon and widens into a vast curtain, slowly billowing into the ionospheric winds. A tinge of translucent pink collects, gains density, and transforms itself into a red nebula, as if the curtain has caught fire in the cold overhead. A vast, ethereal dance of light and color spreads above him. Tonight, the aurora borealis battles the full moon to rule the Yukon sky.*

Farther on in the book Balzar paints another picture of what it's like out there when he sets off down the Yukon River on a trapline dogteam borrowed from Wayne Curtis: *Sometimes in the outdoors, like at the bottom of the Grand Canyon or hiking in the high mountains of the Brooks*

Long Hard Trails and Sled Dog Tales

Range, I've found myself dizzy from the enormousness of space. Against the majesty of the surroundings, I've felt shockingly reduced. In other circumstances, however, something quite different happens to one's sense of self and space. Once I sailed across the Pacific in a sloop. In this largest of wildernesses, I was surprised to see that I didn't shrink. Instead, the world around me did. Everything came down to the compact sixty-five foot deck of the sailboat and the narrow path it cut through the sea. Now, as I travel the Yukon River in winter, the sensation is something of the same. The buckled ice crust, the trees, hills, mountains, and sky stretch before me--but in abstract, distant monochrome. My worldly reality lies inside all the puffy layers now encasing me, cocoonlike. Sounds are muffled. I am shielded from the cold and the harsh touch of the wind, even as ice slowly builds around my face and neck. I am acutely aware of my own body working as its own efficient furnace. I can hear my heartbeat. Mine is the tiniest of worlds, the self alone.

Donna and I rolled into Dawson City just before noon and pulled over just down the street from the easily-seen race headquarters. Right behind us was the checkpoint with its large yellow banner spread across the street welcoming the teams to a much-needed 36-hour layover, and we could tell from the gathering crowd that something was about to happen. We walked around a bit, asking questions and getting our bearings, and learned that we'd arrived just ahead of the first musher, who was expected into town shortly. We said a quiet word of thanks to the businessman at Pelly Crossing for helping us arrive in the nick of time, and then quickly started bedecking ourselves in our winter gear right there beside the car.

I remembered that when my daughter Jody and I had traveled this road and crossed the Yukon River on the free ferry a few years before, we'd seen an impressive cliff face along the riverbank at the north end of town. I'd been hoping the trail would take the mushers in front of that cliff, because I knew it would make a good photo opportunity. Sure enough, the trail ran right along the eastern shoreline, under the cliff face, and we were there just in time to get set up and ready. We drove down to the boat ramp and walked across the road for a good view downriver.

Once again I found myself wondering what it was like out there, and recalled that Mark had pulled an excerpt from one of our interviews with Lance and shared it on the weblog: *Lance Mackey talks about the Yukon Quest trail from Circle City to the Yukon River: "...the Yukon is spooky, to say the least...When you get out in the middle of the Yukon on a tiny dogsled, with nobody else around, you get a sense of how small you really are. And that in itself is... scary..."*

Sitting there watching downriver for the approaching team, we quickly decided that one of us should be up at the checkpoint, so when the musher came into view – it was Lance in his easily recognizable red snowsuit, of course – I took a few quick photos and then left Donna to shoot his arrival on the river and I drove back up to the checkpoint. I'd just gotten into position when his team came into view, wearing their bright red dogcoats and led by Hansome and the only female in the team, the long-legged Lippy, who'd been with Lance on his three previous Quest wins. They trotted under the banner, slowed and then stopped at the officially recorded time of 1:01 pm. One dog, Willy, who'd torn a hamstring, was riding in the basket. The crowd quickly closed in and the questions started flying, cameras flashed and microphones were extended to catch every word. I recognized the big gray Larry, midway in the team, and told him he was a good boy and doing a great job. Lance graciously spent a few minutes with the crowd and the reporters, then he swung his weary team around in the street and retired to the dog campground on the other side of the river.

Ken Anderson, who had lost two hours in a penalty for not properly signing out of the Chena checkpoint, arrived half an hour after Lance, at 1:34 pm. Theresa's post at the Northern Light Media weblog told the story:

It was a long morning of waiting at the Dawson City checkpoint, but it was worth it. Three-time Champion Lance Mackey glided into town just a minute after 1 p.m. with 12 dogs in harness and one in his basket.

Spectators, who began gathering at the checkpoint before 5 a.m., stampeded from the building when the call came, "team spotted!"

The faded red glow of Mackey's parka gradually came into focus as he traveled down the Yukon River and finally onto Front Street and into the cheering throng. Mackey was chatty and alert, and very hungry. He joked that he'd use his four ounces of gold nuggets—his winnings for arriving first at the halfway point—on matching jewelry to a nugget stud on his earlobe, part of his winnings from another Yukon Quest.

No sooner did the celebrity musher whisk his team off to the dog yard with his wife and dog handler, Tonya, when "team spotted!" rang out again. Ken Anderson, who Mackey claimed he hadn't seen more than eight hours earlier in Fortymile, breezed into town just 33 minutes later. His yellow sunglasses couldn't hide his swollen and sleepy eyes. He tried to sound upbeat, but he was tired. The brilliant white snow he'd been facing for so many hours had taken its toll. He said he had a difficult time coping with so much light.

Both mushers reported a difficult trail the whole way to Dawson City. Mackey said most races allowed him to sit in his sled for awhile to rest. This year, he got knocked out whenever he tried. The terrain slowed him down by four hours compared to his time in 2006. "I've done it a lot faster than this," Mackey laughed.

The two can relax now for 36 hours, the mandatory layover time in Dawson City for all Yukon Quest competitors. The scattered start times from Fairbanks will be corrected at their departure from Dawson City. Anderson will leave seven minutes after Mackey in the wee hours Saturday. Michelle Phillips and Dave Dalton are expected to arrive next in Dawson City. The two stopped this morning at Fortymile and have not left.

The Yukon Quest dog camp was set up in the territorial campground which sprawled along the western bank of the river across from Dawson City. Donna and I drove across the frozen Yukon River on the ice bridge – a strange experience for me, remembering how swift and deep it had looked from the ferry ride a few years previously. There was a large ice block inuksuk in the middle of the river, and another about half a mile upstream – we stopped to take pictures of them on the way back from the dog camp, and one of those photos eventually became the logo for Northern Light Media.

We parked at the campground entrance, among the dogtrucks which had unloaded their tents and camping gear and dog care equipment, and were now clustered along the short plowed distance of the snowed-in dead end road. We walked the half mile or so to Lance's camp, arriving just ahead of the Quest veterinarian team. Lance's handlers, his wife Tonya and a friend, Kate Schaefer, had set up a comfortable camp, with a long open-ended tarp tent for the dogs, filled with straw, and an Arctic Oven tent in a large area cleared in the knee-deep snow, with camp chairs, a fire ring, and firewood at the ready.

Lance spent some time talking with a vet who was going over the dogs, talking about the trip up the river ("Horrible, just horrible, the worst I've ever seen out there!"), his dogs having a bout of diarrhea ("self-inflicted, from eating beaver meat, it's too rich for them..."), and how his dogs would get excited when they'd see a cabin ahead, thinking they were going to stop, and that he would talk to them and encourage them for several minutes after passing it to get them refocused on the trail.

Lancee told Tonya which dogs needed the red pills she was dispensing out of a large baggie ("Zorro needs one, and Battel needs one, and Dred...") and she repeated the names back to him for confirmation, "Zorro, Battel, and Dred," and then she knelt beside Zorro, deftly lifted his muzzle and slipped the pill into the back of his throat with a swift practiced move. She rubbed his muzzle affectionately before moving on to Battel.

Administering his pill didn't go as smoothly. She put the pill down his throat, but he wriggled away and spat the pill into the straw. Tonya seized it and pried his mouth open, stuffed it far back in his throat, and held his muzzle, laughing, "He's got it now!" and then explaining "You have to push it way down, man, they'll go 'aagh' and hack it right back up!"

Long Hard Trails and Sled Dog Tales

We spent an hour or so watching Lance as he and the veterinarians went over his teammates, checking each dog for tender spots, soreness, chafing, and other possible problems. It was fascinating to see how much went into caring for the dogs, and we sat in the straw under the big blue tarp for a long time after the vets left, as Lance applied ointments to his tired team's feet. He told us about who was doing well, who was being watched a little more closely, and who was being dropped at that point. Lance looked every bit as tired as his dogs, but he tended each one with seemingly infinite patience.

After a while Donna and I hiked back to the car, past all the unpeopled campsites set up and awaiting the arrivals of their teams. We re-crossed the ice bridge, stopping to take photos of the big ice inuksuk and the one farther up the river, and then took a quick spin around Dawson City, marveling like the tourists we were at the old Yukon capitol's many gold rush era buildings. In its glory days this was a bustling city of 40,000 souls, including, for a time, both the poet Robert Service and the author Jack London. Between the two of them, Service and London had left a considerable literary legacy, and their talents had no doubt helped shape the dreams of many who travelled to this remote and distant place. Robert Service often put a romantic spin on the harsh realities, and softened the extremes of landscape and weather with lines like these:

I've stood in some mighty-mouthed hollow
That's plumb-full of hush to the brim;
I've watched the big, husky sun wallow
In crimson and gold, and grow dim,
Till the moon set the pearly peaks gleaming,
And the stars tumbled out, neck and crop,
And I've thought that I surely was dreaming,
With the peace o' the world piled on top.
-The Spell of the Yukon

Jack London took a different tack. There was a passage in London's novel, *The Call of the Wild*, which had enchanted me since the first time I read it, and the city we now drove through was the real-life setting for the fictional account of events in the life of the great sled dog Buck who, at this point in the story, ran in the traces of a courier for the Canadian Government, bearing important dispatches:

...they pulled into Dawson one dreary afternoon... Here were many men, and countless dogs, and Buck found them all at work. It seemed the ordained order of things that dogs should work. All day they swung up and down the main street in long teams, and in the night their jingling bells still went by. They hauled cabin logs and firewood, freighted up to the mines, and did all manner of work that horses did in the Santa Clara Valley. Here and there Buck met Southland dogs, but in the main they were the wild wolf husky breed. Every night, regularly, at nine, at twelve, at three, they lifted a nocturnal song, a weird and eerie chant, in which it was Buck's delight to join.

With the aurora borealis flaming coldly overhead, or the stars leaping in the frost dance, and the land numb and frozen under its pall of snow, this song of the huskies might have been the defiance of life, only it was pitched in minor key, with long-drawn wailings and half-sobs, and was more the pleading of life, the articulate travail of existence.

The most compelling chronicler of life in Dawson City, however, was Pierre Francis De Marigny Berton, CC, O.Ont, BA, D.Litt., a noted author of non-fiction, especially Canadiana and Canadian history, as well as a popular television personality and journalist, an accomplished storyteller, and one of Canada's most prolific authors. Pierre Berton's contributions were such that when he died in 2004 the Canadian Prime Minister, Paul Martin, wrote, *His ability to chronicle the life and times of our great nation was without peer. His love of Canada, its people and its history, and his personal attachment to the North (were) vividly expressed in his numerous books and writings as a journalist.*

Berton, who was born in Whitehorse and raised in Dawson City, wrote *The Klondike Fever: The Life and Death of the Last Great Gold Rush*. The witty excerpts he selected as chapter headings for his table of contents relate a wealth of history in succinct phrasings, such as these for Chapters Two, Three, Nine, and Eleven:

- *How Dawson was born, Circle City died, legends were lived, and fortunes won without the world being the wiser*
- *Of treasure ships laden with gold by the ton and bearing the germs of an endemic disease called 'Klondicitis,' which drove a continent to madness*
- *How Dawson City, flooded first by water, then by men, was transformed into a glittering metropolis of the north, where sounds of the human carnival were never stilled (except on the Sabbath)*
- *Nourished by gold, the 'San Francisco of the North' runs wild for a year, burns itself out, and enters its long decline*

Pierre Berton's mother, Laura Beatrice Berton, was a 29-year-old kindergarten teacher who, in 1907, left her comfortable life in Ontario to teach in Dawson City, and then made it her home for the next 25 years. *I Married the Klondike* is her classic and enduring memoir, and her publisher describes the book and Laura Berton's years in the North:

When she first arrived by steamboat in Dawson City, Berton expected to find a rough mining town full of grizzled miners, scarlet-clad Mounties and dance-hall girls. And while these and other memorable characters did abound, she quickly discovered why the town was nicknamed the "Paris of the North." Although the gold rush was over, the townsfolk still clung to the lavishness of the city's golden era and the young teacher soon found herself hosting tea parties once a month, attending formal dinners, dancing the minuet at fancy balls and going on elaborate sleighing parties. In the background a famous poet wrote ballads on his cabin wall, an archbishop lost on the tundra ate his boots to survive and men living on dreams of riches grew old panning the creeks for gold.

Donna and I had reserved a room at the stately El Dorado Hotel, recommended by someone who'd been on the Yukon Quest many times, and we weren't disappointed when we settled into our home away from home. It was clean, comfortable, quiet, and on the ground floor, which made unloading all our gear easier than we'd been anticipating. I went to check out the restaurant and lounge and found Lance surrounded and being interviewed by a pack of earnest reporters. I listened in on some of the stories he told, but it was nice to just sit in a comfortable chair and watch the show; I knew we'd be talking with him at length later. When things wound down I moved over to Lance and Tonya's table and we chatted about the dogs and the cold and some repairs Lance needed to make to his sled, which had taken a beating on the Yukon River's jumble ice. There was talk about the weather and the trail, both what lay behind and what was still ahead, and of later watching a friend take on the local challenge of the infamous "sour toe cocktail" at a bar down the street. Theresa had posted an interesting article on the 'trail behind' at the Northern Light Media blog:

Three-time Champion Lance Mackey said upon his arrival in Dawson City that the Yukon Quest trail so far was the most difficult he'd experienced. Fresh in his mind as he said this was no doubt the harrowing trail leading him into Eagle Checkpoint, now 147 miles (237 kilometres) behind him. As photographs on the Quest website can attest, jumble ice on the rivers were big and "ugly" according to volunteer trail groomer Eric Cusmutto of Fairbanks. This is Cusmutto's first year volunteering his time, his energy and his snowmobile, not to mention more than $1,000 in costs for gear, upgrades to his sled, including installing steel studs on the sled's rubber tracks, and the repairs it must now undergo. The broken ice chunks, caused by the warming and cooling of the river, which causes the ice crust to break and the pieces to surge and jut into the air, were up to four-feet thick and piled higher than a house at the edges of the riverbank. For the previous three weeks, 60-below temperatures had made it impossible for the trailbreakers out of Central, AK, to groom this section of trail. Cusmutto and two other volunteers on snowmachines are shocked at what they find on this yet-unbroken pathway on the Tuesday that Mackey would travel it. Besides the jumble ice, there is a 15-foot cavern "like the depths of hell" in the middle of the river and open water in several places.

Long Hard Trails and Sled Dog Tales

Further up, the trio encounters "giant mushrooms" of snow and ice, most likely caused by rocks beneath the water preventing sections of ice crust from falling when the surface ice warms and sinks, Cusmutto guesses. At one point while struggling to groom a trail, Cusmutto feels the ice give beneath his sled; he floors it and barely gets out of there before sinking. When he watches Mackey maneuver the same terrain later, it appears the musher and his dogs were "making better time" than the snowmobiles. Yet another natural phenomenon that made Cusmutto shake his head.

The friend who'd recommended the El Dorado hadn't steered us wrong; it was a good place to be in the thick of things as the teams slowly filed into town. The hotel manager presented Lance and Tonya with a complimentary room, and many of the mushers, handlers, and media crews seemed to be staying there. The lounge had free wireless, so Donna and I spent some time catching up with email while Lance and Tonya had dinner with friends. Being Valentine's Day, we weren't surprised when they wrapped up the visiting and announced they were going to check out Dawson City's nightlife. *Yukon News* reporter Genesee Keevil captured Lance's attitude that evening in an article for the tabloid *Yukon News*:

Lance Mackey should have been sleeping.

But after winning four ounces of gold for being the first musher into Dawson, Diamond Tooth Gertie's tempted the three-time Yukon Quest champ.

"On my way into Dawson, I was thinking about how I'd spend the 36-hour layover," said Mackey, downing a glass of Crown Royal at the Eldorado Hotel late Thursday night.

"I was going to spend 10 hours eating, 10 hours sleeping and 16 hours on dog care," he said.

"But I don't have many issues with my dogs.

"So now I'm thinking, I'll spend 10 hours on dog care, 10 hours drinking Crown Royal and 10 hours at Gerties."

I didn't stick around long enough to see if he followed through on his

43

new plan; settling into a warm bed made more sense to me.

After breakfast the next morning Donna and I once again drove across the frozen Yukon River, past the towering inuksuk, and parked beside Ken Anderson's big Windy Creek Kennels trailer. We hiked through the campground noting that more teams had arrived, and we took photos of several. We watched a team skirting the far shore and traveling under the cliffs into Dawson City. Half an hour later the same team pattered down the campground road to its campsite, the musher visibly happy to have made this checkpoint and a well-earned rest.

Lance wasn't anywhere around, but we shot photos and filmed video footage, trying to capture the essence of what we were seeing while also portraying the overall sense of the place and the scenes before us. Donna shot several minutes of the sleeping dogs in their open-ended tarp tent, zooming in on Boycuz as he stood, turned, and laid back down again; on Pimp as he opened an eye to survey the visitors and then closed it again; on Larry sleeping soundly, barely moving; on Lippy, her chest rising and falling and steam rising from her like an ethereal cloud. The scene was of peaceful slumber, and we soon left the dogs to their rest.

We knew there was a musher's briefing on the rest of the trail back at race headquarters, so we headed back to Dawson and made our way into the small meeting room. This was the first time I'd gotten a good look at many of the mushers, and they were a surprisingly young, very serious-looking lot. As the race officials droned on in turn about weather and landmarks and what to expect on the trail ahead, I found myself wondering what makes a person decide to take on the challenge of this lifestyle, this sport, this all-consuming passion. I found myself recalling the wild joy of driving a team of huskies who raced along the wooded trails of another lifetime. They were big furry trapline dogs, and they weren't particularly friendly, but they were well-behaved, and I loved the infrequent opportunities I had to hook them up and go flying across the snow.

Suddenly, in a moment of revelation, I realized that only a few twists in the trail had kept me from potentially joining the ranks of these mushers decades before, and for a quick moment I wished I'd stayed the course with the team I'd once known and loved. It was a fleeting wish, and I was happy I'd essentially traded that team of huskies for a small herd of horses which had, in effect, helped Mark and I raise our five children. Instead of snow and ice and cold frozen adventures with dogs, our kids grew up riding their horses through sun-filled days and moonlit nights in the forested mountains of eastern Washington state. It was a trade-off, one lifestyle for another, but now here I was back with the dogs again, having somehow come full circle.

I'd never really looked at it that way until then, but the realization and sudden perspective made me smile to myself. I'd loved our horses as much as the kids had, but somehow the dogs just always called me back. Over the years we'd owned many horses in Alaska, but dogs just made more sense in the north country. And now that our kids were all grown and the older horses had been turned out to permanent pasture, I had two big Alaskan huskies at home, and a good strong sled.

The remaining time in Dawson City went by quickly. Donna and I spent some time exploring the town on Friday afternoon, checking out some interesting-looking shops and stores for gifts and souvenirs. We enjoyed a nice dinner at the comfortable Riverview Inn early Friday evening, then found Lance and Tonya back at the El Dorado lounge. I taped an interview with Lance in the nearly empty hotel restaurant; the manager graciously turned off the overhead music for me, and Lance talked for almost an hour.

Interview with Lance Mackey
El Dorado Hotel, Dawson City, Yukon Territory
February 15, 2008

Me: The first question I'd like to ask is if you can tell us a little about the dogs you have with you.

Long Hard Trails and Sled Dog Tales

Lance: Okay, the two leaders I had coming in here were Hansome and Lippy. Let's see, then there's Hobo and Battel, Boy and Foster, Rapper and Pimp, Dred and... uh... I think that's all of 'em. There's a dozen, I'll leave here with twelve. I came in with thirteen but one had a little hamstring injury, his name's Willy... Yeah, so there's twelve. Oh! And my main leader, Larry! How could I forget Larry? Actually I haven't used him in the lead this trip just because I have others that need to basically take his spot in the next couple of years, so he's here for backup if I need him, but I haven't really needed him this year. And he's a little bit irritated with that because that's his spot. But when he goes in lead he knows that it's important and he's there for a reason, so he's pretty proud, his head comes up and his chest sticks out. He knows he's The Man.

Me: Can you tell me a bit about the trail coming into here?

Lance: There were sections of it that were good, but only sections. For the most part, from the starting line til here, has been the most demanding trail I've ever been on. Physically, you know, you don't just stand on your sled and ride the sled down the trail, you have to drive the sled, you have to manhandle it around the corners, which takes some energy out of you, and when we started this race it was 50-plus below, so first you've got all your clothes on and you're sweating, and then you get to a good section of trail and you're not sweating and you're standing on your runners and you're just froze solid...

So it's been a little bit frustrating, and that's part of being successful, you have to keep those things together, you can't go off frustrated and throwing a little fit, yelling and crying, because the dogs pick up on those things, so as miserable as it can be - or was - I still try to stay positive for the animals, and because of that they stay upbeat, they don't really know any different. They know what I teach them, and if I teach them that soft snow and miserable times are not always miserable... and we did this in training, so when they get out here this is nothing new to them. That's why when they came in here they were still upbeat, standing up, wagging their tails... And it's important to me to know that my job has been done in pre-season training, and out here there's nothing that's gonna surprise 'em.

Long Hard Trails and Sled Dog Tales

What's surprising to me is what's happening, they're suprising me with their stamina and their enthusiasm and their endurance is just incredible, so it's a real pleasure to drive them.

Me: What about the trail ahead? You've been over it before, do you think there will be any surprises or do you know what you're getting into?

Lance: I do know what I'm getting into, and here not too long ago today we had a nice trail report from the Canadian Rangers, and they made it sound like a paved highway! One small section of overflow, which is minimal compared to what this race can produce - and has. So that's real nice to know. And minimal hills... Well, I won't say minimal, we still have King Solomon's Dome, and it's not real steep, it's just long, it's a good long climb.

So I'll leave here with twelve dogs, eleven big males and one female, and I'm not worried about the hills. I'm looking forward to the hills, for the simple fact that the team right behind me, Ken Anderson, is a bigger guy, he has a smaller dogteam, smaller sized dogs... Leaving Eagle he was right with me - for a few minutes. By the time we got over the hill he was quite a ways behind me. So I'm pretty calm about the fact that he won't stay with me in the hills.

Donna wanted to be riding on Lance's sled when he made the midnight run from his campsite through the campground to the re-start area on the banks of the Yukon, and once Lance got over his surprise at her unusual request he agreed, cautioning her that if she fell off en route he wasn't going to stop his team and help her back aboard. With steely determination she agreed, so shortly after midnight we checked our cameras, bundled up warmly, and took our places for the 1:40 am restart of the race. My agreed-upon place was at the westside ferry landing, to film him coming up the river from the campground and out along the river trail in front of the lights of Dawson City. Looking the situation over as I dropped Donna off at the campground, I hoped I could get some good footage in the dark light conditions.

I later posted a brief update at our weblog:

47

Long Hard Trails and Sled Dog Tales

Lance Mackey and his team headed out of the dog encampment and down onto the Yukon River at 1:40 this morning. With the lights of Dawson City to his left, he followed the trail markers right up the river past town, heading for a long 200+ mile run to Pelly Crossing - the next place we'll catch up with him. The notorious 4,002' King Solomon's Dome lies between here and Pelly Crossing; when I asked Lance about that last night he told me it's not all that steep, but it's a long wearying uphill grade. There's a dog drop at Scroggie Creek, and many mushers stop for a hot meal at Stepping Stone, then Pelly Crossing, where we'll pick up filming the teams again.

The next morning we explored the town a little more, photographed Robert Service's cabin on 8th Avenue, where the Bard of the Yukon lived between 1909 and 1912. We visited a couple of gift shops, then drove back to the west side of the river again to film Brent Sass leaving the campground dogyard. Donna held her camera on him for a long approach from where he'd dropped down onto the river from the campground, poling smoothly to help the dog along. He wound his way through the gathered photographers, shouted a hearty "See you all in Whitehorse!" and directed his smartly running dogs across the ice road, between the orange and white striped barriers, and back down onto the frozen river. Somewhere up ahead of him were Lance Mackey and Ken Anderson...

Long Hard Trails and Sled Dog Tales

CHAPTER FOUR

Pelly Crossing, Yukon Territory

The checkpoint at Pelly Crossing was in front of the Selkirk First Nations Curling Rink building, a large gymnasium with a small kitchen and comfortable facilities, with tables set up for the media teams, and plenty of space for the mushers to spread out their sleeping bags and catch a few hours of sleep. The checkpoint manager, David Bennett, a wiry, friendly man who had been born and raised in Pelly Crossing, spoke with us for about ten minutes, explaining his duties and how the village had moved from its original location near Fort Selkirk, a Hudson's Bay Company trading post at the confluence of the Pelly and Yukon Rivers, when the Klondike Highway was put through in 1950.

The Pelly River looped around the town, and the mushers would be crossing it just before entering the checkpoint. Driving around to orient ourselves, Donna and I admired a very picturesque small log church on the bluff above the river, right beside the trail the mushers would use to come off the river. We considered trying to include it in our video footage, but with darkness fast approaching it finally made more sense to use the big checkpoint lights for illumination.

Lance didn't make it into the checkpoint until very late, as he'd gotten lost for three hours on the outskirts of Dawson City. He later admitted: "It's my own damn fault. I was running without a headlamp, looking at the moon, and I didn't see the trail markers. I should know better, because I've done it before in the same area."

Two years earlier he'd taken a wrong turn and travelled at least five hours out of his way, almost losing the race to former Quest champion Hans Gatt. Mackey sighed, "Let's just say, I know the backside of Dawson real well."

This time, not far out of Dawson City, Lance took another sidetrip up a dead-end trail and back down again, which cost him three hours and put Ken Anderson in the lead. Then they played a cat-and-mouse game; when Ken didn't see any tracks on the trail leaving Dawson he figured Lance had gotten lost, but then he wondered if he'd gotten lost as well. He later admitted "There were markers, but it was like the Twilight Zone..."

When Anderson camped just beyond Solomon's Dome, Mackey caught up with him, having made a long ten hour run to make up for lost time. Mackey explained that he "wanted to know where Ken was at," and then he cut two hours of rest time to stay ahead of his Fairbanks neighbor. When Mackey stopped to rest at Stepping Stone, a hospitality stop 35 miles out of Pelly, Anderson tried to sneak past him, but Lance had parked his team right on the trail and as soon as Ken's team went by Lance rejoined the chase. Anderson acknowledged Lance's faster team, explaining "He gains about half an hour on me in an eight hour run, so I'm also cutting rest."

Arriving at the Pelly checkpoint shortly after midnight, Anderson's dogs appeared exhausted. They laid down and waited with their noses on the snow for him to go through his drop bags and fill his cooler with hot water. When Mackey arrived half an hour later his team looked more lively, but as he rummaged through his drop bags and snacked the team, Lance was still concerned about having cut their rest times to stay in the running with Ken.

"Their attitude is not like it was last year at this time," he said. "They're normally screaming and barking to go."

As he zipped up his sled bag and got ready to leave the checkpoint, the team finally sprang to life, barking and lunging into their harnesses.

"Now that's more like it," Mackey grinned, as he walked down his string petting and encouraging each dog in turn.

My reports for our Northern Light Media weblog captured the attitudes of the front-running mushers:

Ken Anderson blazed through the Pelly Crossing checkpoint at 12:35 am Sunday morning, with 11 dogs, saying on the way in that he was pushing on through, but he was dropping one because it was a young, inexperienced dog. He asked when Lance left Stepping Stone and when a reporter asked if he thought he had a lead he said no, he said he'd wait to see Lance's run time between the checkpoints.

Lance Mackey was only 40 minutes behind Ken Anderson coming into Pelly Crossing, his dogs were bouncing and jumping and wolfing down their snacks, obviously enjoying the thrill of the chase!

When asked about his three hour detour, Lance kind of laughed and said he was "getting to know the backside of Dawson pretty well..." He said he knew he was on the wrong trail when it dead-ended up a mountainside, but he didn't seem too concerned about the wrong turn. He left Pelly Crossing half an hour behind Ken..

The next checkpoint is McCabe Creek. On the Yukon Quest site's "Mushers Guide to the Yukon Quest Trail," John Schandlemeier describes this part of the trail as a "brush, lakes and burn area" and predicts a "relatively fast, easy, 30 mile run to the McCabe Creek Dog Drop." Then 39 miles to the Carmacks checkpoint.

Donna and I drove back to the point on the Klondike Highway where we knew the teams would be running alongside the road, just before they crossed the road and dropped into the McCabe Creek dog drop. We pulled into a wide spot and got out to admire the northern lights extending from horizon to horizon in a broad band of blue-green curtains.

There was no sound other than the muffled tinkling of the car engine cooling, and no lights except for a cherry-red signal light on a hill not far away. We were alone in the Yukon, in the middle of the night, waiting for dogteams.

We retire to the car, Donna starts it up and lets the heater run to warm our cold cheeks and noses, and then we settle in to wait. The surrounding countryside is easy to see. It's not bright by any means, but we can see the trees and hills around us clearly enough. And the red light, of course.

Finally, around 3:10 am, we detect movement far up the trail. We can barely see the moving forms, but slowly it becomes clear that a dogteam is approaching.

3:13 am, it's Ken Anderson's team, and he briefly turns on his headlamp as he approaches us. We're not sure why, because surely he can see us as clearly as we can see him, and it's bright enough for Donna to shoot good footage of his passing, although the dogs are just blurry little beings. I step onto the highway and take a still shot of his team; later I'll see several pairs of glowing eyes in the ethereal picture. Ken calls a soft "Hey" as he goes by, and Donna returns "Hi!"

3:41 am, half an hour later, we see movement up the trail again and smile at each other, knowing it's Lance. We stand at the road's edge as he passes and Donna captures his fast-moving team with the same blurred effect and the now-familiar runners-over-the-snow sound, like a far-off train smoothly rumbling past.

4:04 am, we move down the highway a few miles to the crossing point and, knowing Ken will have already passed, settle in to wait for Lance. It's easy to spot him this time as he approaches with his headlight on. Just past us he calls a sharp "Gee!" and the leaders swing up onto the highway, head for the trail markers on the other side of the road, and disappear down into the ditch, the scratching sound of Lance's sled runners on the pavement still echoing back to us. We head for Carmacks, where hot showers and warm beds await our arrival.

CHAPTER FIVE

Wauconda, Washington

At what point does one recognize that a life-changing event has occurred? When do the roadsigns, which must have been there all along, move into focus and begin to awaken the realization that something is amiss, or askew, or not quite as we thought? Sometimes the warning signals are mistaken for other, more benign messages. And sometimes the heart simply doesn't want to know - or accept - what the head probably figured out a long time ago.

During the course of publishing our magazine Mark and I had weathered more than a few political storms. We'd been outspoken and aggressive in our defense of family and educational freedoms, and our no-

nonsense, no-holds-barred stance had often seen us quoted in the national media. We'd been central figures in the formation of three national organizations, lending our publication and our website as rallying points for key discussions and preliminary planning. We had been oft-quoted advisors as legal cases wound through the court systems in many states, and we had been at the forefront of legislative battles which resulted in new laws for educational freedoms. Over the course of a quarter of a century we worked alongside thousands of people who bravely changed the future of both public and alternative education in this country, and in the process we made innumerable friends, and a handful of enemies.

Fast-forward for a moment: In a news column which ran in the August, 2010 issue of our magazine I commented on a situation which had been brewing for some time between Heather Idoni, who lived in Michigan, the owner of a respected online bookstore; and Mimi Rothschild, in Pennsylvania, the owner of a chain of online learning programs:
"Heather has also been the target of an ongoing campaign by Mimi Rothschild to discredit her for taking a principled stand against Mimi's notoriously unethical business practices, and now Heather is embroiled in a lawsuit brought against her by Mimi."
It was a short, concise statement describing the situation as I saw it. This was not the first time Mimi Rothschild's name had crossed my radar, and the previous run-ins had already left a bad taste in my mouth. I felt there was something seriously amiss, but with an overly full schedule I had neither the time nor the interest to pursue it any further. I silently wished Heather good luck and promptly forgot about the situation.
With frequent travels between our homes in Washington and Alaska it was difficult to keep track of anything which didn't relate directly to keeping the magazine edited and published. Notices, notifications, and other paperwork often ended up filed and soon forgotten. No doubt that is what happened to the first rumblings of my being enjoined to the lawsuit against the bookstore owner. There may have been moments of utter

disbelief that such a thing was happening, but eventually the reality of the situation made itself clear: I was named by Mimi Rothschild and her husband, Howard Mandel, as a defendant in their lawsuit filed in the Philadelphia Court of Common Pleas, charged with defamation which had resulted in "...substantial damages, including, but not limited to: (a) loss of standing in the community, (b) damage to their reputations, (c) severe emotional upset (Rothschild and Mandel); (d) loss of marital consortium (Mandel), and (e) loss of business."

I kept reading and re-reading the charges, not quite believing what I was seeing, and not sure whether to be irritated or amused. I'd heard the term 'frivolous lawsuit' before, but never in a million years thought I would be embroiled in one over something so seemingly inane. Who *was* this Mimi Rothschild and what the *hell* was her problem?

As our interest in sled dog races and the mushing community evolved, Mark and I developed another website in the fall of 2007 to support our growing involvement and our new business, which we named Northern Light Media. Drawing on our many years of experience with the Internet and the still-new phenomena which would become known as social media, we live-blogged races, provided excellent photo coverage, and created a new column for Alaska's premier online newsmagazine, *Alaska Dispatch*.

Titled *Team and Trail*, the column featured news and commentary of interest to the mushing community, along with articles about the history of mushing, interesting personalities in the sport, slideshows related to mushing, and detailed reports on the major races. Everything we wrote for *Alaska Dispatch* was cross-posted to our Northern Light Media website, and the resulting traffic was rapidly moving our site to the top levels of Internet search engines. Mark and I were once again successfully melding our respective talents and expertise into a dynamic new enterprise.

The decision to produce a video about the champion dog musher Lance Mackey was made in late 2007, as other opportunities for our new business were also breaking. At dinner one evening our friend Donna

Long Hard Trails and Sled Dog Tales

Quante asked if we'd like to go to Nome. The 100th anniversary of the All Alaska Sweepstakes was going to be run in late March, after the finish of the 2008 Iditarod, and Donna was the videographer for the epic event; she would be producing a commemorative DVD about the history and the 100th anniversary running of the race. After much discussion with her and the webmaster for the All Alaska Sweepstakes, our friend Theresa Daily, we signed on to produce a book about the Centennial race, and Mark would use our new video camera to shoot B roll footage for Donna's video documentary. In return we received round-trip tickets to Nome and media access to the historic race. We didn't have enough experience under our belts to fully understand the significance of the event, and we only knew the mushers, judges, race officials and other key players by their reputations. But we were quick learners, and our enthusiasm and our hard-won professionalism made up for our shortcomings.

As I held down the fort at our home in Wauconda and kept the magazine business humming along, Mark and Donna drove to Lance's home north of Fairbanks and interviewed the intrepid musher who'd rocked the sport by winning both the Yukon Quest and the Iditarod back-to-back, with almost the same team of dogs. It was an achievement which would change how many mushers looked at the abilities and potential of their dogs, and Lance's candid discussion of his record-breaking run was a highlight of our film. Mark sent me the audio interview for transcribing and developing the filmscript, and I keyed on a section where Lance was talking about communicating with his dogs. Mark asked him if he thought they understood what a special job they'd done, and as I listened to the now-familiar gravelly voice describe the end of the Iditarod, I felt a broadening smile cross my face:

Well, you know I honestly believe Larry, if anybody understood what was about to happen, he did. And the reason I say this is... You know, every year I've got kind of a routine when we see Nome, I stop, I pet 'em all, I give 'em all loving and tell 'em that when we get to the finish line there's not going to be time to thank them and whatnot, because there's going to be a crowd of people, so I do it out on the sea ice, or I do it on Cape Nome or something.

This year I pulled over top Cape Nome, and we'd been in the race - in the hunt - since the beginning. But I never get... I never... It's not over 'til it's over. You know, I've had incidents where I've got lost miles from the finish line. So I had a nice lead when I left White Mountain, and I knew I was in a good position, but still, I had 70 miles to go.

So anyway, I get to Cape Nome and there it was, nobody's behind me, so I stopped, and I petted everybody, and I gave them all kisses and stuff... And by now I'd already been crying for many miles, because... the emotion was just overwhelming, I couldn't hold it.

So anyway, I got to Cape Nome and I knelt down beside Larry, and he was kind of looking down there like he knew where he was at. And I told him, 'You know, I know you know where you're at, you've been here many times, the one thing I don't think you realize is that we're here first this time.'

And I honestly believe he did know that we were there first this time, because he was looking down the hill with his ears back and like 'why're we stopping, let's get this over with...' and then when I told him that he just kind of looked at me and had this look like 'yeah, I know what we're doin'...' He just had this look, and um... I know he knew what we were about to accomplish.

And he confirmed it when we got to the finish line and they put him up on this pedestal and he sat there so tall and so proud, just looking around, and he made sure everyone took pictures, and he even sat there with his eyes closed, half falling asleep, trying to... I mean, he knew that this was his time. Whether he knew that he was there first or not, I don't know if he knows that, but he knows that he accomplished something pretty special.

While the inevitable naysayers were insisting that his string of victories were merely coincidence and a run of uncommonly good luck, Lance was justifiably proud of his accomplishments and the unprecedented media attention his team had won by doing what had been considered impossible. But he was quick to point out what he rightly considered his greater achievement. It came when Donna interjected a question toward the end of the interview, asking Lance about his predictions for 2008. Lance's reply was guarded and reserved, and is especially interesting in light of his still-to-come history-making victories:

Obviously number one is just to enjoy what I'm doing. That's the most important to me, I can't understand doing something you don't like doing, it's just too damned expensive. But as far as performance?

Lance nods his head, thinking about his answer for a moment.

I'm realistic about this. One of the main reasons I'm racing in the Quest, Iditarod, and the Sweepstakes. My goal is the top three in the Quest, top ten in the Iditarod, and I'm gonna win the Sweepstakes. That's my goal. But realistically? It's a dog race and anything can happen.

So I'm not banking on any of them. If I could do well in one of the three, that's a good year. And by keeping that kind of an attitude, as opposed to saying I'm going to win one of the three, or I'm going to repeat last year's performance, I think that's ridiculous. But I think keeping a level head like that and being realistic, my finishing position will be better than I predict.

I've been asked many times, since last year, what do I do to beat last year's performance? And being the Quest and the Iditarod are the two biggest races in the world, it's hard to top that, except... to do it again. That'd be the only way. And I'd love to! I'd love to repeat that! If I even come close, that'd be a great year!

And then he revealed the attitude which would win him the honored title of 'The Dogfather' in the 2010 Iditarod:

But more than anything, I want my team to look the way they did at the finish line this year. People are still talking about that. Not that I won both races, but how the team looked at the end. And that, to me, is something special, because it's not just from the fans and the media, it's from my competitors. When my competitors can basically suck up their pride a little bit and admit that my team looked better than theirs - and that's hard to do! Even myself, I want to brag about my team, my dogs and the way they look, but for my competitors to take note of that, and to comment on it, that, to me, is priceless!

I'd love to have another trophy. I'd love to have another new Dodge truck. But more than anything, I love to hear the comments people make about how my team looks.

CHAPTER SIX

Whitehorse, Yukon Territory

At the Carmacks checkpoint that morning Donna and I joined the now-familiar media people in the comfortable community center, which had been appropriated as the hub of activity for the race. We uploaded photos and I wrote race reports, and we kept an ear open for signals that a musher was nearing town. A report which later ran on the Yukon Quest website explained what happened next:

"Ken Anderson and Lance Mackey are keeping Yukon Quest watchers on their toes. To everyone's shock, the two rivals swooped into Carmacks at 10:40 and 10:43 a.m. They weren't expected to arrive until around 1 p.m. or even later, as everyone expected them to stop for a much-needed rest somewhere in the 66 miles (106 kilometres) between Carmacks Checkpoint and Pelly Crossing Checkpoint."

When the 'musher in sight' signal came at 10:35 am we hurried out to the high bank along the frozen Yukon River and tried to determine who the incoming team belonged to. As I wrote for our Northern Light Media website later that morning, the resulting discussion among the gathered watchers was amusing: "Ken?" "Or Lance?" "It's Ken... No, it's Lance!" "No... that's definitely Ken!"

It turned out to be Ken Anderson, who brought his ten dogs to a smooth stop in front of the community center as the race officials and vets gathered around to perform their duties.

Seemingly within seconds the cry came, "Another team!" and we knew it would be Lance. His team swung up off the river and past most of the officials, who scrambled after him as Lance finally brought his dogs to a halt, entering an arrival time three minutes after Ken's.

The formalities over, both teams were led around behind the community center to the area designated for them. As we filmed and photographed, Lance removed booties and harnesses, applied salves and ointments to tired paws, pushed pills down dog-throats, snacked his dogs and prepared to cook their food, keeping up a running commentary about what he was doing all the while. Chores done, he retired to the community center for a quick meal, and then disappeared into a room marked "Mushers Only."

I later posted this to our Northern Light Media website: *Lance Mackey straggled out of the quiet room for mushers at the Carmacks checkpoint around 5:15 pm, followed by Ken Anderson a moment later. Both wandered down the hall and settled into chairs beside a row of lockers as reporters gathered to hear their upcoming strategies. Ken spoke almost inaudibly into the mike, perhaps because Lance was pulling on his boots less than a dozen feet away?*

Lance headed outside and as he pulled his coat on and collected an armload of gear he said he and Ken had a 'sort of mutual understanding' that they'd both spend eight hours here. Then Lance smiled and said, 'But I'm keeping an eye on him.'

Lance and Ken both left the comfortable Carmacks checkpoint within minutes of each other: Lance at 7:20 and Ken ten minutes later at 7:30. Lance's parting comment was 'ten minutes is all I need...'

There was only one more checkpoint between Carmacks and the end of the race. Braeburn Lodge, an official checkpoint since 1999, was a potentially challenging 77 trail miles away, 100 miles from Whitehorse. A mandatory eight hour rest would be taken at the home of the enormous Braeburn cinnamon buns before the final non-stop push to the finish.

When Lance pulled into the Braeburn Lodge checkpoint at 5:53 the following morning, Ken had fallen behind, running with three fewer dogs than Lance's team and arriving at 6:12 am. Clearly Lance's team was faster, but the question on everyone's mind in Braeburn was could he hold the lead and win an unprecedented fourth consecutive Yukon Quest?

Around 9 am I posted this report to our Northern Light Media website: *The Braeburn Lodge checkpoint is a cozy small place, warm and friendly and full of good smells - those tremendous cinnamon buns, you know - and when Donna and I got in Lance was happily plowing through a big plate of three eggs, ham, toast and 'a whole field of potatoes!'*

As he ate, Race Marshall Doug Grilliot was telling him about the trail ahead, including a bad bit of unavoidable overflow 18" deep on a lake a little over 12 miles out. The Canadian Rangers are running four to five hours ahead of the mushers to check and clear the trail, but no one was optimistic that they'd be able to do anything about the overflow - although tongue-in-cheek comments are still going around the cafe about building a 'floating bridge' or just 'draining the lake...' Lance commented that he really didn't like overflow...

Lance plans to drop one dog - maybe two - here in Braeburn. He said Pimp has a sore shoulder and is holding him back, and he was considering dropping Dred as well and just going with his trusted veterans. When Tonya commented that he'll want to put veterans in the lead when he gets to the overflow, Lance countered that when he gets to that point he'll be the veteran!

Lance thought it would take about 14 hours to get to Whitehorse; he can leave here at 1:53 pm, and Ken Anderson will be 15 minutes behind him. He admits that Ken will be pushing him hard and that he'll have to kick and run a lot to stay ahead of him. From here to Whitehorse it'll be an exciting sled dog race!

The trail from Braeburn to Whitehorse followed the Old Dawson Overland Trail for 70-some miles across lakes and through rolling timbered hills, before dropping onto the Takhini River for approximately 20 miles, which led to the broad Yukon River for the final ten miles into Whitehorse.

Regarding the reported overflow conditions on the trail, I posted this report to our website: *A trail report just came in from someone who'd snowmachined out from the Whitehorse end. They said there are two bad overflow areas, one 4 to 5 miles out of Braeburn, knee deep and about 100 meters (300') wide, then another the same depth and length about an hour further on. The Canadian Rangers are just getting ready to leave here and we overheard one say they'll try to find a way around the overflows and mark the trail for the mushers.*

Lance was in a jovial mood as he prepared to leave the checkpoint that afternoon, rolling around in the straw with his dogs much to the delight of the onlooking photographers. He pulled his snowhook precisely eight hours after arriving, at 1:53 pm, having dropped one dog. Ken followed him promptly when his own eight hours were up, also dropping another dog and checking out at 2:12 pm. The race was on!

Donna and I enjoyed the afternoon drive through the beautiful Yukon wilderness, and upon arrival in Whitehorse we checked into the RiverView Hotel, directly across the street from the finish line near the White Pass & Yukon Route train depot. We caught up with email, enjoyed a leisurely dinner, then took a quick nap and prepared for the long night ahead. The frontrunners were expected to finish sometime after midnight.

Long Hard Trails and Sled Dog Tales

There was a party mood under the Yukon Quest banner as people jostled for position. Our media badges gained admittance to the finish chute for Donna and I, and we chatted amicably with the gathered handlers, wives, judges, vets, and other media crews, most of whom we now knew by name. It was bitingly cold, but spirits were high as people murmured speculations about which team would arrive first. At the end of the chute Lance's wife Tonya chatted easily with Ken's wife Gwen Holdmann, but it was obvious each was hoping to see their husband's team cross under the banner first.

Reports began coming in that a team had been spotted, and the tension in the chute became palpable. Everyone peered into the darkness until finally the bobbing light of a headlamp came into view, approaching the finish chute, and the enthusiastic crowd of almost five hundred fans held their collective breath – was it Lance? Was it Ken? Lance? Ken?

It was Lance. We held a victory celebration of sorts over pizza and beer at Flipper's Pub, reliving Lance's record-setting fourth championship and barely daring to hope that his team might repeat the performance in the Iditarod, only two weeks away. Donna and I filmed an interview with Lance in the lobby of the hotel the next morning, then spent a couple of hours filming the dogs as he fed them and chatted with well-wishers and passers-by. Two teenage girls came up to him with copies of the *Whitehorse Star* with his face almost life-sized on the front page, and he stopped to read the caption before posing with the two for a fan photo.

After the dogs were taken care of Donna and I headed downtown to do some shopping, and as we were taking photographs of each other in front of the Klondike Gold Rush Prospector's statue, Lance and Tonya crossed the street and invited us to join them for a drink.

We headed for a nearby lounge and whiled away the rest of the afternoon talking of races past and future, and as the liquid relaxation took hold, Lance shared a daydream of someday owning a place near Unalakleet. There was a serene smile on his rugged face as he talked about that faraway country.

Donna and I didn't stay for the Finish Banquet. After breakfast the following morning we packed our bags and headed for home, to get ready for the upcoming Iditarod and the All Alaska Sweepstakes soon after it finished. We learned later that it would've been well worth staying for the Finish Banquet festivities, as noted in this official media report from the Yukon Quest:

WHITEHORSE, YUKON (February 23, 2008) – The 2008 Yukon Quest Finish Banquet had it all, including a marriage proposal by 10th Place musher William Pinkham to his dog handler and girlfriend, Jodi.

But it was probably four-time Champion Lance Mackey's emotional response to being chosen for the 2008 Veterinarian's Choice Award that will stay in everyone's mind when the 25th Yukon Quest is but a distant memory.

Mackey, 37, was his upbeat and humble self while accepting his prize for First Place for the fourth year in a row.

"I don't think this is ever going to get old... I am absolutely blessed with a beautiful family, a beautiful wife, a beautiful dog team and people who support all of our madness," said Mackey,

He praised the Second Place finisher and his only rival in this race, who also happens to be his neighbour in Fairbanks, AK. "Ken Anderson, you put on a hell of a race, made it exciting, kept me on my toes. It's hard to keep up with a high-caliber team like that."

But when the surprise announcement came that Mackey had been chosen by the Yukon Quest's team of 14 veterinarians for his superb dog care on the trail, the man they call "invincible" was visibly shocked and shaken. "This means more to me than winning this damn race," said Mackey. In his earlier acceptance speech he spoke at length about his dog team and how, "for whatever reason they go out of their way to please me."

Mackey's fourth win this year is a Yukon Quest record. He confirmed plans to run the Yukon Quest next year with the goal of achieving five championships in a row.

Anderson, 35, who also received the 2008 Rookie of the Year Award, was less committal. "I will be back next year if I can."

In just a week's time, both Anderson and Mackey will compete in another 1,000-mile race, the Iditarod.

In 2007, Mackey became the first person in history to win the Yukon Quest and the Iditarod in the same year. The world will be watching to see if he does it again—and whether Anderson can steal this championship away from him.

Chapter Seven

Willow, Alaska

Back in Wasilla again, I helped Mark edit the Lance Mackey documentary while we prepared for the 2008 Iditarod and All Alaska Sweepstakes races. It took me a bit to get the hang of editing video, but once I figured out the process it was fun and enjoyable, and not unlike editing for print production. Maintain the storyline, edit out the unnecessary parts, and keep the whole thing focused on the subject, which in this case was Lance and how he'd become not only a champion musher, but one who was radically shaking up the way races were run. His uncanny ability to go longer and farther than other mushers, and his dogs' remarkable willingness to match his seeming tirelessness, were creating a noticeable stir in the media.

The *Anchorage Daily News*, Alaska's largest newspaper, featured Lance on the cover of a special full-color glossy insert for the 2008 Iditarod. With his head thrown back in a jubilant victory howl, forefingers of both hands extended high under the famous Burled Arch, Lance was relishing his moment in the sun. It was the same Bob Hallinen photo which had graced the front page of the March 14, 2007 issue of the *News*, under the title "Idita-Quest Champ, Mackey Makes Mushing History," and for which the caption had noted that "Mackey became the third member of his family to win the race. His father, Dick, won in 1978, and his brother Rick won in 1983."

The 2008 insert's cover text read: "Double Trouble?" And the question on everyone's minds was right there in print: "Can Lance Mackey repeat his remarkable victories and start a new dynasty?"

It was heady stuff, being part of his media team. We all had media badges which granted behind-the-scenes access to the Ceremonial Start on Anchorage's snow-packed Fourth Avenue after the gates had been closed to the public. We filmed Lance dropping his dogs, feeding and checking them, and then harnessing the team in readiness for the ceremonial 11-mile run through the closed streets and along bike paths of Anchorage. Campbell Airstrip was the end of the run, and Mark was the designated driver for Lance's dogtruck, which would leave when he did to be in place for the re-loading at the airstrip. With bib number six Lance would be among the first to go out under the banner which marked the start of this showy beginning for the epic race. The next day, Sunday, the real race to Nome would begin in earnest 70 miles north of Anchorage, on the thick ice of Willow Lake.

With 95 teams in the 36th annual running, the raucous sound of thousands of excited huskies straining at their harnesses and trying to gain traction mingled with the muffled road of the crowd, which echoed between the buildings on Fourth Avenue. The temperature was 20 above and the entire scene before us looked like something out of a travelogue: the colorful teams, the gaily dressed fans, the mushers in their ceremonial gear, the handlers and volunteers and officials and sponsors and the media teams like us, hurriedly trying to capture all of the sights and sounds of the frenetic event.

We met Lance's graciously smiling Idita-Rider, Janet Tremer from Cooperstown, Pennsylvania, and her husband Walt. They were major sponsors of Lance's Comeback Kennel, and Janet had won the online auction bid to ride as Lance's passenger on the annual canine parade across Anchorage to the airstrip. Tucked snugly into the sled, she grinned broadly as the signal came for Lance's team to start advancing up the street to the the starting chute.

Mark snapped a few last photographs of the team and then bounded back to the dogtruck to begin weaving his way out of the start area, while I headed for the start chute ahead of Lance's team, ducking under elbows and sliding between local and national media people to be in a good position to film their departure.

The front page of the *Anchorage Daily News* that morning once again featured head shots of six of Lance's dogs, this time labeled 'Leaders of the Pack.' Larry, Hobo, Rapper, Hansom, Foster, and the lone female Lippy had all been with Lance in his previous Iditarod victory, and had also been part of his team in the 2007 and 2008 Yukon Quest wins.

The article accompanying their photos, by ADN reporter Kevin Klott, explained: *Even if the Comeback Kennel doesn't four-peat, if all six cross the finish line in Nome they could set a new standard for dog durability.*

The article went on to explain why Lance's superstar, the legendary Zorro, was missing from the ranks: *Zorro, Mackey's most-prized dog and the kennel's main stud, nearly died of pneumonia in last year's Iditarod. Veterinarians didn't hold out much hope for the male leader after he got sick. A year later the 9-year-old had regained enough strength to finish the Yukon Quest.*

Long Hard Trails and Sled Dog Tales

"It's incredible," Mackey said Thursday, "A lot of veterinarians are still shaking their heads... that he's still able to run."

Zorro's final race will be the All-Alaska Sweepstakes, a 408-mile race that takes place two weeks after the Iditarod in Nome. Mackey hopes Zorro and the rest of his team will have enough juice in the tank to propel them to the $100,000 winner-take-all championship, the largest winning payout in the history of Alaska sports.

Early the next morning Mark and I were on our way to the wide spot in the Parks Highway called Willow, for the re-start on Willow Lake. Flashing our media badges, we made our way to Lance's dogtruck and met Donna and Theresa already chatting with Lance and the crew and snapping photographs. In the number six starting position, Lance would be among the first of the 95 mushers to hit the trail, so he was wasting no time in making sure everything was ready to go.

We watched as dogtruck after dogtruck rolled down the hill past the Willow Community Center and out onto the frozen surface of Willow Lake. I recognized a few teams from the Yukon Quest, but we were still novices to this game and mostly just took it all in in wide-eyed silence.

The television crews interviewed Lance and filmed his dogs, and Mark and I smiled to ourselves as he shared the same well-rehearsed answers we'd heard the day before. "Larry needs no introduction; he's finished nine 1,000-mile races..." "Hobo's my speed, when I put him up front he makes my whole team go faster..." "Hansom's the only dog that goes back to my Dad's breeding, so he's kind of sentimental to me..."

We met Lance's mom, Kathie Smith, and friends who'd come from near and far to wish him well. At some point in the process Mark pulled the paper plate which had Lance's starting position written on it in black marker off the dogtruck's windshield. He wrote the names of the sixteen dogs, in the order they were harnessed and clipped into their places on the gangline, on the back of the paper plate: Zena and Rev up front in lead, Hansom and Larry right behind them in swing, then Hobo and Lippy, Paulie and Dred, Rapper and Pimp (my favorite after the venerable Larry),

Foster and Raunchy, Hayden and Boycuz, and then Stitch and Fudge in wheel.

When the time came to line out the team we helped hold them in place until Lance said he was ready to advance to the starting chute. We wished him good luck, Mark shook his hand and I gave him a quick hug, and then he was off, making his way across the lake to once again take his place under the start banner in the chute.

As Lance's beautiful team trotted confidently across the ice, heads turned to respectfully watch them pass by. Breaking records and setting precedents once thought impossible, they were already on their way into the mushing history books, and whenever people gathered to share stories of the legends of the sport, Lance Mackey's name would be among the first spoken.

Mark and I finalized the documentary and got it ready for production, with a striking photo of Lance coming up the Yukon River and into Dawson City on the cover, his dogs looking bright and alert, with their jaunty red coats and Lance's red snowsuit contrasting nicely against the snow. Donna had done the voiceover for the introduction to the video, and Kyf Brewer, a professional musician and longtime friend of hers, had sent us a CD of beautiful original music for the score.

With the documentary finally finished, Mark and I turned our attention to wrapping up our May-June issue of the magazine, to clear our slate for the upcoming All Alaska Sweepstakes. We ran our standard selection of good articles and informative and entertaining columns, the latter provided by a reliable staff of long-running columnists. Mark and I edited and published the magazine, but at this point, with far more good content coming in than we were able to print, we were not writing anything for inclusion.

Around this same time we received a phone call from our office manager, Stacy, an old family friend who was keeping things running smoothly at the magazine office, which was located adjacent to our home in Washington state. Stacy had received a phone call from Mimi Rothschild, the charter school academies owner, who was trying to contact me. According to Stacy, Ms. Rothschild was very upset with me over a situation which had transpired the year before, and she was claiming that I was publishing untrue and malicious things about her and had cost her millions of dollars in damages and untold other losses.

The truth of the matter was quite different, and well-documented on the Internet. It involved, among many people, several of our current and former magazine columnists, and a national organization for homeschooling families which we had helped create a few years before, the American Homeschool Association.

There had been a running online battle with Ms. Rothschild which boiled down to knowledgable people trying to find a way to share news and information about her multitudinous and seemingly spurious business enterprises, and Ms. Rothschild blocking those efforts at every turn and threatening legal action against everyone who so much as mentioned her name or any of her many business fronts.

We learned over the course of this conflict that Mimi Rothschild functioned under several aliases, including Mimi Roth and Miriam Mandell. She also claimed to be a child's rights advocate and to have authored a total of seven books on children's education, and she was the founder of several online homeschooling academies, including The Einstein Academy, The Jubilee Academy, The Grace Academy, The Narnia Academy, and The MorningStar Academy, all of which were aggressively marketed to Christian homeschoolers. There were multiple complaints filed against her academies at online consumer advisory sites, and favorable reports about any of her handiwork were very thin and difficult to find.

My response to Ms. Rothschild's attempts to contact me through Stacy were the same as they had been a couple of years previously when she had tried to contact me: I advised her that I was not interested in private communication with her, and that there were multiple open forums for discussing any grievances she might have. The woman was becoming a time sink and an emotional drain, and I advised my entire staff to avoid engaging with her if possible.

The 2008 Iditarod was exciting for fans from the beginning, with five former champions and teams from three foreign countries in the race. During his 24-hour mandatory layover in the remote checkpoint of Cripple, four-time champion Martin Buser amused everyone except the officials when he gave his IonEarth tracking device to an Iditarod Air Force pilot headed back down the trail to McGrath. Fans watching the race online via the tracker results were confused by readings which apparently showed Buser's team traveling south along the Iditarod Trail at 130 miles per hour!

The race teams jockeyed for position and by the time Lance Mackey and Jeff King arrived at the Ruby checkpoint, just past the halfway point, they were in first and second position respectively, and the always canny Jeff King had begun good-naturedly heckling Mackey. As he drove his 16-dog team into the parking area, Jeff asked Lance if he was worried yet. It was a belated comeback to Lance's comment in Unalakleet the year before that "King should be worried," but Lance just laughed and said no, he wasn't worried. They were both, however, setting up for an epic battle to the finish line.

The unusually warm weather was taking a toll on the dogs, with temperatures between 30 and 40 degrees during the day. The mushers were running their teams in the cool of the night, and Lance had made a marathon 14-hour night-time run from the halfway checkpoint of Cripple to the Yukon River, where, as the first musher to the Yukon, he enjoyed a six-course gourmet meal spread before him by the Millennium Hotel, and collected $5,000.

By the time the two teams crossed the Kaltag Portage and rolled into Unalakleet, King was in the lead, and he took the trophy and $2,500 in gold nuggets as the first musher to reach the coast. Behind the two front-runners was a chase pack made up of determined champions, including five-time champion Rick Swenson, four-time champion Martin Buser, and three-time Yukon Quest champion Hans Gatt. The 2004 Iditarod champion, Mitch Seavey, was in the running, as was Lance's nemesis from the Yukon Quest, Ken Anderson, and no one would make the mistake of underestimating the racing abilities of Ramey Smyth or Zack Steer. Lance noted that the scenario in Unalakleet was almost the same as it had been the previous year, and then he added with a confident smile, "We all know how that story ended."

Anchorage Daily News reporter Kevin Klott kept the suspense going with his colorful tales from the trail. In an article boldly titled "Mind games in play as leaders seek an edge," he wrote from Koyuk: *Icicles dangled from the mustache of defending Iditarod champion Lance Mackey on Monday afternoon as he pulled into this village on the coast of frozen Norton Sound with a four-time champion on his heels.*

The two had just traveled 45 miles from Shaktoolik along windswept ice, fighting a ground blizzard, below-zero wind chill and a nasty headwind. With visibility less than a mile, the two ran close together along the flattest terrain on the 1,100-mile Iditarod Trail. Despite snow swirling around him, Mackey could turn his head and see King's team in the distance.

As they spread straw and heated water for their dogs' meals the two champion mushers sparred with the reporters, each still trying to outfox the other with misleading information about the condition of their dogs or what their intentions were. It was an old ruse, tried and true, and these two were masters at the peak of their game.

Remarkably, Jeff King was still running all 16 dogs he'd started with. Lance's team was down to 12. Veteran *Anchorage Daily News* reporter Craig Medred explained what happened next: "...there was no doubt King's dog's were faster. But at the end, when the mushers were confronted by two difficult climbs, Mackey's gritty canines showed their stuff.

On the trail from Elim to White Mountain on the Bering Sea coast, climbing up over the 1,000-foot summit in the Kwiktalik Mountains that mushers know as 'Little McKinley,' Mackey put time on King's dogs. And again in the Topkok Hills out of White Mountain on the stretch run to

Nome, he pulled away, building on what had been a 57-minute lead at the 8-hour mandatory White Mountain stop.

Lance had gained much of that wide lead in a crowd-pleasing surprise move at Elim, when a cagey plan bluffed his competitor into thinking he was settling in for a nap, so Jeff settled his team in and did likewise, but then the ever-shrewd Mackey quietly crept out of the checkpoint, motioning for the media and checkpoint personnel to keep quiet, and got almost an hour's jump on the sleeping King.

Steve MacDonald, of KTUU Channel 2 in Anchorage, interviewed Lance and Jeff on March 12 and they both had some interesting comments about the episode. Steve opened with the question, *"You told Channel 2 early this morning that the race was won in the village of Elim. Take us back to the checkpoint, tell us what happened. Did you really sneak out of there?"*

Lance Mackey: *"That's exactly what happened. We had to take advantage of a situation. I couldn't outrun him on the trail, that was pretty obvious. It was time to pull out some old tricks and see if they work and low and behold, they did. We caught him napping and I took advantage of it."*

Steve then turned to Jeff and asked: *"Jeff, did he get the drop on you and what was reaction when you found out Lance had left?"*

Jeff King: *"Well, he sure did get a jump on me there. It was amazing, 50 minutes earlier in the race it wouldn't have had quite the impact it did in Elim.*

"Lance and I had teams that were pretty well matched at that point in the race; it would have been hard for either one of us to shake the other without a maneuver like that.

"I was pretty disappointed in myself. Earlier that day, back in Koyuk I lied down closer than normal to Lance and I had my feet on top of his boots that he had drying next to the stove. I knew that the guy might sneak out on me and he was going to have to take his boots to move. Later that night I didn't pay enough attention to the very same situation.

"Fact is Lance led this race pretty much from Takotna. I had an awesome race but I can't begrudge who got here first. He had a heck of a run."

Lance once again loped down Front Street with his team in first place, and this time he silenced the people who'd claimed his first victory was merely "a fluke" or somehow "just luck." He won $69,000 and the keys to another new Dodge pickup, but he also won a place in the lore of mushing. In winning both the Yukon Quest and the Iditarod in the same year, with most of the same dogs, Lance had done the impossible, and now, a year later, he'd done it again.

CHAPTER EIGHT

Nome, Alaska

With the 2008 Iditarod in the record books it was time to turn our attention to the long-anticipated centennial running of the All Alaska Sweepstakes, the oldest organized long distance sled dog race in the world. In fact, the only sporting event in the state older than the Sweepstakes was the Alaska Baseball League's Midnight Sun Game.

There had been informal races since the beginning of man hitching dogs to a sled, but the Sweepstakes, 408 miles from Nome to Candle and return, was the first sled dog race to feature a codified set of rules.

It was a richly historic event, the race which made Leonhard Seppala and Scotty Allen famous. And we were part of the official media team which would be recording the centennial event in photographs, on video, and in a book.

Donna Quante was the videographer, recording the event on film, and Mark was shooting the B roll, or backup video. I was taking photographs and recording copious notes for the book. Jan DeNapoli was also taking photographs, and hers would form the core of the book I would later write. Jodi Bailey, a champion musher from north of Fairbanks, was recruited to help design and maintain the spreadsheet which became the online leaderboard, a far cry from the blackboard at the Board of Trade saloon which tracked the early Sweepstakes races.

Our friend Theresa Daily, a retired musher turned web designer and media guru, was the webmaster for the race; she had organized the media coverage and was our connection to the race committee in Nome. Mark and I and Donna arrived at Theresa's home in Chugiak with enough gear and luggage to outfit a small army, and we'd mailed several boxes of food, more clothes, and extra batteries to Nome ahead of ourselves.

The flight to Nome was spectacular, a bright sunny day, and I loved watching the peaks and valleys of the Alaska Range pass below us. The rivers looping and snaking across western Alaska were endlessly fascinating, and then the sea ice on Norton Sound, with huge blue leads, or open water, parting the ice... It was a whole new world, and I was mesmerized by the beauty of it all. And then suddenly Nome was under our wings, and I marveled at how small it looked against the frozen edge of the Bering Sea.

Nome! The gold rush city, stuff of dreams, a place my mom had always wanted to see, and I tried to take it all in so I could adequately describe it to her when I got home. She'd given me a black and white print of the town as a tent city, and I'd studied it often in the previous weeks, scarcely believing the luck which was taking me to see that storied town for myself.

Nome's legendary Leo Rasmussen met us at the airport, and chuckled as he eyed our small mountain of baggage. But he gamely helped load it into the back of his SUV and we set out for a look at the town. Because Mark and I and Donna had never been to Nome before, Leo gave us a celebratory tour of the town's highlights, pointing out the cemetery, the harbor, the house Leonhard Seppala had lived in, the largest gold pan in Alaska and the statues of the Three Lucky Swedes who'd found gold.

Leo regaled us with bits of local lore and pointed out the roads to Teller to the north and Council to the east, both seventy-some miles away over roads which were snowed in now, and he told us what to expect in the days ahead as everyone got ready for the big race. Then he delivered us to our home in Nome, the elegant Aurora Inn, with its strangely out of place and somewhat antebellum white facade; not what we'd expected to find in this northernmost town with the rugged reputation. But we were delighted with the executive suite reserved for us, as it was very spacious and quite comfortable, with two bedrooms, a full kitchen and living room, and a lovely bay window overlooking the Bering Sea.

Group consensus gave Mark and I the bedroom also facing the sea, and it was lovely to wake up and look out over the ice and bask in the very history of the place. I found myself thinking of Mom often, and her black sweatshirt with 'Nome' embroidered across the front, and I decided I would bring her with me to this storied place someday...

The following days were something of a blur, as we attended the many events leading up to the race start. The whole town seemed as excited as we were about the race, and it was fun meeting the officials, the mushers, the townspeople, and the other people who'd traveled to Nome for this great commemorative race. The purse was the richest ever offered for a sporting event in Alaska, a jaw-dropping $100,000.00, winner take all.

We were surprised to learn that only 16 teams had entered to vie for the purse, but among them were champion mushers whose race records left no doubt that they were there to win, including Lance and Jeff. It was interesting that both had agreed there was no rivalry between them in Steve MacDonald's KTUU interview, when he'd queried them about what many people were wondering: "Is Mackey and King becoming a rivalry like we saw between Rick Swenson and Susan Butcher?"

Lance replied first: "I hope not. Nothing personal. He's a competitor; I want to beat him just as badly as he wants to beat me. I don't think it's going to become a bad relation sort of deal."

Jeff concurred: "I've raced Lance's dad and his brother. It's easy for me to remember that this is the third Mackey I've raced. It brings back a lot of memories. Lance was 10 years old when I was racing his dad back up in the Cold Foot, that's a little bit of a shock for me."

Lance's reply underscored the age difference between them: "I grew up watching these guys race so I've got a little idea of what it takes to try and outrun them."

In their book *The Cruelest Miles* cousins Gay and Laney Salisbury set the stage for the upcoming race by describing the situation in turn-of-the-century Nome, Alaska:

From the beginning, Nome depended on its dogs. Teams were drafted into service as mail trucks, ambulances, freight trains, and long-distance taxis. The demand for sled dogs was so high, particularly in the northern gold rushes, that the supply of dogs ran out and a black market for the animals sprang up in the states. Any dog that looked as if it could pull a sled or carry a saddlebag-whether or not it was suited to withstand the cold-was kidnapped and sold in the north.

Skilled dog drivers were in high demand, and his well-known travels and exploits earned A.A. "Scotty" Allan a reputation as a dog man of the highest caliber; he was reputedly able to train almost any dog into reliable service as a sled dog. In the early years of the Sweepstakes, Scotty Allan won most of the races, and for many years his teams were considered the best in Alaska. In his 1931 autobiography titled *Gold, Men and Dogs* he told a harrrowing tale of the 1910 Sweepstakes race, when he literally "fell off a mountain" when a snow ledge gave way beneath his team and he and his team rolled over two hundred feet down a nearly vertical drop, but they gathered themselves and finally arrived at the finish line with "five dogs hitched, two in the sled, and three tied behind."

The course set for the All Alaska Sweepstakes was a tough one, traversing the width of the remote Seward Peninsula from south to north and back again. Nome Kennel Club President Esther Birdsall Darling described the trail in her promotional booklet, *The Great Dog Races of Nome*: *The route varies consistently - from hour to hour - from narrow passage between towering ice hummocks of the Bering Sea to wide plains of unbroken snow; from the steep slopes of Topkok Hill, to the desolate, storm-swept waste of Death Valley; from the pleasant winding road through wooded Council district, to the trackless and treacherous ice on rivers and lakes.*

Archdeacon of the Yukon Hudson Stuck also described the country in his 1914 book, *Ten Thousand Miles with a Dogsled*: *Traveling, like so many other things, is very different on the Seward Peninsula. The constant winds beat down and harden the snow until it has a crust that will carry a man anywhere.*

A little later, after describing the local meteorological peculiarities, he continues: *So a striking difference in travel at once manifests itself; in the interior all the snow is soft except on a beaten trail itself, while in the Seward Peninsula all the snow is alike hard. The musher is not confined to trails-he can go where he pleases; and his vehicle is under no necessity of conforming in width to a general usage of the country-it may be as wide as he pleases. Hence the hitching of dogs two and three abreast; hence the sleds of twenty-two, twenty-four, or twenty-six inches in width. My tandem rig aroused the curiosity of those who saw it.*

Of the trail from Candle to Council the Archdeacon wrote: *For a while there would be travel such as one sees in children's picture-books, where the man sits in his sled and cracks his whip and is whisked along as gaily as you please - such travel as I had never had before; but there was no pleasure in it - the wind saw to that.*

The other legendary musher of the All Alaska Sweepstakes was Leonhard Seppala, whose contributions to the All Alaska Sweepstakes, to dog mushing, and to the development of the Siberian Husky cannot be overstated.

In *The World of Sled Dogs*, author Lorna Coppinger wrote ten years after Seppala's death in 1967: *No dog driver has the status, the reknown, the respect of his colleagues as does Leonhard Seppala.*

Leonhard Seppala's reputation was created by his victories in the All Alaska Sweepstakes, but the intrepid musher went on to play a pivotal role in the 1925 Serum Run to Nome, when his famous racing leader, Togo, led Seppala's team through a blinding blizzard and across the treacherous frozen Norton Sound.

In his classic history of the Nome Kennel Club, written around 1990, Nome historian Howard Farley described the first year of the All Alaska Sweepstakes race: *The All Alaska Sweepstakes got its start in 1908. The first race was a very slow race. It was run in about 100 hours, perhaps a little more. The contestants were basically freighting - type teams, which is why the times were slower.*

A fierce blizzard contributed greatly to the slow times of the inaugural race. A newspaper article in the *San Francisco Chronicle*, dated April 25, 1909, was written by Frank M. Hertzer, described as the first white man to cross the Seward Peninsula. He wrote of the beginning of the race: *About forty miles from Nome one of the severest blizzards of the season was encountered, the temperature dropping to thirty below zero, with the wind blowing from the north at a velocity of about fifty miles an hour.*

So violent was the storm that of the ten racing teams, six were forced into Brown's road house and held there for nearly twenty hours. Of the remaining four, one lost a dog by freezing to death in the storm; another was lost, going as far as Bluff without discovering his whereabouts; and the third was forced to remain at Topkok.

Hertzer went on: *After having been delayed some twenty hours at Bluff, and when the storm had somewhat abated, three of the teams pulled out together, with three others following shortly afterward, and then the race again began in grim earnest.*

On the return from Candle to Nome the race was even more furious and exciting than on the trip up. 'Could dogs and men possibly last without sleep and rest? Could the terrific speed at which they were coming be maintained? Was it possible that human and canine endurance could withstand such a strain?' were questions which everyone was asking of his neighbor.

Throughout the long nights and days the crowds never left the bulletin boards. The entire population seemed to be perfectly willing to do without food and sleep until the race was finally determined. As was remarked by an old racer from the States, "The two-minute sensation of a Tennessee or Kentucky Derby was prolonged for five solid days!"

In 1909 the time was decreased a little by a Norwegian immigrant named Louis Thrustup, who was driving a team owned by a Russian fur trader, William Goosak. The dogs were from Goosak's homeland, Siberia, and they were much smaller and lighter than the typical large freighting dogs which the miners and mail team drivers were running in the Sweepstakes race.

They garnered a lot attention from the mushers and spectators in Nome, being "thick-coated, prick-eared, tough-footed, swift little foxy-looking dogs." They were the forerunners of today's Siberian Husky.

The record which was still standing at the time of the Centennial race was set in 1910 by dogs also imported from the Siberian side, by the Scottish nobleman Fox Maule Ramsay. Impressed with the 1909 teams, he traveled to the Anadyr River area of Siberia and brought back around sixty of the remarkably fleet and hardy dogs.

Long Hard Trails and Sled Dog Tales

Ramsay entered three teams in the 1910 All Alaska Sweepstakes, including one he was driving himself. But it was another of his teams, driven by a man known as 'Iron Man' Johnson, which took the number one position with a time of 74 hours and some odd minutes.

Howard Farley noted, *Down through the years, until 1918, the All Alaska Sweepstakes continued with great mushers like Scotty Allan and Leonard Seppala trying, trying and trying to break that record of Iron Man Johnson's. Leonard Seppala was to win the race three times and Scotty Allan was to win it three times, but in all their trying they could not best the record of Iron Man Johnson.*

The All Alaska Sweepstakes races were held until after the first World War was over, and then interest in sled dog racing waned with the decrease in gold mining in the Nome area, which meant the dogteams which hauled supplies to the mines and gold from them were no longer necessary. Shorter races still tested the mettle of dogs and men, but no Sweepstakes races were held until 1983, when the 75th Anniversary race was won by Rick Swenson, the only five-time Iditarod champion. His partner in that race was Sonny Lindner, who'd been called "a dog musher's dog musher," and who would go on to win the inaugural Yukon Quest the following year. Lindner had placed in the Iditarod top ten five times and now he was back for the 2008 Sweepstakes race, once again teaming up with the venerable Rick Swenson.

Pre-race festivities included the Sweepstakes Queen contest and her official coronation, the mushers' bib drawing and taking their official photos, an art fair displaying many beautiful and unique creations, another fair for the native artisans and craftsmen, and the hilarious hi-jinks of the Nome Follies, with music, dancing, oration, history, a sing-a-long and can-can girls, followed by a preview showing of the new city of Nome promotional DVD, 'There's No Place Like Nome.' All in all it was a fun and exciting few days leading up to the ceremonial start.

Long Hard Trails and Sled Dog Tales

Mark and I were continuing the monitor the situation with Mimi Rothschild and her threats to sue, but it still didn't seem like anything more than the somewhat outlandish machinations we'd seen from her before. It appeared to us that she used controversy as a desperate form of advertising and promotion, keeping her name in the news and in front of people whatever the cost in terms of reputation. We were reminded of the old newspaper quote, "I don't care what they say about me as long as they spell my name right."

The day of the race appreciative fans formed the start chute down Front Street, standing shoulder to shoulder with no barrier between them and the teams, just as the crowds of 1908 had done. They roared their approval as Sweepstakes Queen Janice Doherty was ceremoniously pulled to the starting line by her team of Husky Men. The traditional burled arch had been placed backwards and draped with the gold and green banner of the All Alaska Sweepstakes proclaiming "100th Anniversary March 26, 2008 $100,000 Winner Take All."

The honorary team, first one out at 10:00 am sharp, was for Peter MacManus, a respected teacher and dog driver from the village of Ambler who'd been killed in a plane crash along with all of his dogs while returning from the 1983 race. The driver and passenger were his grandsons, Peter MacManus and Jayson Russell, there to honor their grandfather's memory.

And then the sixteen racing teams - two women and fourteen men - were sent off one by one at two minute intervals, in a scene just like one described in *The World of Sled Dogs* by Lorna Coppinger: *The noise of the dogs was deafening as they barked incessantly, reflecting the excitement around them, and more than ready for the trail. The drivers busied themselves nervously around their teams, checking again the harnesses, the lines, the long sleds.*

Donna had chosen the end of the street from which to shoot her video footage, just where the teams made a sharp right turn and then headed down a snowy ramp behind the Subway restaurant and onto the Bering

Long Hard Trails and Sled Dog Tales

Sea ice. A seasoned filmmaker, she knew ahead of time that some dramatic action was likely to take place there as the fresh and furiously racing teams rounded the corner.

Mark was given the chute position, and he crouched a team's length in front of the starting line, his video camera meeting each team as it came into the chute, following it through the countdown, and then he would nimbly step out of the way, still filming, as the team gathered itself and tore away down the street.

The footage he secured in the process became the core of the commemorative video, putting the viewer face-to-face with the jumping, barking, totally focused and animated dogs. Seeing his incredible video footage one can feel the tension as the dogs strain to get going, and then at the musher's signal they scramble and dig into the snow, sending it flying behind them as they lunge into their harnesses and set to work. For someone who'd never held a video camera a few short weeks previously it was brilliant shooting, perfectly executed.

With the teams on their way up the trail we settled into our roles as race reporters, getting immediate updates from the race officials and from the ham radio operators who were tracking the race from checkpoint to checkpoint. Jan and Donna flew out to the Council and Haven checkpoints, securing more photos, video, and reports from the trail, while Mark, Jodi, Theresa and I kept websites and the leaderboard updated, press releases and new reports going to the media, and phone calls and emails from fans around the world replied to. It was a heady and exciting time, and we felt lucky to be in the middle of so much history-in-the-making.

As an introduction to the trail for race fans, someone had taken the time to type up a flyer and copies were printed and distributed from Nome's mini-convention center, which served as race headquarters and the central location for events and activities. The flyer read, in full: *So what about this All Alaska Sweepstakes route, designed by creators of the Nome Kennel Club to make for such a tough race?*

Most of us will probably never get all the way up that direction, so let's hear a description from 'The Cruelest Miles':

For the first fifty miles, the trail ran east along the blustery coast and up Topkok Mountain, a steep, 600-foot incline rising up over the sea. It turned inland and climbed steadily through willow and cottonwood bush, then across creeks and rivers to Council, a mining settlement 80 miles from Nome. The route snaked through valleys, tiptoed along ridgetops as narrow as a sled was wide, and sloped off into half-mile-long drops. Then, about 120 miles into the race, the trail entered Death Valley.

If the musher had survived this far, he climbed a glacier to cross over the Continental Divide--the boundary line separating the Pacific and Arctic Ocean watersheds. Thirty miles farther lay the turnaround mark, the village of Candle, which was situated near Kotzebue Sound on the north shore of the peninsula. An exhausted and sleep-deprived driver would have to turn around and face the same terrible 204 miles all over again...

Hudson Stuck, Archdeacon of the Yukon and author of *Ten Thousand Miles with a Dog Sled: A Narrative of Winter Travel in Interior Alaska*, had minced no words in describing the route in his 1914 book: *A savage, forbidding country, this whole interior of the Seward Peninsula, uninhabited and unfit for habitation; a country of naked rock and bare hillside and desolate, barren valley, without amenities of any kind and cursed with a perpetual icy blast.*

Into this unforgiving maw had plunged the 16 teams of the 2008 All Alaska Sweepstakes Centennial Race.

Chapter Nine

Seward Peninsula, Alaska

The weather had been on everyone's minds as the Sweepstakes race neared; Jeff King's blog reported that the race would be "challenging," and noted that the wind would be "the critical key in the trail conditions for the race."

An article in the *Anchorage Daily News* just before the race start was titled "Sweepstakes trail conditions are a concern," and the depth of snow in the outlying areas was expected to create problems for the teams on the trail. There were questions without answers, and speculation about just how bad it might get was rampant.

Early reports of the trail up north had mentioned "feet and feet and feet of snow," and a fifty-foot crevasse of collapsed trail. An oft-told tale circulated of trail breakers who'd found one of their own out alongside the trail and when they asked him where his snowmachine was he replied "I'm standing on it!"

Long Hard Trails and Sled Dog Tales

The only Alaskan sporting event older than the All Alaska Sweepstakes was the Alaska Baseball League's Midnight Sun Game, which had been held in Fairbanks since 1906; the Iditarod ran for the first time in 1973, and the Yukon Quest was founded in 1984.

An article for the *Anchorage Daily News* noted that the early-day races were run on "a well-packed survey trail - used daily by dog sleds and horse-drawn carriages to travel from one mine to the next." This Centennial race would be run on a long-abandoned route over a trail put in just for this event.

From our comfortable suite at the Aurora Inn we downloaded photographs and wrote articles and news releases about the start, and from time to time we walked the length of town to the mini-convention center to get updates from the race officials and the ham radio operators who were tracking the progress of the mushers. We talked with the wives and handlers who stayed in Nome, and the race organizers and support teams whose jobs did not entail being out on the trail.

We visited the Nome Library and listened to Howard Farley, who had run the 1973 Iditarod, talk about the history of the races; and we photographed the trophies, banners, timesheets and old leather harnesses of the historic first races in Nome.

Esther Birdsall Darling wrote in her book, *The Great Nome Races: The route varies constantly — from hour to hour–from narrow passage between the towering ice hummocks of the Bering Sea to wide plains of unbroken snow; from the steep slopes of Topkok Hill, to the desolate, storm-swept waste of Death Valley; from the pleasant winding road through wooded Council district, to the trackless and treacherous ice on rivers and lakes.*

From Nome, the trail wound across the Seward Peninsula, 204 miles to the old gold mining town of Candle, named for nearby Candle Creek. According to a booklet titled *The Fairhaven Gold Placers, Seward Peninsula, Alaska*, by Fred Howard Moffit (U.S. Government printing office, 1905), the news of some very rich placer gold finds on Candle Creek drew miners in the late fall of 1901:

Long Hard Trails and Sled Dog Tales

News of the strike spread quickly and was followed by a stampede of miners in the late fall, so that the entire creek was soon taken up and scores of men with rockers busied themselves in cleaning out the richer and more readily worked portions of the gravels. As high as an ounce of gold per day was paid to shovelers on some claims.

Moffit's booklet also explained the origin of the name: *Candle Creek is said to have received its name from the fact that in the springtime, when the prospectors first saw the stream, the willow twigs along its banks were covered with a thick coating of ice, and suggested the name because of their resemblance to candles.*

Before I'd started reading and studying in preparation for this race, I had no knowledge of this part of the state, aware only that Nome had been a gold rush town of the first order. I hadn't known there were actually multiple gold rushes on the Seward Peninsula, or that gold was still being actively mined there: *Harrington (1919) estimates that by 1917 $325,000 of gold (at $20.67/ounce) had been taken from Candle Creek. It is estimated that production from Candle Creek has exceeded 600,000 ounces of gold since 1901 (Williams, 1998).*

Three-time All Alaska Sweepstakes Champion A.A. "Scotty" Allan described the route to Candle in his classic autobiography, *Gold, Men and Dogs* (G.P. Putnam's Sons, 1931): *It was selected because the trail to it from Nome goes over all kinds of country, from sea ice to high mountains, with rivers, tundra, timber, glaciers, and everything else in the way of mental and physical hardships en route. We knew there wouldn't be any doubt about the excellence of a dog or driver that covered it.*

In her booklet and official souvenir history of the race, titled *The Great Dog Races of Nome Held Under the Auspices of the Nome Kennel Club, Nome, Alaska,* author and 1916 Nome Kennel Club President Esther Birdsall Darling described the "why" of the race: *It was early seen that not only would the races furnish much of the winter entertainment, but that there would also be a consistent effort on the part of the dog owners and dog drivers to improve the breed of sled dogs, which up to this time had* been but little considered; an effort to instill into all dog Users an intelligent understanding of the accepted fact that care and kindness to their dogs bring the quickest and surest returns from all standpoints. This has resulted in the development of such a high standard for dogs that not alone is their worth acknowledged throughout Alaska, but their supremacy is conceded the world over.

Leonhard Seppala, who would, like Scotty Allan, win three Sweepstakes championships, became a living legend in Alaska, and in his own autobiography, *Seppala, Alaskan Dog Driver*, written with Elizabeth Ricker, he described a harrowing event which took place during his first Sweepstakes race:

The wind drove us on at a great rate of speed. The snow was whirling in front of my face, suffocating me so that I could hardly get my breath at times. Judging by the time we had been on our way, I figured we ought now to be close to the coast, but I knew that unless I hit Allen Creek and Topkok cabin I should run a chance of falling over the cliffs which ran in succession along the shore.

We were racing southward at a breakneck speed when suddenly there came a lull between puffs of wind and I saw that I was very close to some high, steep place, and as I peered ahead I could see way down below the ice hummocks of the Bering Sea. Suggen was close to the edge of the precipice. I jammed both feet on the brake as we sped downward headed for destruction, but the crust was icy and smooth and I was not able to hold the team. I brought out my emergency steel bar and rammed it into the crust through the hole in my brake made for that purpose, bringing the dogs to a standstill. By that time we were on a steep incline close to the edge of the cliff. I tried to call Suggen back to turn the team, but the wind, which was now blowing furiously again, made it hard for him to hear.

Finally Suggen responded and tried to swing the team, but the young dogs wanted to go with the wind. My first plan was to leave the dogs and the sled and crawl up to safety, but it was so slippery on the crust that my Eskimo mukluks could get no hold, and the more I thought it over the less I could consider leaving my dogs to face such a tragic fate. I thought that perhaps by scrambling up the hillside I might be able to see landmarks, but as soon as I climbed a few feet the wind blew me back to the sled, and my several attempts proved utterly useless. Apparently our fate rested with Suggen. I saw the ice hummocks several hundred feet below, and I thought with horror of what would happen if the steel bar gave way. But the crust was hard an so far it still held. I pictured my sled, my dogs, and myself falling down the two-hundred-foot precipice to the rocks below. It had often happened that people had been lost here and were never heard of until the snow left in the spring, when they were found frozen and mangled on the rocks and ice hummocks.

I spoke again to Suggen, still trying to call him back to me. He did his best to respond, making several efforts to turn, but still the young dogs refused. I kept shouting, and finally the four dogs behind him got the idea, and as Suggen turned the others followed. To my great relief I saw that little by little the whole team was turning, scrambling back up the hillside, digging their claws into the crust, headed toward safety. By some miraculous chance they were able to pull the sled and me up the incline, but I had no feeling of safety until I reached the top, for it seemed that at any moment the strong wind blowing against them might send them sliding back over the precipice. I kept shouting words of encouragement as every dog scratched and pulled, while I used my steel bar to push the sled along–and at that it was slow progress.

Checkpoints and stops along the trail route would include Fort Davis, Hastings, Safety Roadhouse, Solomon, Topkok, Timber Road House, Council, Boston Creek, Telephone Creek, Camp Haven, First Chance, Gold Run and Candle, names which alluded to the history which was being relived as the dogteams made their way north. Race Marshal Al Crane offered the opinion that Esther Birdsall Darling's classic book, *Baldy of Nome*, provided as good a description of the trail as any source available, and a photocopy of the book was kept on the counter at the mini-convention center. Thumbing through the section where the Great Race takes place, my eye caught a description of Scotty Allan's team with

Long Hard Trails and Sled Dog Tales

Baldy in the lead: *At times the hard smooth trail wound like a silver ribbon under the pale glow of the Aurora. Then, with flying feet, they sped along the edge of deep gorges, up steep slopes, and over the glare ice of rivers and lakes.*

I thought about the sixteen teams out on that trail, crossing that same country, and I wondered at the circumstances which had brought me to be in this place at this time. Even as the events were unfolding around me I sensed a kind of epic achievement, a feeling that this was a time like no other in my life had ever been, or was ever likely to be again. To be sharing it with Mark and our friends just seemed like a dream come true, and I shared that dream in my journal:

So here we are in Nome, the teams are off to Candle and the reality is starting to sink in. Nome! Here I am in Nome, Mom's dream destination, and it's nothing like I expected and everything I'd hoped it would be! We are walking historic streets, stepping where Leonard Seppala and Scotty Allan stepped, and I spend a lot of time just staring at the old buildings and trying to imagine what it must have been like in their time. I'm taking lots of photos to share with Mom, I'm going to enlarge and frame several of the best ones and give them to her for her birthday this year - she'll be so excited! Someday I'd like to bring her up here and we can explore some of the outlying areas, and if it's summer maybe we can even look for gold on those fabled black sand beaches.

Many of the people who were volunteering for the race had also been present at the last running of the Sweepstakes in 1983, and their stories of that 75th Anniversary race made the current race easier to track for those of us who were tasked with taking the mushers' progress to fans and followers.

I quoted the volunteers liberally in my news posts and blog entries for our Northern Light Media, and I tried to keep a progression flowing which would later aid my work on the book about the race. I sprinkled photographs throughout my posts and articles, and response and feedback from readers was good.

The race officials had made a special effort to contact relatives and descendants of anyone who'd been involved with the earlier Sweepstakes races, and their attempts had been successful. In addition to the grandsons of Pete MacManus, Ruby Hollembaek, granddaughter of Percy Blatchford, was present for the Centennial run. Percy Blatchford had come into second place behind Scotty Allan in the second All Alaska Sweepstakes race, held in 1909. The Blatchford family would later make a special presentation to one of the mushers: the Blatchford Spirit of the Race Award.

Fred Haswell, a great nephew of Esther Birdsall Darling of the Darling and Allan Racing Kennel, winners in 1909, 1919, and 1911 with Scotty Allan driving, was in Nome for the race.

Carrie Shelley, the great-granddaughter of Johan Hegness, the very first winner of the All Alaska Sweepstakes in 1908, was present; she brought a suitcase full of photographs to the Nome Museum and announced that her great-grandfather's ashes would be moved to the Nome cemetery.

Three children of Carl Charles Johnson had made the trip to Nome for the Sweepstakes race. Johnson had raced in the 1910, 1911, and 1912 Sweepstakes, placing third in the 1911 and 1912 races. To commemorate his races his children, Gene Johnson, Helen McClellon, and Lillian Stevenson, were in Nome, and they told us many engaging stories one afternoon in the comfortable lobby of the Aurora Inn.

As the ongoing reports of the mushers' progress up the trail were received at Race Central there would be a flurry of activity, deciphering the news and comparing where the mushers were in relation to each other. Safety, Solomon, Topkok, Timber, Council....

The Council checkpoint was another gold rush community, founded in 1897 when placer gold was discovered in nearby Ophir Creek. Within a year there were more than 10,000 residents, but most of them left when even larger quantities of gold were discovered near Nome around the turn of the century.

Long Hard Trails and Sled Dog Tales

We listened to the reports coming into the Communications Room at the back of the mini-convention center as the ham radio operators talked with their contacts at checkpoints up the trail. There were no roads where the mushers were going now; the only access was via airplane and snowmachine. And dogsled, of course.

Boston, Telephone, Haven.... the reports kept coming in throughout the night. Teams passed each other, juggling for position, trying to deduce each others' strategies. First Chance, Gold Run, and then the turnaround point at Candle, where the checkpoint was in the old Fairhaven Hospital.

Several years later I was given an essay by one of the judges at the Candle checkpoint, Joe May. He'd written it for inclusion in my book about the race, which I was revising and updating.

As it happened, I received Joe's essay while traveling with a friend, and as we read it that evening in an old log cabin alongside the Maclaren River it was easy to envision the scene Joe's writing vividly brought to life:

Fairhaven Hospital, Candle. Built at the turn of the 20th century, it stands resolute, square, and unadorned–like the miners who built it. Constructed of salvaged barge timbers, it stands apart from a gaggle of crumbling cabins on a hillside above the Kiwalik River–as if in quarantine. The linoleum in the pantry is stamped 1902–as would be the cornerstones of important buildings in New York, Paris, or London.

Much of the history in its walls is as lost to time as the gold from the nearby creeks and the men who dug it. Left behind is an aura and vacuum that susceptible minds are easily seduced into filling with ghosts and shades from Candle's past–the moilers and mushers of London and Service.

Race officials, vets, checkers, timekeepers, and a cook, used the hospital as a bunkhouse and headquarters for the half-way checkpoint of the 2008 Sweepstakes race. The Fagerstrom and Sherman families, owners of the property and seasonal residents of Candle, volunteered as volunteers. Peggy Fagerstrom and Mike Sherman, siblings and Alaska Natives with roots in Candle, had been born in nearby Kiwalik and wove the past into the present. Mike's wife Dorothy cooked for the crew; caribou ribs and moose stew. Mike did "water, wood, and turned frozen sheefish into sushi." Peggy Fagerstrom was "house mother" and her husband Chuck, a man of infinite calm, was keeper of the official time sheet and custodian of the bubble of time that so engulfed us all.

Of an evening, supper done, stories told, sleeping bags unrolled–a single lantern hissed and wrestled with shadows in the far corners of the lower room. An unseen presence stirred and claimed the attic spaces for its own–in spite of murmurs from downstairs watch-keepers. Rafters shifted, floorboards creaked, and vagrant williwaws whispered a cryptic refrain in the eaves, "time to go...time to go...time to go." A plaintive dog wail from the river–or was it an errant echo from the hills, a hundred years lost, seemed to say, "we're ready–get your ass down here."

It was no stretch to imagine Iron Man Johnson, Scotty Allan, or Leonhard Seppala padding about an upper room in stockinged feet– careful not to wake the competition–gathering up dried harness, parka, and mitts in preparation for another go at the trail–with always a notion to steal a march.

Listening intently, one could easily imagine a footfall in the dark stairwell–the muted squeak of a rusty hinge as the outer door closed ever so softly–and the receding crunch of mukluks on the crisp, midnight snow– hurrying away, down the hill–down the hill to the waiting dogs....

Wavery windows, crooked doors.
Papered walls and slanted floors.
Ugruk sole upon the stair,
Sepp's a-stealin'
light as air.
     ~Joe May

By Thursday morning, March 27th, Lance Mackey was overtaking Iditarod veteran Jim Lanier near the First Chance checkpoint, 165 miles into the race and only 39 miles from the turnaround point at Candle, and much to the entertainment of fans, Jeff King and Lance were keeping up

Long Hard Trails and Sled Dog Tales

their sparring match which had started during the Iditarod. Early Friday morning, March 28, the three front-runners had made it back down the trail to the Camp Haven checkpoint on the return trip, with 140 miles still to go. Racing under the northern lights, Jeff had wrested the lead from Lance and was now followed closely by 2004 Iditarod champion Mitch Seavey, Lance having faded back to third place. The three leading teams raced on, through the Telephone and Boston checkpoints, to Council on the Niukluk River, 85 miles from the finish line in Nome.

Our new friend Jan DeNapoli, a photographer from the Fairbanks area, was in Council and photographing the teams as they arrived at and departed from the scenic checkpoint. She took a magnificent photo of Lance's dog, Zorro, standing proudly in his signature red-and black Mackey team harness, his teammate Fudge alongside and both dogs looking quite ready to hit the trail again. Zorro was Lance's foundation stud, a beautiful black-and-brown Alaskan husky with cream-colored highlights. He'd been a key part of Lance's Yukon Quest team, sat out the Iditarod win, but was now back for Lance's race for the All Alaska Sweepstakes trophy.

Jeff King left the Council checkpoint first that afternoon, but just before 9 p.m. that evening, about a mile from the Safety checkpoint, 22 miles from Nome, Mitch Seavey's tough little Kenai Peninsula dogs passed him and started gaining ground. Two and a half hours later Mitch's team crossed under the burled arch in Nome, winning the $100,000 purse and shattering the race record which had stood for 98 years. The crowd gathered on Front Street was jubilant, even those of us who'd been rooting for other teams found much to like about the quiet Mitch's remarkable win. His mustache covered with frost, trail-weary but happy to be the champion, Mitch posed for the cameras with his leaders, Payton and Ditka, and accepted congratulations from the race officials, fans, volunteers, and media personnel. After several minutes he headed for the dog lot at the end of Front Street with his team, and the crowd turned its collective attention back down the trail, awaiting the second place team.

It was Jeff, also sporting a frosty mustache, arriving ten minutes later. He was somewhat more subdued than usual, understandable as he'd not only just run 85 miles almost non-stop, but he'd also just missed the winner-take-all prize; his take was the $11,224 raised by the All Alaska Sweepstakes queen, Janice Doherty. $88,776 short of Mitch's purse for first place. Jeff gamely posed for the obligatory photos and answered questions from the crowd, but like Mitch, he quickly took his team down the street to the dog lot.

Once again heads swiveled in the direction of the race trail.

CHAPTER TEN

Nome, Alaska

There had been reports of Lance's team being hit by a snowmachine near Safety, but details were sparse and unclear; no one really knew what had happened, or even if the report was true. It was scary news, as mushers and dogs had been killed in collisions with the fast-moving snowmachines; two weeks earlier, during the Iditarod, a dog in musher Jennifer Freking's team had been killed when a snowmachine plowed into her dogs on the Yukon River.

The small crowd waiting under the burled arch peered into the darkness, down the street festively lit with Christmas lights strung crossways from utility poles in a zig-zag pattern, and wondered what could have happened out on the trail.

Long Hard Trails and Sled Dog Tales

It was almost two in the morning before Lance's team appeared on Front Street, but a crowd almost as large as that which had met Mitch and Jeff were assembled and loudly cheered him across the finish line. We stood back respectfully as the race formalities were done, Lance signed the finish timesheet, judges checked the mandatory gear in his sled and counted the dogs - one was in the sled basket: Zorro. Lance and Race Marshal Al Crane went over the dog, Lance explaining what had happened. Zorro seemed alert and interested in what was going on around him, and no one sensed any reason for concern other than Lance and his dogs suffering through the needless collision.

With the finish formalities over, Lance turned his attention to his fans and spent close to an hour talking about his dogs and the race, posing for photos, signing autographs and answering questions. In a moment of sheer exuberance at being part of the history-making race, I asked Lance to put his signature across the shoulder of my full-length white parka, and after asking me if I was really sure I wanted him to, he scrawled his familiar signature across my coat with a Nome Kennel Club green felt pen.

Lance's son Cain and handler Braxton took the team down to the dog lot, but Lance, true to form, stayed to visit with his fans. He didn't dwell on the accident; he chatted about the race, the trail, the weather, his dogs, and what he might have done differently given the opportunity.

A bunch of us finally retired to the adjacent Board of Trade saloon for drinks and Lance spent another hour laughing and visiting before the exhaustion of the race finally caught up with him. Those of us who'd been with him saw no reason for concern; he seemed the same as he had at the end of the Yukon Quest, happy to be off the trail and sharing some well-earned good times with his friends.

The news the next day hit everyone like a thunderbolt: Zorro had been severely injured in the accident and was being flown to Anchorage for possible surgery. An *Anchorage Daily News* reporter, Kevin Klott, had flown to Nome at his own expense to cover the race, and he wrote about the situation in an article for the *News*:

Long Hard Trails and Sled Dog Tales

"NOME -- An unidentified man driving a snowmachine early Saturday morning crashed into the back of the dog sled driven by two-time Iditarod champion Lance Mackey during the All-Alaska Sweepstakes and seriously injured a key animal in his Comeback Kennel.

Mackey broke down in tears Saturday, telling how his most-prized dog, Zorro, was critically injured as the canine was riding in the sled's basket from Safety to Nome -- less than 22 miles left in the 408-mile race."

Several of us walked down to the dog lot later that day and looked at the damage to Lance's sled. He explained that Zorro had been riding in the sled bag due to a sore shoulder, and was probably asleep when the sled was struck. Lance said he tried signaling the driver of the snowmachine by flashing his bright headlamp at him, but the snowmachine plowed into the sled at what Lance estimated to be 60 miles an hour. Lance said he jumped aside about 30 feet from the site of the impact, then ran to help his tangled and injured dogs, swearing at the driver all the while.

Lance explained how the snowmachine had literally impaled the sled bag with its runners, hitting Zorro, who was trapped inside. Mark took notes and created a photo interpretation of the damage, labeling the broken stanchion and showing where the snowmachine ski had slid into the bag and struck the dog. We worked with our friend Theresa Daily, the webmaster for both the Sweepstakes race and Lance's Comeback Kennel, as well as being Lance's public relations manager, to put together a press release and an official statement about the accident. Even as we worked, however, things were changing, and it would turn out that Lance and his wife Tonya would fly to Anchorage that night to accompany Zorro on to Seattle, missing the Sweepstakes finish banquet and possibly forfeiting his third-place prize money.

The banquet was a splendid affair reminiscent of the early days of the race, with a vintage menu replicating one of the original finisher's dinners: Salmon with herbs, bacon-wrapped tenderloin, peas with pearl onions and garlic mashed potatoes. Strawberries, macaroons and ladyfinger cookies were the dessert, and entertainment from the stage kept everyone smiling until time for the awards ceremony.

Musher after musher was called forward to receive their beautiful green-and-gold finishers' certificates. Two mushers had dropped out of the race on the trail, and one was still out there, pursuing a lifelong dream. There were twelve finishers present at the banquet, and each musher shared a little about his or her journey:

Kirsten Bey, who said her dogs were "just a recreational team" but still finished 13th: *"...just the thrill of a lifetime trip and I'll never forget it! The dogs were incredible..."*

Kari Miller, ex-Californian and mother of eight, 12th place: *"I'd like to thank my family... I think this is a memory we'll always cherish."*

Connor Thomas, finishing 11th, had been a checker in the 1983 race: *"What a race! I don't think I've ever had as much fun in a dog race as this one was; I loved seeing the country!"*

Fred "Moe" Napoka, driving the Tuluksak School team to a 10th place finish: *"It was a wonderful race and I thank all of you!"*

Aaron Burmeister, a Nome native and 11-time Iditarod finisher, 9th place: *"One of the pilots in Candle asked me if I'd seen any wolves, and I said no, and he said there was a big pack of wolves headed this way..."*

Ramy Brooks, 1999 Yukon Quest champion and five-time Iditarod Top Ten finisher, in 8th place: *"I think that this race, of all the races I've ever run, really exemplifies what its all about.... the whole community raising $100,000; just extraordinary!"*

Cim Smyth, son of two legendary mushers and a seven-time Iditarod finisher, came in 7th: *"Thank you for putting on this race..."*

Jim Lanier, veteran of a dozen Iditarod races with never a scratch, and the only musher who had also run the 75th Anniversary Sweepstakes Race in 1983, in 6th place: *"I made a study of Seppala's run in 1916, and I planned my race after that run. I did exactly what Seppala did, I stopped the same places and I rested approximately the same length of time. So I thought that if I followed that schedule with my dogteam and we had a pretty good trail, I could trace the race. And I did! I actually out-Seppalaed Seppala!"*

Ed Iten, a Kotzebue musher who'd won the Iditarod's prestigious Leonhard Seppala Humanitarian Award only two weeks earlier, came into Nome again in 5th place: *"It was just a real treat! I don't think we'll ever get four days of the weather we just had again..."*

Sonny Lindner, whose kennel partner Rick Swenson had won the 1983 Sweepstakes race, took 4th place, and as he accepted the purse money from Sweepstakes Princess Dana Sherman he commented: *"I would'a voted for her!"*

Lance Mackey was on his way to Seattle with his injured sled dog, but he had prepared a statement before he left, which was read onstage by Theresa Daily, blinking back tears: *"I wish to thank all the people who made the most incredible start chute I ever went out of. At one point it seemed to be only three feet wide, hands were hitting both shoulders, trying to high five as I passed by, and the excitement of the crowd brought tears to my eyes. It was truly an unforgettable memory..."*

Jeff King, the four-time Iditarod champion who came in second for the second time in two weeks, shared a tale of the trail: *"We took a break at Robert Thompson and Amos' camp on Telephone (Creek), and it was a pretty interesting evening. A large gray wolf lay dead outside the wall tent of the checkers, smoke was coming out of the woodstove, and they were both very generous and friendly. and as I took care of my dogs, my crew showed up, and we had a chance to go in and try musk ox stew with these guys..."*

There were several special awards presented between the individual mushers' awards, such as the Percy Blatchford Spirit of the Race Award to Cari Miller; and the Allan Alexander "Scotty" Allan Humanitarian Award for excellence in dog care during the race to Sonny Lindner. And then it was time for the first place award.

Mitch Seavey had out-raced several of the best mushers in the sport to claim the prestigious three-foot-tall silver loving cup as the 2008 All Alaska Sweepstakes Champion. His race time was inscribed below his name: 61 hours, 29 minutes, 45 seconds. A new race record would stand in the Nome Kennel Club's record-book.

As part of his acceptance speech, Mitch shared a story which would go down forever in sled dog race lore: *"Late in January I was still deciding whether I wanted to try this race or not, and it just so happened that Janie and I were in the airport waiting area, to get on a flight to another race, and another musher asked me, 'You think you're gonna win that Sweepstakes?' and I said, 'Well, you know, after the Iditarod and everything, and in the spring, and I know my back's usually kinda sore, and I'm busy.... If I run that 408 mile race up there I don't know if I'll be enjoying it too much out there.' And this musher looks at me and says, 'You gotta get over that!' And I said 'Yeah, I guess you're right!' So that musher was Jeff King, and I appreciate that!"*

Mitch then had his lead dog, Payton, brought onto the stage for the traditional bestowing of a wreath of yellow roses and green leaves - the Nome Kennel Club colors.

The symbolic honor reportedly dated back to the 1910 Sweepstakes race when John "Iron Man" Johnson won and the exuberant crowd threw a horseshoe-shaped garland of flowers around his neck. He removed them and placed them on the leaders of his team, Kolyma and Sandy, declaring 'I didn't win the race, the dogs did!'

After the excitement of the historic race and the festivities of the finish banquet, it was time to begin gathering ourselves for the trip home. At the race headquarters and around town there was a somber feeling of finality coupled with the sense that we had all been witness to a historic race, and perhaps the last of its kind. Most who knew the situation agreed that there would most likely never be another All Alaska Sweepstakes race, for how does a small community like Nome top a purse of $100,000?

We followed the news about Lance and Zorro in the national media, for the story of the much-loved Yukon Quest and Iditarod champion's accident, and the grave injury to his intrepid sled dog, had become front-page news across the nation. Zorro was examined by a veterinary neurologist in Seattle and underwent an MRI to fully evaluate his spinal injuries. The results suggested that despite significant trauma to his chest and spine, he was expected to achieve a full recovery.

Theresa opened a Paypal account for donations to Zorro's mounting vet bills, and we all watched in fascination bordering on disbelief as the balance quickly grew far beyond our wildest expectations. It was a tribute to a great musher who had always taken the time to be there for his fans; now his fans were there for Lance and Zorro.

Finally the morning came when we shuffled our luggage downstairs and headed for the Nome Airport and our flight home. It seemed as if everyone had booked the same flight, and the time passed quickly as we all shared final goodbyes and best wishes. Then through the security gate and we walked out across the tarmac to board the famous Alaska Airlines Salmon-Forty-Salmon, with its hundreds of times larger-than-life fish mural. It seemed like a fitting way to end the adventure.

There was a postscript to the story, however, which I wrote about for our Northern Light Media website:

Everyone was on the plane and getting comfortably settled when Theresa Daily received a phone call and announced that the final musher, Nome's own Jeff Darling, was in the Safety checkpoint, 22 miles from town. We all applauded his progress and left Nome delighted to know that he was finally so close to home and his hard-won Sweepstakes finish. We hoped a good crowd would be there to meet him, and several of us admitted that we'd thought about staying for a later flight and probably would have if we'd known he was so close.

Fast-forward to Anchorage. A large group is gathered in the airport concourse to say good-byes before heading down to gather baggage and go on their separate ways. Race Marshal and Lead Judge Al Crane takes a phone call from Nome: Jeff Darling is 100 yards from the finish line!

Al held up his cellphone and the dozen or so people standing in Anchorage cheered Jeff to the burled arch from 1,000 miles away! Jeff was clocked in at 11:56:11, taking the traditional Red Lantern and 14th place, a very fitting end to the last great race.

CHAPTER ELEVEN

Wasilla, Alaska

With the race season winding to a close, Mark and I focused our attention on the promotion of our new video about Lance. We attended open house events with Lance, distributed copies to bookstores and gift shops, and drove to Fairbanks for a showcase event at the Alpine Lodge, which was planning to place Lance's Yukon Quest sled and some of his gear on permanent display in their lobby. Mark created an almost life-size photograph of Lance with his team and mounted it on fiberboard, and we bought a large easel to display it prominently near the hotel's front desk.

We spent an afternoon at Lance's place, talking and planning as Mark helped him with some brush-burning and I played with the many small housedogs of uncertain lineage which raced around waiting for Lance to stop working. Finally he took a break and settled onto the deck of his porch, stretching out his lanky frame in the warm spring sun, and the small dogs took that opportunity to pig-pile on top of him, much to the musher's delight.

Long Hard Trails and Sled Dog Tales

That trip marked my second visit to Fairbanks. The first had been in the early seventies to surprise a family friend who was bar-tending in the Mecca Bar on Second Avenue, a booming pipeline haunt which left me with a decidedly less than favorable impression of the town.

This trip presented a very different view of the city, and I enjoyed meeting Lance's friends and watching the boisterous welcomes which greeted him wherever we went. He was clearly a hometown favorite, and when we stopped at a downtown restaurant for lunch he was hailed by the owner who proudly displayed his newest photo of Lance on the establishment's wall.

We took wholesale orders for hundreds of *Appetite & Attitude* DVDs, and left Fairbanks feeling like we'd made a good call in filming Lance. His string of race awards seemed endless: Copper Basin 300: 1st place in 2005 and 2006; Yukon Quest: 1st place in 2005, 2006, 2007, and 2008; Iditarod: 1st place in 2007 and 2008; plus he'd won the 2002 Iditarod's Most Inspirational Musher Award - and won it again in 2007; he won the Yukon Quest's Dawson Award in 2006; the Iditarod's GCI Dorothy Page Halfway Award in 2007; the Iditarod Millenium Hotel's First to the Yukon Award in 2008; the Iditarod's PenAir Spirit of Alaska Award in 2008, and the Yukon Quest's Veterinarian's Choice Award for Excellence in Dog Care on the Trail in 2008. A note about that last award appears on Lance's website: "When the surprise announcement came that Lance had been chosen by the Yukon Quest's team of 14 veterinarians for his superb dog care on the trail, the man they call 'invincible' was visibly shocked and shaken. 'This means more to me than winning this damn race,' said Lance. In his earlier acceptance speech he spoke at length about his dog team and how, 'for whatever reason, they go out of their way to please me.'"

At home in Wasilla, we settled into catching up with the magazine business and helping our son Jim and his girlfriend, newly arrived in Alaska from Washington state, in their search for a suitable home to buy. It was fun touring homes and considering the possibilities, and eventually they chose a small cabin with enormous potential for expansion and development. We spent the summer fishing at the usual favorite places, and as summer wound down Mark got ready to head down to Washington to take care of our home and rental before winter. We gathered everyone for one last fishing trip to Willow Creek and enjoyed a relaxing day of hanging out at the creek and celebrating the three August birthdays in the family: myself, my son John, and my granddaughter Ally, all with birthdays within a week of each other. It had become an annual tradition to go camping and fishing in mid-August to celebrate, and this year was no exception. I drove Mark to the airport that evening, and as he headed off to find his flight it occurred to me that he hadn't wished me happy birthday, but I brushed it off as lost in the excitement of the trip south.

A month later, on a bright September day, I drove north to the Willow area to do some photographing and play with my Alaskan Husky, Chena. Exploring a little-used dirt two-track road I'd never been down before, I came across an old homestead on the shore of a lake, obviously long abandoned and in advanced stages of decay. A cabin built of logs and plywood stood on a slight rise above the lake, with a full porch across the front and a view to the Talkeetna Mountains across the water.

An old Airstream trailer sat behind the cabin, covered in thick green moss and shot full of mindlessly-aimed bullet holes. Newspapers on the cabin floor were dated in the 1970's, and scattered around amongst clothes and pieces of what had one time been furniture were interesting food tins and packages from that era.

Circling the cabin I came across part of an old wood cookstove half buried in the ground, and another, smaller woodstove in pieces nearby. It looked as if someone had been trying to move the stoves but for some reason stopped at this point and abandoned the project. They were rusty and weather-worn, but looked solid beneath the ravages of time and the seasons.

This cabin had been someone's Alaskan dream, and it was easy to see they'd invested a lot of hard work into the old homestead before letting it go. Flowerbeds and a garden area were visible, barely, and broken-down parts of a rail fence showed someone had once cared about the appearance of the place. I spent an hour or so just wandering around, with Chena ranging in circles around me, but when a light rain started falling I decided it was time to head for home.

I stopped by Mom and Dad's on the way, got interested in a TV show they were watching and stayed for dinner. I told Mom about the old homestead, and as expected, she wanted to go back with me the next day. Mom had always loved exploring old places, and we'd spent many happy hours digging for old bottles, rusted tin cans, tools and similar relics over the years. I left their place late, looking forward to an adventure with her the next day.

The following morning I was cleaning away the dishes after breakfast when my sister called; Mom wasn't feeling too well, could I come up there right away? The tone of her voice conveyed an urgency which meant RIGHT NOW, so I stopped everything and drove the five miles to Mom and Dad's home. Mom was having pains in her chest, and trouble breathing, and after a short discussion we decided it best to take her to the emergency room. I remember bits and pieces of that drive: My sister calling ahead to the emergency room and asking Mom to confirm her date of birth; Mom asking why my Jeep was vibrating as we crossed Hyer Road, was something wrong with the alignment, and I assured her it was just a rough patch in the highway; a homemade banner hanging from the overpass as we crossed the highway back toward the hospital; the stark outline of the mountains to the south...

I pulled up to the emergency room door and ran inside for a wheelchair; my sister and I were helping Mom into it when two staff persons came out and took over. I backed away and watched - I'd seen this happen many times with Dad, this was just another 'better safe than sorry' visit, and we'd probably have to put off that trip to the old homestead for a couple of weeks.

I was listlessly thumbing through an issue of the *Reader's Digest* when a nurse came out and said I should come back with her; my sister was already there. The tone of voice told me to brace myself, and when I walked into the room the doctor bluntly told me that if I had anything I wanted to say to Mom now was the time to say it. It took a brief moment for the meaning of his words to sink in, and I felt my knees start to buckle under me. Now I was understanding what he'd said, but it didn't make any sense to me. Mom couldn't be dying, we'd just shared dinner the evening before and we had plans for today...

The doctor motioned us outside the room and explained something that meant, in effect, that Mom had suffered a major heart attack. That pain in her chest, the trouble breathing...

I called both my brothers and told them to bring Dad, something was wrong, and I called my sister in Washington state, and I called Mark. While I was making those calls I overheard that a LifeFlight helicopter was on its way to take Mom into Anchorage, to the bigger hospital, so there was still hope, they were doing everything possible. I went back into her room and stood beside Mom and held her hand and talked to her, told her I loved her, but I didn't know if she could hear me or not. I'd never been through anything like this before and I didn't know what to do, what to say, but I was doing and saying things anyway, even as I reeled and tried to focus on what the doctors and nurses were doing to my mother.

Finally the staff told us we should start for Anchorage, because it was a 45 minute drive and the helicopter would only take a third that long. They wheeled Mom out on a gurney and we kissed her and I told her to keep fighting, that we'd see her in Anchorage, and then somehow I got my legs to carry me out of the hospital.

My sister Sandra and my brother Bill rode into Anchorage with me, and as we neared the Muldoon Road exit Bill said I should take that route to the hospital, that there was a new back way to the hospital which should be quicker. I'd never gone to the hospital that way, and for a brief moment I considered arguing with him and taking my usual route down Boniface Parkway, but I turned the wheel and left the highway.

Pulling up to the stop sign, I waited for traffic to clear and then pulled in behind a large white SUV. As we rolled to a stop at the first stoplight on

Long Hard Trails and Sled Dog Tales

Muldoon Road Bill pointed at the license plate and said "Look at that!" The plate was from Virginia. Mom's name. What were the chances?

We followed the SUV all the way to our turnoff to the hospital, parked and made our way inside, spent a few minutes getting our bearings and asking where we should go, and then we were walking down a long hallway toward the emergency area when we met Dad's heart surgeon, Dr. Peterson. Recognizing us, he immediately took control of the situation and ushered us into a closed waiting room, then went looking for information about Mom.

When he returned a few minutes later he gently broke the news that she was gone. At that point I remember being grateful that this kind man had been the one to tell us, and I was grateful that we were all together in a place where no one was watching, or would interrupt our grief. I felt an especially deep gratitude that Dr. Peterson was there for Dad. Of all the doctors in all the hospitals in Anchorage, there was no one I'd rather have had with us that day, and since then I've often wondered about the serendipity of meeting him in the hallway just when we needed him most.

My sister flew up from Washington and we all made it through the funeral arrangements somehow. Mom's sister sent two stand-alone sprays of flowers and we talked about Mom's favorites, what we should have at her memorial and funeral. Pansies were a favorite, and nasturtiums, and roses of course. Mom loved all kinds of flowers and a few years earlier when she and I had taken a trip to northern California it had delighted her no end to fill the car with armloads of beautiful flowers! I'd taken one of my favorite photos of her on that trip, holding a big bright purple bloom up to her cheek and smiling broadly. I could see in that smile the California girl my Dad had fallen in love with over 60 years before.

One bloom that we all knew she loved was one she'd raved about after a trip to Hawaii: the Bird-of-Paradise. Looking quite like a tropical bird with a long colorful beak, it was a difficult flower to find in Alaska; none of the flower shops we contacted had it in stock, and ordering some would take too long. We settled for every other kind of flower we could find, and

I took a large colorful bouquet of my own sweet peas to the funeral in a fine crystal vase.

As the wife of a career soldier Mom was entitled to be buried in the Pioneer Cemetery on Fort Richardson, and on a sublimely beautiful fall day we followed the funeral home's hearse across the flats, over the rivers, along the base of the Chugach Mountains that Mom had so loved, and onto Fort Richardson. A memorial service was held in a lovely stone building that Mom would have admired, and then we waited for a brief interlude as she was buried. That done, we drove to the very back of the cemetery, a location Mom would have approved of near the trees and with a beautiful view of the freshly snow-capped mountains. Termination dust, we'd always called it. The words had a new meaning now.

We stood at Mom's grave, uncertain what to do next, and I placed my vase of sweet peas on the fresh dirt. Then I heard a gasp, and someone pointed, and I looked... One row back and two graves over was another new gravesite. The name was Virginia Ellen, the same as Mom's name, and there was a fresh bouquet on the grave with a bright Bird-of-Paradise rising above the other blooms. I felt my knees give way again...

We talked about that incident and others for a long time. Walking across Mom and Dad's driveway a few days later I stooped to pick up a quarter someone had dropped and it turned out to be a Virginia state quarter. What were the chances?

I tried to convince myself the chances were actually pretty good, as someone would have saved a quarter with Mom's name on it. The white SUV with her name on the license plate was harder to explain, and the rare flower and her first and middle names on another grave were harder still. Dad's favorite doctor being at the hospital could have been a happy circumstance, or something else entirely. To me it felt as if someone was trying to tell me something, and I found it all comforting and reassuring. If this was how things worked I could see how religion might become a popular way to explain or make sense of the world. Suddenly it didn't seem like too much of a stretch to think there were greater powers in control of things.

The one shattering disappointment had been Mark. I asked him - begged him - to come back for Mom's funeral, as I didn't feel I could make it through the days after her passing without him, and I knew the boys and especially Dad would welcome his being here. But he said no, and I struggled to understand why.

I found these words somewhere and wrote them in one of my journals: *The key question to keep asking yourself is are you spending your time on the right things - because time is all you have.*

Mark returned to Alaska just before Thanksgiving and we settled into routines of work and spending time with our kids and grandkids. The race season kicked off again in December with the Sheep Mountain 150 just before Christmas, and I enjoyed a trip to the race start with Donna and Theresa.

We held our annual family Christmas dinner party and everyone had a good time, but there was a huge hole where Mom had been. After everyone went home Christmas night, Mark and Dad and I sat up for hours watching old John Wayne movies we'd all seen a dozen times before.

The first weekend of January Mark and I photographed the Knik 200 race, laughing and enjoying the excitement of trying to figure out where to get the best shots of the mushers. We filmed the first half of the start from on the lake, getting some great chute photos, and then moved to the old townsite of Knik for the remainder of the field, photographing the mushers against the backdrops of the venerable Knik Hall and the log Bjorn cabin. We stopped for dinner in Wasilla and at that point it seemed as if finally all was right with the world again.

The Copper Basin 300, often referred to as 'the little Iditarod' for its challenging terrain, was the following weekend, and we decided I would drive up and cover the race alone while Mark worked on the magazine, our websites, the video and other business. I left around 4 am and arrived at Wolverine Lodge on Lake Louise, where the race was starting, around 9 am. As I pulled up to the picturesque lodge overlooking the lake I snapped a photo of the thermometer inside my Jeep showing the outside temperature was 42 below.

Lance was entered, along with his family friend and longtime handler, Braxton Peterson. Also running was Lance's new protoge, an Alaska National Guardsman named Harry Alexie, from Kwethluk, Alaska. The Alaska National Guard was leasing a team from the Mackey Kennel in a program implemented to challenge guard members and to encourage new recruits. Harry's Guard unit also joined in when possible, following Harry to the sled dog races, handling his team at the race starts, checkpoints, and race finishes.

I donned my cold-weather gear and walked down to the lake, listening to the loudspeaker repeatedly telling me how cold it was, and photographed the teams as they harnessed the dogs and got ready to race. Once I got into the rhythms of the start I didn't seem as cold, and I filmed most of the teams leaving the chute and heading for the far shore of the lake.

Back at the lodge after the start I ordered soup and a sandwich and talked with Lance's wife Tonya and a few other people about the dogs, the course, and things unrelated to racing. I was in no hurry to leave, as I knew the teams would be in the remote backcountry until the next morning. I stopped in Glennallen and spent a few hours at race central in the American Legion hall, downloading photos and writing articles, and sent some good race reports to our website which were picked up and linked to by Theresa's Go Mush website, Lance's Comeback Kennel site, and a few others. I was gaining traction as a roving race reporter.

The next day I drove to Paxson and got many good photos of the teams crossing Meier's Lake and coming into the Paxson checkpoint. The drive was beautiful, through rolling forested hills with the eastern peaks of the Alaska Range on the horizon, and I wished someone were there to share the trip with me. I didn't mind being alone in the back country, but I did wish I wasn't alone.

That night I once again stopped at race central to download photos and write race reports; our Northern Light Media website was gaining a reputation as a reliable source of race news and updates. it seemed that my first-hand reports and quickly uploaded photos were paying dividends and making the time and expense of the trip worth the effort. Besides, I was learning the lay of the land, the players involved, the terminology and the small details which could only be gained by being at the checkpoints. I was paying my dues, so to speak.

Not wanting to spend money on a motel room for the few hours I wouldn't be on the trail, I splurged on a long leisurely dinner at the Caribou Cafe and then drove most of the way back to Wolverine Lodge and slept in my Jeep with the motor running. It was really no different than the many times I'd pulled off the road and slept when traveling between Alaska and Washington, and I actually slept better in the comfortable reclining seat of my Jeep than I would have in a cheap motel bed. It was a plan which would become routine for me while covering future races.

At Wolverine Lodge the next morning I met Tonya again and we drank coffee and talked and listened to race reports all day. She said they were looking for a new kennel logo and we talked about possible designs. She wanted something simple, a musher against the mountains with the northern lights overhead. She shared an adorable photo of her with a friend's dog which had been taken at the Gin Gin 200, and at 4:41 pm Lance came in first to win the 2009 Copper Basin 300. National Guardsman Harry Alexie placed well, coming in ninth out of twenty-six entries to win the "Rookie of the Year" Award.

Lance decided to withdraw from the 2009 Yukon Quest, saying a number of things factored into his decision. One was Harry Alexie being signed up for the Iditarod, which would take Lance's time and attention to prepare for, and another was his stepson Cain running the Junior Iditarod, his last Junior race. Lance would miss being there if he was on the Yukon Quest, and he stated, "I'm a father first, and I have never been able to watch Cain run the Junior Iditarod. I have always been off running races myself. It's important to me. I have nothing to prove to anyone, and I think I have my priorities straight."

Chapter Twelve

Circle, Alaska

On February 19th I drove to Fairbanks for the end of the 2009 Yukon Quest. I found free Internet at a Barnes & Noble bookstore cafe on the north side of town and spent several hours drinking good coffee and catching up with business. I slept in my Jeep again that night, went back to the Barnes & Noble for a ham & cheese croissant breakfast and more online work, then ordered a large hazelnut mocha and headed for Circle.

I found an NPR radio station, KUAC, and was happy to hear frequent updates on the race from Dan Bross, and a long thought-provoking poem at one point by Robert Frost with the ending line, "One could do worse than be a swinger of birches."

Ah, yes.

The country I was driving through held me spellbound with its sheer vastness, hills rolling away in the distance from the top of Cleary Summit, old gold dredges and gold camps and log cabins beside lakes.... The pavement ended and I was on an improved gravel road. This seemed like a magical, mystical land, and I savored the long drive up Twelvemile Summit. Near the top I drove into a cloud bank and all I could see were short dwarf-like spruce trees on the bank above the road, telling me with their size and sparseness that I was at a great elevation.

Then down out of the cloudbank and another twenty miles of spectacular scenery before I found myself at Eagle Summit, with a 20-foot snowbank on one side and a sheer drop-off into nothing on the other. I slowed my Jeep to a crawl and eased across the pass, scared to look at the vast emptiness to my left, trying to hug the right side of the road but keeping an eye on that towering snowbank.

On the other side of the pass the country opened into a broad valley which fanned out into seemingly endless lands beyond. I stopped the Jeep and stood staring at the strange new land for a long time, wondering what was out there. This was the storied land of gold miners, freighters, trappers, and the intrepid mushers of the U.S. Mail. I'd been excited to visit Nome for the Sweepstakes race, but this was a place which evoked a quite different feeling, more somber, almost reverent. This land beyond the fierce mountain passes seemed deserving of a level of respect I hadn't felt for a place in a long, long time.

I passed through the small town of Central without stopping–I would check it out on the return trip–and I drove the last thirty winding miles of dirt road to the village of Circle on the Yukon River. At that time I didn't have more than a passing knowledge of the history of this part of Alaska, but I knew Circle had played an important role and had once been the largest gold mining town on the Yukon River, pre-dating the famous Klondike Gold Rush by several years.

There was no gold mining at Circle, it was just the closest river supply point for the mines back near Central, and the town became a hub for many of the gold camps throughout interior Alaska. Named because the founders thought it was located on the Arctic Circle, the town is actually about 50 miles south.

Long Hard Trails and Sled Dog Tales

The 2,000-mile long Yukon River flows past the end of the road in the center of town, and as I nosed my Jeep up to the snowbank overlooking the frozen scene I couldn't help feeling like I'd arrived at a destination I'd been searching for a long, long time. The history was palpable here, the untold thousands of men and women who'd passed through here before me included distant relatives about whom I knew very little other than their having been here on their way to find their fortunes. I felt like in some strange, difficult to describe way, I'd found mine, and I sat there for a long, long time staring out over the ice and snow at the end of the road.

The front-running mushers weren't expected into Circle until close to midnight, so I wandered around the small village getting my bearings and finally found the school, where food, showers and place to throw down a sleeping bag were available, and a classroom had been set up for the media to work. The actual checkpoint was two blocks away at the fire hall, but there were no amenities there for anyone except the race staff and the mushers. I walked through to get the lay of the landscape, spent a few minutes standing around the bonfire outside and listening to the trail talk, then took my gear back the schoolhouse and staked out a student-sized desk to set up my computer.

My first website post from Circle was titled '300 Miles of Mushers,' and explained how the Yukon Quest teams were stretched across nearly 300 miles of remote backcountry trail. The judges and veterinary team members were at the Circle checkpoint, awaiting the first teams, but unpredictable weather conditions and accumulating snowfall made it difficult to predict when the first mushers would arrive. I drove back down to the river and sat there watching for a long time, then decided to spend the night there rather than in the warm schoolhouse gym. The riverbank just seemed more like where I wanted to be, and it was relatively warm, only minus ten, and I had a good Arctic sleeping bag.

Several months after this race I would become a columnist for the online newsmagazine *Alaska Dispatch*, and the first words I wrote were about this very night:

Long Hard Trails and Sled Dog Tales

"February 2009. Circle City, Alaska, on the bank of the Yukon River. Somewhere around midnight. I'm trying to see through the darkness upriver, watching for the faint telltale beam of light from a musher's headlamp making his way to this Yukon Quest checkpoint. Whoever this musher is, he'll have travelled several hundred miles from Whitehorse, across some of the most remote country in the great northland, following old mail routes and gold rush trails over mountains, across frozen lakes, and down the mighty ice-bound Yukon River. He'll be roughly three quarters of the way home when he reaches this checkpoint, but the roughest ride is still ahead: the double whammy of Eagle and Rosebud Summits, grueling climbs of over 3,000 feet from this current riverside elevation. Looking up at the stars -- no northern lights tonight -- and then squinting back up the river one last time, I turn and head for my warm sleeping bag."

    Canadian William Kleedehn arrived at 10:46 pm, followed by Hugh Neff an hour and a half later. I recognized Kleedehn's name, the musher described in Brian Patrick O'Donoghue's book, *Honest Dogs*: *...an Austrian expatriate now living in the Yukon. Although he'd lost one leg in an accident years before, Kleedehn, the thirty-eight-year-old owner of Limp-a-long Kennel, had finished as high as eleventh in two previous Quests. Numerous victories in shorter sled-dog races made him a long-shot threat to win.*

    I recognized Hugh Neff as the musher Lance had introduced to Donna and I in Whitehorse the year before. We'd been eating breakfast when Hugh and his girlfriend Tamra Reynolds came in and sat at the table next to ours, and for the next hour or so we listened to the two mushers exchanging stories about the trail and their respective runs. We met Hugh and Tamra again at the Iditarod start, and spent some time with them at the All Alaska Sweepstakes after Hugh scratched. I liked Tamra, a quiet girl but obviously very knowledgeable about the dogs. I was still forming an opinion about the more quirky Hugh.

Long Hard Trails and Sled Dog Tales

Mushers continued arriving at the Circle checkpoint: Jon Little, Sebastian Schnuelle, Brent Sass, and the Canadian girl I recognized from a video about women on the Quest: Michelle Phillips. The video was *'Dog Gone Addiction,'* and several of us had attended the Alaskan premiere at the Bear Tooth Theatre in Anchorage and met the filmmaker, Becky Bristow. Becky was an adventurer herself, and talking with her after the film had played a part in my wanting to become a filmmaker.

As the teams came and went throughout the day I got some great photos and took notes which I would translate into posts and articles about the race later. My friends from the Sweepstakes race, Jodi Bailey and Jan DeNapoli, were in Circle, and it was fun to talk with them as they waited for their teams to arrive. We bought dinner from the Circle schoolkids at the cafeteria–turkey with all the trimmings–and I opted for a hot shower that night before setting in for an all-nighter on the computer.

The next day I drove back to Central, a picturesque wide spot in the road with a colorful history. In 1893, three years before the Klondike gold rush of 1896, Jack McQuesten, a trader for the Alaska Commercial Company, grubstaked Creole miner Peter Pavlov, better known as "Pitka," and his brother-in-law, Serge Cherosky. The two found traces of gold in a stream called Molymute, a tributary of the upper reaches of Birch Creek, the snaky-winding waterway I'd crossed on the only major bridge between Central and Circle.

Birch Creek began in the Crazy Mountains west of Central and the only access was across the swampy, mosquito-infested Yukon Flats, but the gold was there, and as the 1800s came to a close the increase in river traffic to the region compelled the Alaska Commercial Company to add new steamers to service the Birch Creek and nearby Fortymile gold districts. Central became a convenient place between the mines and the river landing at Circle, and a community sprang up.

The news in Central was that Hugh Neff had closed the gap on William Kleedehn, pulling into the Central checkpoint three minutes ahead. But the bigger news was later reported by KUAC's Dan Bross:

Long Hard Trails and Sled Dog Tales

After 8 days of pretty smooth going, news that Hugh Neff was penalized 2 hours for mushing on the road into Central instead of the race trail came as a shock. The penalty for not staying on the trail isn't defined in the rules and left up to the discretion of the race Marshall. It's hard to say what's fair in such a situation, but if the penalty was lined out in the rule book, well than at least you could say it's the same for everyone. The subjective penalty determined in Neff's case, begs questions...why not a $ fine? Why 2 hours in such a close race? When questioned about the penalty, Race Marshall Doug Grilliot said it was meant to be disciplinary, as much as make up for any time Neff (2nd position) might have gained on then race leader William Kleedehn, by gliding along the icy road surface.

There were more surprises in store, as fierce winds on Eagle Summit played havoc with the race plans of Kleedehn, Neff and Little. Sebastian Schnuelle, who'd been a ways behind the front of the pack, found less daunting weather on the summit and gained an edge which he built into a slim win, crossing the finish line in Fairbanks just four minutes ahead of Hugh Neff.

Dan Bross revisited Hugh's penalty in his commentary on the finish: *Wow! What a finish! Congratulations Sebastian, Hugh, and Jon on their record breaking finish times, and everybody else, especially the dogs, for their hard work, and driving spirit in this year's Quest.*

That said, the finish was bitter sweet. Sure the Schnuelle's edging Neff by 4 minutes was a record close finish and very exciting, but it wouldn't have been that way if Neff hadn't been penalized two hours for choosing to run on the faster road surface, instead of the trail on the way to Central. Opting for the road was wrong, and Neff admits it, but was two hour penalty given the closeness of the race, fair discipline? I don't know. If he was back in the pack or at least farther behind the winner, it would've been no big deal, but sadly the penalty affected the outcome of the race. Not sure where to go on this, but other mushers tell me it's not the first time a racer has run on the road in this section. I guess this year's incident and penalty had more to do with the circumstances and the fact that several people witnessed the violation.

Long Hard Trails and Sled Dog Tales

It wasn't the first win which would be characterized as bittersweet, and hardly the last. I was learning a side of this sport which I'd missed all those years ago when I sat in on those formative Iditarod meetings, and I found myself wishing I hadn't lost two and a half decades of involvement with this game. I had a lot of catching up to do, and I knew the only way to do it was to stay involved, to keep meeting and talking to people, and to stay on the trail as much as possible.

The race was won, but it was far from over; teams were still spread out back up the trail, and after the long drive back to Fairbanks I took a left just north of town and headed out Chena Hot Springs Road to watch the back of the pack come in.

The checkpoint was about thirty miles out, at the Twin Bears Camp, a rustic Adirondack-style collection of cabins on a small frozen lake. Parking at the camp was reserved for judges and the vet team, everyone else parked out near the main road and walked about a half mile around the lake to the camp.

I pulled in next to the big motorhome with Jamaican flags and banners on it, not sure yet what that was all about, and put on my snowboots. I'd learned a little about the Jamaican musher, Newton Marshall, back in Central, when I'd met my friend Susie Rogan in the parking lot. She was heading out to the Mammoth Creek road crossing to check on her partner Hans Gatt's progress, and I jumped in with her to chat on the 20-mile trip.

She said something about Hans mentoring a fellow from the island of Jamaica, leasing him a team and training him to run the Quest, and I realized it was the same guy who'd greeted me with a disarming smile at the Sheep Mountain 150 several weeks earlier. I mistook him for a media reporter, only to be surprised later when he pulled into the start chute behind a team of Hans Gatt's fast dogs!

A few weeks later I had mentioned the incident in a website post: *One of my fondest memories of the 2008 Sheep Mountain 150 a couple of months ago is stepping out of the cafe and seeing a brilliant smile coming toward me across the parking lot. The smile broadened and announced with excitement, "Isn't it a Beautiful Morning!" It wasn't a question, it was a pronouncement, punctuated with capital letters and a huge exclamation point!*

    The Twin Bears Camp was a wonderful place to take photographs, and the day was beautiful, so I spent most of my time watching the last half of the race while visiting with friends. Jan DeNapoli, who'd been with us in Nome for the All Alaska Sweepstakes, was there, helping with the dropped dogs, and at one point we jumped in her truck and drove the 30-mile round trip to her place for some medical supplies the checkpoint needed. I marveled at Jan's beautiful big log home, classically Alaskan, and met her father, a friendly and welcoming man. Jan's beautifully-kept homestead included dozens of sled dogs and a couple of horses, and seeing her in her own environment just confirmed my feeling that she was an old-school Alaskan of the first caliber.

    Back at the Twin Bears Camp I took photos of the incoming teams and the mushers hauling water, tending their dogs, and doing their checkpoint chores, and I snapped a great shot of judge Karen Ramstead, a purebred Siberian Husky breeder and distance racer from Alberta, Canada, enjoying the sunny scene with Mike Ellis, whose Team Tsuga Siberians were creating a stir. In 2008 Mike and his team of 14 AKC-registered Siberian Huskies had finished the Yukon Quest in 12 days, 9 hours, and 58 minutes, finishing in 11th place out of a field of 24 teams and setting a new record for a purebred team. Mike and his team had also won a handful of awards at shorter races, including the prestigious Humanitarian Award at the 2009 Copper Basin 300 in January. He and his wife Sue were moving their kennel to Alaska from New Hampshire.

    I knew Karen Ramstead through my friend Donna Quante, who had filmed Karen and her beautiful North Wapiti team of purebred Siberian Huskies as they trained for and entered the 2005 Iditarod, resulting in the documentary DVD *'Pretty Sled Dogs.'* I'd met Karen at an open house the year before, and her warm smile and contagious enthusiasm about her dogs made me an instant fan. She was from Perryvale, Alberta, described in Wikipedia as "a hamlet in northern Alberta in Athabasca County, located 104 kilometres (65 mi) north of Edmonton." It had a 2006 census population of 10, "living in three dwellings." I assumed at least one of those dwellings was Karen's.

As the sun went down and the temperature dropped those of us at the checkpoint wandered inside to warm ourselves near the barrel stove. Booties were arranged on the floor around the stove, drying, and mittens, gloves, scarves and other gear were hung from lines overhead or draped over handy nails on the walls. Several picnic tables made up the seating, and judges, vets, volunteers, fans, and a few trail-weary mushers were sitting in various groups and assortments around the room.

After a while someone said something about two mushers who hadn't checked in yet, and someone else asked for clarification. It was two women who'd been bringing up the back of the race for the entire trip, Iris West and Becca Moore. There was discussion of whether they might be in trouble or not, but the general consensus was they'd made it this far, including over most of the big summits, and they'd probably be fine. Sure enough, just before 5 pm Iris mushed into the checkpoint, and almost an hour later Becca made it. An eight hour mandatory rest would make it easy for them to finish the next day.

Jan had invited me to sit with her at Wayne Hall's table for the finish banquet, and that gave me an excellent opportunity to be a good position to get great photos of the awards ceremony. I enjoyed meeting Wayne and his wife, Scarlett, and Jan introduced me to a number of people whose names I soon forgot. One I remembered meeting, sitting at the table next to ours, was Brian Patrick O'Donoghue, author of *Honest Dogs*, which I'd been keeping in my Jeep as a sort of reference to the trail. His vivid descriptions of the country during the 1998 Yukon Quest were echoing what I was seeing for myself first-hand: *The brush ceased as we passed between broad, white mounds, gleaming in the midday sun. It was another gold mining camp. The machinery, glimpsed through thick cloaks of snow, appeared of fairly recent vintage. Winding through what I presumed was*

Long Hard Trails and Sled Dog Tales

piles of either tailings or rock slated for processing, I was struck by the contrasts between the Quest's image as a solitary wilderness trek and these repeated excursions through industrial sites.

I had likewise been surprised to see the amount of man's incursion into that country beyond Fairbanks; I'd never known there was so much history out there until I literally drove into it. On the way to Central I'd been mystified by a huge brown pipeline which paralleled the road for miles and miles, until finally I came to an interpretive sign which explained that it was the 90-mile-long Davidson Ditch, built in the 1920's to supply water to the gold dredges from the upper Chatanika River. In the late 1920's watchmen were employed to patrol its length, perpetually examining the pipeline for leaks and problems. In the winter, it was patrolled by dog team, and All Alaska Sweepstakes champion Leonhard Seppala was employed in this capacity and named the chief watchman of the ditch. I would later learn that Seppala and his wife had, for a time, lived in a cabin near the gold camp of Chatanika.

When I got home we had only a couple of weeks to get magazine business squared away before the madness of the 2009 Iditarod engulfed us. The Lance DVD was selling steadily, aided by some outstanding reviews and steadily increasing distribution points. The organizers of two large sled dog symposiums ordered several cases of them, and the feedback we were receiving was enthusiastically approving.

Mark and I drove up to Willow for the start of the 2009 Junior Iditarod; Lance's step-son Cain Carter was hoping to win on the final attempt for which he qualified–the following year he'd turn 18 and would be racing with the other adults. The year before he had come achingly close; he was neck and neck with Jessica Klejka at the finish, but her lead dog's nose had crossed the finish line two seconds ahead of his lead dog.

The next day we returned to Willow to watch a jubilant Cain race under the banner and into first place. Lance and Tonya were justifiably proud of the young musher, and it was fun to be there and enjoy the moment with them.

Chapter Thirteen

Anchorage, Alaska

The first week of March was filled with friends and fun as the preparations for the 2009 Iditarod got under way. Friends were making plans to gather in Anchorage and I volunteered to help drive several who would be arriving at the airport without transportation to the race events.

One visitor I was greatly looking forward to seeing was Betty Walden from Texas, whose infectious good nature had won me over the year before. Betty was a retired teacher and had followed the Iditarod for many years; she knew the race lore and legends, and the histories of most of the mushers, and she had well-thought-out opinions of the rest of them, so spending time with her was always a delightful treat!

Another Texan, graphics artist Sarida Steed-Bradley, was a 1972 West Anchorage High School graduate, and she had designed a beautiful full color patch for Lance's inimitable lead dog, Larry, for a group of online friends who'd taken to calling themselves The Larry Appreciation Society.

While we were in Nome for the 2008 Sweepstakes race, Sarida had emailed her draft of an idea for the patch and we all had a good time playing with the design and then showing it to Lance for approval. The whole plan was to sell the patches as a fundraiser for his kennel, so Lance was behind the idea, and Sarida had finalized the design and had the patches made. It was all great fun, and proved so successful that eventually several other patches for Lance's Super Dogs were designed and made available.

Now, after 37 years away from Alaska, Sarida was returning for the 2009 Iditarod. On her weblog, *Return to Alaska, A Journey North*, Sarida gave an indication of what the trip would mean for her: *Alaska has called me back. Over the past year and many months I've found my thoughts and dreams turning north as if magnetized like a compass needle. I'm almost ready to go.*

Sarida had another reason besides the Iditarod for traveling to Alaska. Her favorite uncle had perished while crossing a stream on a hunting trip in August, 1966. She wrote on her blog: *Among the souvenirs I plan to pack from my trip in March is some Alaskan dirt, pebbles, mud or such. I can't bury him in Alaska, but next time I'm in Arkansas, I can bury some of Alaska with him.*

Sarida had shipped two trunks to me ahead of her trip north, and I met her at the airport and delivered her to her hotel. We had plans to make a trip north on the Glenn Highway to the area where her uncle had been lost, but first there was a race to get started.

The first event of the Iditarod was the vet check at the Iditarod Trail headquarters log cabin near Wasilla, and I offered to be the Texas Taxi driver for my friends Betty and Sarida. I picked them up in Anchorage and we drove back out to the Valley, talking all the way. It was a fun and relaxed day of meeting old and new friends, talking with the mushers, photographing the dogs and just enjoying the anticipation in the air. The vet check was where I'd first met Lance in 2007, when my friend June Price introduced us and then snapped a photo of me with the guy who would notch his first Iditarod win less than two weeks later.

We were beginning to wonder if Lance was coming to the vet check when his big red truck pulled into the parking lot and stopped near us. Sarida was just beside herself with excitement, and she filmed Lance dropping his dogs with a running commentary about each one, delighted to see how Lance just let the inimitable Larry run free while he fastened the other dogs to their truck chains. She wrote later that she'd overheard someone say to Lance, "I think she's more excited to meet Larry than you." And Lance replied, "That's the way it should be."

Still, Sarida was not immune to the well-known Mackey charm, as she wrote later on her blog: *I've worked with the famous and semi-famous during my years knocking around backstage. I've loaded guns for Howard Keel, bought fruit for Van Johnson, been on a video shoot with Willy Nelson, built stages for Shamu the Killer Whale and never felt any excitement for performers. Lance Mackey has me star-struck.*

Lance was at the height of his glory, having won four Yukon Quests and two Iditarods; silencing the nay-sayers who'd called his first Yukon Quest/Iditarod win a fluke or just happy coincidence. It was in fact a feat which was considered almost impossible by many and was deemed one of the most impressive feats ever by a musher. Lance had been nominated for two ESPY awards, the prestigious Excellence in Sports Performance Yearly Award which was presented by cable network ESPN to recognize superior athletic achievement. He didn't win the award, but just being nominated was an unequalled honor and a first in the mushing community.

Back at the Millennium Hotel in Anchorage for the media meeting, we had a chance to meet other friends, garner cool freebies given out by the sponsors, watch a clip from the official race video, and listen to an hour's worth of promotional spiels interlaced with a little good advice about how we media types should comport ourselves. We also got our official Iditarod media badges, plastic identification cards which were our magic pass to stay on Fourth Avenue after the fans were sent outside the fence, with the same entitlement at the actual race start in Willow. After the formalities several of us retired to the hotel restaurant and lounge, The Fancy Moose, for lunch and further visiting, which had become standard practice through the years. It was a good opportunity to see the mushers in a relaxed non-race environment, as they were all at the hotel for other meetings and pre-race formalities, and most of them wandered through the restaurant at some point in the afternoon. That evening the fun would revolve around the Fancy Moose's annual Iditarod trivia game at which valuable prizes would be awarded for the team getting the most correct answers to questions such as "How many official Iditarod checkpoints are there?" and "What was the first year founder Joe Redington ran the race?"

At some point during that evening's trivia game I wandered out to the women's rest room, and before heading back into the noisy restaurant I took a seat in one of the overstuffed chairs in a corner of the lobby. I was checking messages on my phone when an older couple stopped and the man helped a frail-looking woman into the chair opposite me. I couldn't help noticing she wore a Larry Appreciation Society patch on her parka, and when I asked her about it we struck up a friendly conversation which included her husband when he returned. The couple were longtime Iditarod fans Lee and Claudia Nowak from Michigan, who stayed at the Millennium Hotel every year for the race, and we soon became fast friends.

Thursday was the Iditarod banquet, and excitement about the event was running high because for the first time the dinner and start drawing would be held at the magnificent new Dena'ina Center in downtown Anchorage, the largest and most impressive venue in the state. I picked up Betty and Sarida and we drove through a snowstorm to the Center, much to the delight of my snow-loving Texan friends.

After a Millennium Hotel-catered dinner of boneless short ribs with all the trimmings, followed by a cheesecake dessert, the mushers stepped onto the stage one by one and drew their starting positions, then took their places in line to sign posters for the fans. I took photos of the mushers for a while, then spent the rest of the evening just visiting with friends and watching the fun.

Friday there was an open house in Chugiak at the home of Jim and Bonnie Foster, who opened their home to several mushers and their fans each year. It was a gala occasion, made more fun by the friendly dogs who wandered amongst the guests. I enjoyed talking with old friends and meeting new ones, and I especially enjoyed listening to the stories told by several mushers who were present. One musher related an incident which had happened somewhere out on the Yukon River, when another musher was traveling in the middle of the night and heard voices sounding like they were quarreling with each other. He said the musher stopped and called out, hoping to learn how far he was from the next checkpoint, but there was no answer. Another musher, much older, who had been listening to the tale, nodded and said there had been many similar reports over the years of voices in that same area, and it was generally felt they were the spirits of long-departed people who had once lived in the area but were killed in a massacre sometime around the turn of the century.

Saturday all of the teams gathered on Fourth Avenue in Anchorage. The day was warm and sunny, with clear blue skies and no wind for the 11-mile-long street party that was the ceremonial start. There were plenty of photo opportunities, such as past race champions who were seemingly everywhere; former Olympic skater Dorothy Hamill, who was riding in the dogsled of Eric Rogers; and four-time Iditarod champion Jeff King, who was planning to cruise down the streets of Anchorage on skis in front of a huge freight sled while holding a long gee-pole for steering. It was the way heavy gold-bearing freight sleds were handled in the old days on the Iditarod Trail, but it was something new and interesting to the race crowd who were used to seeing mushers behind their sleds.

Lance had drawn number 47 at the banquet, so he would be going out in the middle of the pack. Somewhere near Goose Lake, about halfway through his ceremonial run, a moose decided to confront the musher's team. Lance told the story to a reporter: *"I'm on the trail at the ceremonial start of the Iditarod with my Idit-a-rider in my sled and my Canada Goose sponsor on my drag sled. I come around a corner and we are confronted by this NOT so happy moose. She put her head down, her ears back and decided we were making her mad. I knew this could get ugly, I looked around for some kind of defense tool in case she decided to stomp my* team. *All I saw was this broken branch sticking out of the snow. I grabbed it and I started heading towards her acting like I wanted to eat her for dinner, I was pretty mad...she must have believed me because she retreated and we went on our way."*

A professional photographer from Texas happened to be nearby and captured a photo of Lance and the moose which made the front page of the *Anchorage Daily News* the next morning. It was a classic shot: The moose looking at Lance from about 30 feet away, Lance advancing on the moose with what looked like a 12-foot tree branch, Larry and the rest of the team intently checking out the action but not willing to get involved, and Lance's passengers wide-eyed at the scene unfolding before them.

The next day Betty and I drove out to Eaglequest Lodge at Deshka Landing, on the Susitna River west of Willow, and took a ride in a snowmachine-drawn sled out to a vantage point on the trail about a mile behind the lodge. It was another classically beautiful blue-sky Alaskan day, and we had a fine time photographing the teams as they raced past us. We made it back to Anchorage in time for dinner with friends, and then I spent a couple of hours downloading photos and writing about the start of the race for our website.

Over the next several days I spent a lot of time at the Millennium Hotel, watching the leaderboard in the lobby, visiting the communications room where friends I knew who were working there would give me up-to-the-minute race updates, and just talking with the myriad of friends and acquaintances who passed through the lobby and the restaurant, where I would set up my computer when things weren't too busy.

The 2009 race was a good one, and Lance played it well, as described by race analyst Bruce Lee in his *Eye on the Trail* blog for the Iditarod website, as Lance rolled into the Grayling checkpoint: *This part of the race is a mental game. Just think about the message Lance Mackey has been sending since he left Takotna. He made it to Iditarod without stopping. His message to his competitors was simple "Let's see if your fast is faster than my fast."* Then Lance took his mandatory 8 hour layover in Anvik after feasting on an eight course meal.

Fast forward to King, Schnuelle and Burmeister arriving in Grayling hoping that they might have gained some ground on Mackey in Grayling. Minutes after their arrival there was a light on the river… and yes, it was Lance arriving in Grayling at 10:50 pm. He stopped long enough to get food and straw and he was gone. That's psychological warfare.

This race is far from over. But if there ever was a time for the cluster of challengers who are chasing Lance to gain some ground, the time is now when they're on the Yukon, and before they get to Kaltag. The team that gains the most ground has at least the opportunity to be in position to do battle on the Gold Coast.

By the time he reached Unalakleet, Bruce Lee, the 1998 Yukon Quest champion, felt Lance had the race in the bag: *I'm sitting here on the shore of the Bering Sea in the town of Unalakleet with Lance Mackey's dogs resting by the checkpoint. This coastal village is buried in drifting snow this year. Many drifts are as tall as houses. At this point I think it fair to finally state that this race is now Lance's to lose. That really has been the case since he made his dynamic run over to Iditarod leaving all of his competitors with a huge time difference to make up. He followed that run with two high powered runs to Anvik and Eagle Island. At Kaltag he made sure he was leaving the checkpoint before any of his competitors arrived. This team is truly amazing to watch travel. They seem to never lose steam and I would go as far as to say they are the nicest traveling team I have ever seen.*

Two days later the Iditarod press release made it official: *In 2008, Lance Mackey proved the impossible was possible again. Today, (March 18, 2009) Lance Mackey made an indelible mark on the Iditarod Trail Sled Dog Race, and on his legacy as an Iditarod Champion. The Fairbanks Alaska musher arrived in Nome Alaska at 11:38:46 am under a blue sky with thousands of race fans cheering him on. Mackey (Bib #47)* made his way under the burled arch with 15 very happy, healthy members of his team. Mackey now joins the legendary Susan Butcher and Montana musher Doug Swingley as having accomplished three consecutive Iditarod Championships. He created an impressive gap between himself and the rest of the pack that has not been seen since 2001. This win was, in a word, "impressive." Mackey set the pace in the 2009 Iditarod after taking his 24 hours in Takotna. From that point forward Mackey's teams runs were blistering. He passed all of his competitors and grew his lead each step of the way.

Alaska Governor Sarah Palin called to congratulate Mackey on his three-peat. Iditarod Principal Partner Anchorage Chrysler Dodge owner Rod Udd was on hand to present Mackey with his third Dodge Ram Quad Cab Pick-up truck in a row. Principal Partner Wells Fargo's Representative Loren Prosser presented Mackey a check for $69,000. In addition, Principal Partner ExxonMobil's Representative Bill Brackin, and Principal Partner GCI's Representative, Gary Samuelson presented Lance with the garland of roses for his two lead dogs Maple and Larry.

CHAPTER FOURTEEN

Wasilla, Alaska

In June I flew down to Washington to see our daughter Jody, my sister Sue, and to work on some things around the two places we still owned there. Mark and I seemed to be trading off making the trip south about every three or four months, spending time with Jody, working on moving the stuff we wanted north and getting rid of the vehicles, boats, trailers, furniture, household goods and other detritus of the years we'd spent there. We rented one of the houses out, but the other one we maintained as a place to be when either of us was there. We had many years' worth of old magazine issues and books we'd published archived in the basement, and we had an office manager who worked three days a week in our old office answering the phone, doing data entry, filling mail orders, feeding the cat and watering the plants.

It was fun being in Washington again for about two days, and then I was ready to go home. I enjoyed the time spent with my daughter, and I always had a good time with my sister and her husband, but I longed to be back in the north country with Mark and our sons. We'd bought a large unfinished two-story log cabin on five acres a few years before, and Mark and the boys had worked on it until we were able to sell it for a handsome profit, which we invested in a large two-story shop where the boys could build their automotive business. Now the plan was to ready one of the

Washington homes for the market, and buy ourselves a home in Alaska with the profit from that sale. Meanwhile Mark and I were living in an apartment attached to the shop, and while it was fun to be part of what the boys were doing every day, I was quite ready for a home of our own.

Before we could sell the Washington property we needed to do a little more work on it, and that was why we traded trips south to get the work done. I managed to get a lot cleared out by hauling two truckloads of stuff to my sister's place near Spokane for a weekend yard sale, and not long afterwards I flew back to Alaska with my two young granddaughters, who were going to spend a month with their dad in Alaska.

We spent most of the summer salmon fishing, great multi-family fishing trips to our favorite camping spots, filling everyone's freezer and enjoying salmon feeds almost every night. Mark and I would play marathon games of cribbage and Scrabble, and then he'd go fishing with the boys at midnight because the tide was right.

In early August we took all the grandkids up to Hatcher Pass on a blueberry picking adventure, and I spent two days freezing the berries for winter pancakes and muffins.

On August 14th we went to the Willow Creek campground for a fishing trip and birthday party for two granddaughters. It rained off and on all day but didn't dampen the spirits of the fishermen or the partiers, and it was late in the day before everyone headed for home, full of hot dogs, root beer, birthday cake and good memories.

The next day we took Mark and the Washington granddaughters to the airport and they all flew to Seattle, and it seemed as if our short happy summer was coming to an end. What I didn't know at the time was that it was the end of much more than summer.

That fall I coordinated a conference on the history of mushing in partnership with Tim White, a champion musher, expert innovator, reknowned sled builder and designer of the famed Quick Change Runner (QCR) System, in which an aluminum rail was screwed to the bottom of wooden runners, then lengths of plastic could be slid into the rails, greatly simplifying the process of changing plastic during a race.

In a 2004 interview with Mark Nordman, an accomplished racer and longtime Race Marshall for the Iditarod, June Price had learned that Mark and Tim's friendship extended back to the early 1980's, when they traveled to Alaska together, Tim as racer and Mark as his dog handler: *"Asked to characterize White, Nordman pauses to think. 'Sled dog sports are his life,' he begins slowly. He explains that as being someone whose every thought and action is somehow connected to the dogs. 'Tim White is the ultimate dog man,' concludes Nordman."*

Tim and I had been corresponding by email for several weeks, and in November we brought everything together in a three-day conference. The first day was an informal gathering at the Iditarod Trail Sled Dog Race Headquarters log cabin near Wasilla, where attendees enjoyed coffee and cookies and an evening of friendship and sharing. Joe Redington, Jr., son of the Iditarod race founder, shared a few slides from his family photo albums as an introduction to the presentation he'd brought to the conference, and the speakers and guests who'd traveled to Alaska for the conference were delighted with the opportunity to tour the colorful Iditarod Headquarters log cabin, with its collection of race memorabilia.

The actual conference got underway Saturday morning at the University of Alaska Anchorage, with Tim White giving a presentation on *The Evolution of Working Sled Dog Nutrition and Diets From Prehistory to the Present*. Tim's slideshow presentation traced working and racing sled dog diets, from the ingredients of wolves and of aboriginal people's dogs to the typical modern racing diets in long distance events. Tim explained the diets used during historic expeditions and explained how, under difficult circumstances, things can go wrong when an animal is expected to perform under difficult circumstances without the foods it is adapted to through evolution. An interested audience wrapped up his presentation with a spirited discussion of the various feeds used in the first Iditarod races.

Long Hard Trails and Sled Dog Tales

Carol Beck of Yellowknife, in Canada's Northwest Territories, was the next speaker, and she brought to life the colorful history of the Diavik 150, one of the longest-running sled dog races in the world. Carol was a sled dog racer and had participated in many races in North America, and she and her husband Grant had been co-chairs of the 2008 Arctic Winter Games Dog Sledding Committee.

Kevin Keeler, Administrator for the Iditarod National Historic Trail, brought a wealth of information, beautiful posters, booklets, flyers, and other materials to share with the conference attendees, and he explained how January, 2008 had marked the 100th anniversary of efforts to open the now famous overland route from Seward to Nome. Kevin also gave a powerpoint presentation which provided an overview of the history, route selection and development of the Iditarod Trail, the sleds and types of teams used, discussed the variations in routes, trail marking, a few of the old roadhouses, and explained a bit about what was being done to preserve and protect the current day Iditarod National Historic Trail.

Dr. Linda Chamberlain of Homer, Alaska, was a scientist, author, professor, historian and dog musher, living with her 20 huskies and her husband, Al, on their 45-acre Howling Husky Homestead outside of Homer. Dr. Chamberlain brought a presentation which traced the history of mail delivery by dog teams along the Iditarod Trail and the Kenai Peninsula, based on historical documents from the National Archives and Records Administration, the U.S. Postal Museum, the Alaska State Library, universities, museums and historical societies, interviews, private collections, and an extensive literature review.

Rod Perry, an author, musher, filmmaker, adventurer and self-proclaimed raconteur, brought a colorful exploration of the Iditarod Trail Sled Dog Race, beginning with an impressive freehand drawing of the state of Alaska, which he filled in with rivers, mountain ranges, towns and cities, and of course, the Iditarod Trail. Rod was one of the intrepid mushers making the 1,000 mile trek to Nome in the very first Iditarod in 1973, with his media darling of a lead dog, 'Fat Albert,' showing the way. I didn't remember Rod, but I certainly remembered the photos and articles about 'Fat Albert,' and it was fun to meet Rod and talk about the first race.

Rod had just published a book on the history of the Iditarod Trail, and he explained how there were trails running north from Seward for about 200 miles to the Alaska Commercial post at Susitna Station, a steamboat stop on the Susitna River; and trails which coursed south from Nome, 300 miles to Kaltag on the Yukon river, over a popular route between Nome and Fairbanks; but in between the ends of those routes lay over 400 miles of little-used and rarely traveled terrain.

Joe Redington, Jr. was someone I definitely remembered; I'd been standing on a street corner in Anchorage, loudly cheering him on, when he won the World Championship Sled Dog Race in 1966. Now Joe and his wife Pam made their home in Manley Hot Springs, 160 miles northwest of Fairbanks, but he'd traveled to Anchorage to share the history and legacy of his family. Joe showed and explained photos of his dad's early days in Alaska, his fish camps and boats, dogteams and airplanes, the Redington boys growing up in Knik and at Flathorn Lake, both on the Iditarod Trail; Joe Sr. working for the Army salvaging wrecked airplanes, and summiting Denali with four-time Iditarod champion Susan Butcher and the renowned mountaineer Ray Genet; and my favorites: Joe Jr. winning the 1966 World Championship Sled Dog Race at the Anchorage Fur Rendezvous.

The last day of the Mushing History Conference was held back in Wasilla, at the Grandview Hotel. Joe gave a second presentation consisting of a video he'd put together which combined many of the same slides with some additional images, but the narrator this time was his father, Joe Sr.! It was fascinating to see both the slideshow and the video, to hear father and son each talking about the family photos, commenting on things which happened over the years, ways of doing things, making observations and sharing laughs with the viewers. The stirring tribute to

Long Hard Trails and Sled Dog Tales

Joe's father, 'Redington's Run,' by Alaska's State Balladeer Hobo Jim, ended the video. It was a delightful presentation, and certainly a highlight of the conference.

Another traveler from out of state was Jeffrey Dinsdale, of Quesnel, British Columbia. He'd been involved in breeding and working with sled dogs for almost 40 years, as he and his family had lived in Canada's Northwest Territories, the Yukon and Northern British Columbia.

Jeff had a keen interest in sled dog history; he was involved in the organization of the first Carcross, Yukon to Atlin, British Columbia Mail Run in 1975, and since 1992 he had been involved with the organization of the Gold Rush Trail Dog Sled Mail Run from Quesnel, B.C., to Barkerville and Wells, B.C. In the 1970's and 80's Jeff had worked with the Canadian Kennel Club and the Eskimo Dog Research Foundation during a period when attempts were being made to ensure that these dogs, which are indigenous to the Canadian Arctic, would continue to thrive, and Jeff had published many articles in various sled dog-related publications.

In the early sixties Walt Disney Studios made a feature length film titled *Nikki, Wild dog of the North*, about a half-husky, half-wolf separated from its owner during the gold rush in Canada's Yukon Territory. As a young girl I'd been entranced by the movie, in love with the beautiful husky pup, Nikki.

What Jeff Dinsdale brought to the conference was a story which many people–including me– didn't know: That Joe Redington Sr. bred the dog who played in the title role! Jeff shared the story behind that dog, and all the dogs used in the film, and how they ended up in the kennels of the Royal Canadian Mounted Police, and what happened after that, in a fun and engaging presentation which no one wanted to see end.

Jeff had written the story for his website, *Mushing Past: Nikki was bred by Joe and Vi Redington of Knik Alaska. He was originally named Polar and was born February 4, 1958. At six months of age he was sold to Bill Bacon. His sire was Tok, a Malamute show dog and a fair working animal. His dam was Chena, also a Malamute, of Earl and Natalie Norris stock. Nikki (Polar) had no Siberian Husky blood in him. The Redingtons later sold six other dogs to Bacon, three males and three females. Three were Chena's pups, but three were sired by Tok of a ½ Siberian Husky ½ Eskimo Dog named Belle. Belle's sire was from Greenland and was brought to Alaska by the U.S. Air Force 10th Rescue Unit of Elmendorf Air Force Base. In all it should be noted that over 200 different sled dogs were used in the movie 'Nikki –Wild Dog of the North,' which was released in 1961.*

Jane Haigh was an Assistant Professor of History at Kenai Peninsula College and an accomplished Alaskan author and historian who had written or co-written a number of books of popular Alaskan history, including *Gold Rush Dogs, Children of the Gold Rush, Gold Rush Women, King Con: The Story of Soapy Smith*, and *The Search for Fannie Quigley: A Wilderness Life in the Shadow of Mount McKinley*. In 2008 Jane was honored by the Alaska Historical Society with their annual "Historian of the Year" recognition, and she brought one of my favorite authors to life at the conference: Esther Birdsall Darling.

Nome pioneer and author Esther Birdsall Darling was the woman who partnered with Scotty Allan's kennel, and helped in the creation of the Nome Kennel Club. Esther Birdsall Darling had been responsible for publicizing the first All Alaska Sweepstakes races and writing the race programs, including the booklet and postcards titled *The Great Dog Races of Nome Held under the Auspices of the Nome Kennel Club, Nome, Alaska: Official Souvenir History*, printed in Nome, Alaska by the Nome Kennel Club, 1916.

She was the author of several books on Nome and the All Alaska Sweepstakes races, including the classic best-selling children's book, *Baldy of Nome*, detailing the exploits of Scotty Allan's famous leader. First published in 1913, the book was kept in print by popular demand through the next four decades, and Baldy's descendants, including Boris and Navarre, were featured in additional books by Darling. Jane Haigh's slideshow and discussion of the famous Nome author and pioneer brought a wonderful Alaskan personality to light for the conference attendees, and I enjoyed getting to know Jane herself, author of several books I had greatly enjoyed.

The last presenter in the Mushing History Conference was my friend Chas St. George, Director of Public Relations for the Iditarod. He brought a film preview from the newest Iditarod video project, *Purely Alaskan*, the first in a series of videos highlighting the almost forty years of Iditarod race history. The 90-minute documentary told the story of the race through archived photos and interviews with more than fifty people, including past champions and other mushers, race veterinarians, Iditarod Air Force pilots, volunteers and others.

Chas had brought more than just the film clip; he also brought along a piece of mushing history in the form of a handwritten letter on the first Iditarod Trail Race stationery, printed in a forget-me-not blue color and decorated with a dogteam racing across the top, the Alaskan flag in the margin, and a relief map of the state of Alaska faded into the background behind the writing.

The letter was from Joe Redington, Sr. to Howard Farley of Nome, dated December 9, 1972–a short three months before the inaugural race began. Written in Joe's bold cursive hand, the historic letter read:

Dear Howard,

I thought you might be interested in this race. I need some help on that end. Let me know if you are interested, also I need to know how many teams will run such a race. I plan to enter and several others here in Knik plan it also. We have some teams already entered from the lower 48. Can you get in touch with any of the nearby villages, maybe radio. I would like to put you on our Iditarod Trail Committee, you could do a lot of good on the Nome end.

Let me know how you feel on this as soon as you can.
So long for now.
Joe Sr.

Long Hard Trails and Sled Dog Tales

In an article she later wrote about the conference for *Mushing* magazine, my friend June Price quoted Chas:

"Joe Redington Sr. put it on the line," he said. "He put his mortgage on the line. Journalists were following him around calling him a Don Quixote," he added, but Redington never wavered. "It wasn't about who won," said St. George, "but about the journey," a sentiment shared by everyone there.

Redington's dreams were a huge part of the presentation made by Chas St. George, too. As a set of photos from the Iditarod's past cycled before our eyes in an endless loop, St. George and others in the audience shared their appreciation of Redington Sr.'s ability to pull others into his dreams. Redington appreciated the history of mushing and lived the lifestyle, yet celebrated its adventure, too. Those gathered for the conference weren't about just sharing ol' stories about mushing; they were sharing it in a manner that put it in the words of those who'd lived the journey. St. George acknowledged this, so to speak, noting that the Iditarod's effort to capture its own history isn't about us telling the story ourselves, but an attempt to tell it through the words of those who've experienced this race.

The Mushing History Conference was a lot of work, a lot of fun, and brought many new friends into my life. It gave me a deeper appreciation for the richness and diversity of the history of mushing, not just the sled dog races, but the important role sled dogs had played in the development of Alaska and the north country. A few years later that appreciation would become a book, *Along Alaskan Trails: Adventures in Sled Dog History*.

About a month after the conference I sent a query to the online newsmagazine *Alaska Dispatch* for a regular column about sled dog races and the history of mushing. The publication's logo was a dogteam silhouette, and I figured with the upcoming race season providing an almost endless supply of newsworthy action it would be a good time to start writing for them on a regular basis.

Long Hard Trails and Sled Dog Tales

The publication had begun the year before as an Alaskan news blog, started by former *Bloomberg* and *Newsweek* correspondent Tony Hopfinger and his then-wife, journalist Amanda Coyne. In 2009, Alice Rogoff, a former *U.S. News & World Report* chief financial officer and wife of Carlyle Group co-founder David Rubenstein, bought a majority share in the website, and the organization moved into a hangar located along Anchorage's Merrill Field Airport. The staff had grown to include respected journalists who had previously worked for other Alaska news outlets such as the *Fairbanks Daily News-Miner*, the *Anchorage Press*, local NBC affiliate KTUU and the *Anchorage Daily News*.

My proposal for a column was accepted and I began writing the twice weekly *Team & Trail* in December, 2009. My first column was *Winter in Alaska is Mushing Season*, about how the history of Alaska is inextricably tied to sled dog mushing. A study of how reindeer herds had almost replaced dogteams as the preferred mode of travel in Alaska was next, followed by a review of Becky Bristow's video about three female mushers on the Yukon Quest, and then a wide-ranging series of columns on the upcoming race season. I would write the *Team & Trail* column for four years, after which it became a collection point for mushing-related articles by anyone on the *Alaska Dispatch* staff.

Chapter Fifteen

Fairbanks, Alaska

On January 8 I drove to Glennallen for the 2010 Copper Basin 300, a tough race known as the 'little Iditarod' for its challenging terrain and often bottomed-out temperatures. The next morning I was warmly greeted by my friend Barb Redington, and we enjoyed photographing the start in downtown Glennallen with unseasonably warm weather. The teams were heading west along the Glenn Highway from town, so I was able to leapfrog ahead of them and get some wonderful images of teams with the Wrangell Mountains behind them, and a few great action shots of the dogs and sleds kicking up snow while coming down a fairly steep hill near Tolsona Creek.

I went back to the race headquarters and uploaded photos and race reports to our Northern Light Media website, then joined a friend for a late lunch at the Caribou Cafe. I spent some time talking to handlers and media friends who were still in town, but most had moved up the trail to meet their teams at the more remote checkpoints. I stayed in Glennallen and chatted with my friend Theresa Daily as she managed the race website that afternoon, tracking the racers' progress while editing my best photos and writing an article for my column at *Alaska Dispatch's Team & Trail*:

Long Hard Trails and Sled Dog Tales

The 2010 Copper Basin 300 got underway this morning, with 43 teams leaving the starting chute in downtown Glennallen. In a change from the last few races the mushers headed due west and followed the Glenn Highway all the way to Tolsona Lake Resort, 23 miles away. With temperatures near zero the race began in an icy overcast, but after climbing for a few miles the teams popped out under beautiful blue sunny skies and they raced past throngs of camera-clad well-wishers all along the route.

At 6:00 p.m. the front-runner is Hugh Neff, who splits his time between Tok and and Annie Lake, Yukon. Neff was followed by Zack Steer of Sheep Mountain and Emil Churchin of Anchorage. From Tolsona Lake the mushers headed north and west to Wolverine Lodge on Lake Louise, and then turned east to Sourdough Creek on the Richardson Highway.

The next morning I drove to Paxson Lodge, narrowly missing a moose who decided to dash across the highway right in front of me. The temperature had nose-dived and it was a frosty minus-twenty-five, but the road was good and I enjoyed the drive, listening to race reports on the local KCAM radio, "The Voice of the Copper River Valley." I got a kick out of their opening theme music from the movie *"The Good, The Bad, and The Ugly"* for race reports, and it always set my mind to categorizing the teams in like manner.

Three-time Copper Basin champion Jeff King led for much of the race, but Allen Moore was only two minutes behind him when the teams got back to Glennallen, still twenty-four miles from the finish. Moore was posting faster run times, and it looked like he was going to pass King before the finish, but Moore's dogs got into a tangle leaving Glennallen and King was able to put some distance between them.

As the first musher into the Tolsona Lake finish checkpoint King added a fourth Copper Basin victory with a seven minute lead, followed by Moore, and then Josh Cadzow of Fort Yukon finishing third almost an hour later. Former Yukon Quest champion Sonny Lindner was fourth, followed by Dan Kaduce, Ray Redington, Sven Haltmann, Brent Sass and

Long Hard Trails and Sled Dog Tales

Zack Steer. I didn't stay around for the finish banquet, feeling like I'd already spent too long away from home and other duties. I hit the road for Wasilla, slept at a roadside pullout above the Matanuska River for a few hours, and made it home as the sun was climbing above the Chugach Range. Somewhere along the way I scrawled a rhetorical question to myself in my journal: *What is it I find so damned interesting about this sport? Why do these mushers and their dog teams fascinate me so much? I think it was Mom who started it all...*

Mom had been intrigued by the sled dog races from the first winter we spent in Alaska, in 1965-66. She would take every opportunity to bundle us kids into the car and go find a race to watch, and I remember endless hours of sitting in an idling warm car sipping a cup of hot chocolate and wondering what was so doggone interesting to her about these racing dog teams. Mom knew all the key players' names, like George Attla, Joee Redington Jr., Dr. Roland Lombard, Earl Norris, Gareth Wright, Bergman Sam, Clarence Charlie... She talked about them as if they were real friends, and she knew the race histories and previous winnings of many of them. Dad seemed to humor her passion, but it was easy for me to tell this was something Mom loved and Dad merely abided.

I thought the big furry sled dogs were cool, but I wasn't too interested in the races. I'd usually just bury my nose in my latest book about fictional heroic dogs which interested me much more than the very real canine heroes racing outside the car. Mom obligingly fed my growing passion for classic dog stories and bought me books like *Beautiful Joe, Big Red, Lassie Come Home,* and *Old Yeller.*

I didn't get interested in sled dogs until the winter of 1972, when my then-husband and I were living in a cabin we'd built on 160 acres north of Wasilla. An old friend gave us several sled dogs, and then another friend invited me to a meeting for a new race being planned, a long-distance race unlike anything which had been done before. The idea of racing sled dogs 1,000 miles across Alaska seemed a little crazy, and that might have been what appealed to me about it. There was an element of that heroic story I'd come to love in my classic dog stories, only this was the real deal.

I wrote an article about the next big race for my *Team & Trail* column in *Alaska Dispatch*:

The Yukon Quest International Sled Dog Race starts in Fairbanks on Saturday, Feb. 6, with 24 teams heading for the city of Whitehorse, in Canada's Yukon Territory. The 1,000-mile trail follows the Yukon River, the old highway of the North, retracing the route the prospectors followed to the Klondike during the 1898 gold rush. The checkpoints are like echoes of Alaska-Yukon history: Central, Circle City, Eagle, Dawson City, Pelly Crossing, McCabe Creek, Carmacks... The Yukon Quest is known as the toughest sled dog race on Earth, crossing four mountain summits, including the 4,000-foot King Solomon's Dome, and with temperatures often dropping beyond 50 below. It's a grueling test of man and dog,

There's an impressive field of mushers entered, including the four-time Yukon Quest champion and reigning Iditarod champion, Lance Mackey; the three-time Quest champion Hans Gatt; the first place finisher in the first Quest in 1984, Sonny Lindner; last year's second place finisher, Hugh Neff; and the 2008 second place finisher, Ken Anderson. The 2009 champion, Sebastian Schnuelle, who set a new race record with his run of 9 days, 23 hours, and 20 minutes, is not running this year's Yukon Quest, but is entered in this year's Iditarod, which starts March 6 in Anchorage.

According to the musher profiles the only musher from the Lower 48 is Katie Davis, from Olney, Mont.; but then there's Pierre-Antoine Heritier of Switzerland and two Belgian mushers, Sam Deltour and Dries Jacobs. The rest of the mushers are from Alaska and the Yukon, with the exception of Bart De Marie, of Christopher Lake, Saskatchewan, who, like Dries and Sam, was born in Belgium.

On February 3rd I left for Fairbanks and the start of the 2010 Yukon Quest. This would be my third Quest, and I was getting the race route and the usual players figured out, and the more I learned about the 1,000-mile trek from Fairbanks to Whitehorse, the better I liked this race. There was something raw and visceral about it, something a little wilder than the much more commercialized Iditarod. There seemed to be more of a community feeling to this race, as compared to what I could only characterize as a corporate feel to the Iditarod.

I took my big gray Alaskan husky Chena with me again, in part because I liked having him along, and in part because I knew he enjoyed traveling almost as much as I did. But I also worried about him when he wasn't with me; there was an 8' chain-link fence around our acre and a half property, but the gates were too often left open, and he would go through them and off exploring at any opportunity. Keeping him with me at least kept him safe.

We stopped frequently for short hikes and explored places I wouldn't have even noticed if he wasn't with me. I rarely put a collar on him, as he almost always came when I called him, and on walks he ranged closely and stopped when I stopped. His only bad habit was chasing rabbits; he loved pursuing the fleet-footed little animals, and he often caught them, and when he did he'd stop and eat most of them on the spot, which meant a delay of anywhere from a half-hour to an hour while he enjoyed his meal. Calling him back from a hunt just didn't work, it was the one time he would ignore my recall, but the occasional delays seemed like a small price to pay for his majestic companionship.

We stopped for the evening at a favorite pullout alongside the Nenana River, and I built a small campfire and heated water for tea and soup. It was peaceful there, listening to the silence, and a faint aurora flickered over the mountains which soared above us. I wished Mark was with me, but I didn't mind being alone. I was never really alone with Chena there.

I stopped at the Fairbanks Fred Meyers the next morning and bought fresh batteries and a new SD card for my camera. That evening was the fun and relaxed Mushers' Meet & Greet at the Alpine Hotel, kicking off the official race events. I chatted with friends between photographing the mushers and asking questions about their race plans, meeting a few I hadn't talked to before and wishing I knew more about their race histories, but with my notes and a little online research I was able to write a fairly knowledgeable column for the *Alaska Dispatch* that evening:

The 2010 Yukon Quest International Sled Dog Race starts on Saturday, but Thursday evening the mushers were relaxing and chatting with fans and each other; signing posters, T-shirts, caps and whatever else was presented, enjoying a relaxing low-key evening of camaraderie before the last-minute details come together and they hit the trail for Whitehorse. Of the couple dozen mushers gathered, it was striking how many were either past Yukon Quest champions or had come very close to winning, often multiple times.

A huge draw for the crowd was returning four-time Quest champion Lance Mackey, who made headlines last year when he dropped out of the Quest to focus on the Iditarod. Not only was Lance gunning for his third consecutive Iditarod championship, he was also mentoring National Guard rookie musher Harry Alexie in that race. The result? Lance won again, and his protege finished successfully in 37th place in a field of 52 mushers.

Yukon musher Hans Gatt, who won the Yukon Quest three consecutive times before Lance started his winning streak -- in 2002, 2003, and 2004 -- is back for his eighth Quest bid. Hans says he's counting on his well-seasoned veteran dogs and "a few outstanding newcomers."

Notably missing this year is the reigning champion and crowd favorite Sebastian Schnuelle, who's focusing his team and his attention on the Iditarod this year. After winning the 2009 Yukon Quest, Sab, as he's known to his fans and friends, went on to place second in last year's Iditarod. This years he's made it known that he's aiming to unseat the three-time champ, Lance.

Ken Anderson, who ran neck-and-neck with Lance in the last half of the 2008 Yukon Quest and crossed the finish line only a few minutes behind him, is back again, as is Hugh Neff, who finished four minutes behind Sebastian Schnuelle last year. Hugh placed third in the 2005 Quest; of the seven times he's run this race he's been in the top ten in five of them.

Long Hard Trails and Sled Dog Tales

And the man who won the very first Yukon Quest in 1984, Sonny Lindner, is returning for the sixth time. Sonny hasn't entered the Quest since 1996, but he was never out of the top ten before that. And in last year's Iditarod he was barely out of the top ten, placing a very respectable 11th.

There are plenty of other champions entered, from other races around Alaska and the Yukon, most notably Brent Sass, who's won both the Copper Basin 300 and the Gin Gin in recent years; Joshua Cadzow, who won the 2008 Yukon Quest 300; Zack Steer, who won the 2003 Copper Basin 300 and came in second in the 2004 Quest; and Gerry Willomitzer, who won the tough Percy DeWolfe Memorial, which runs a segment of the Yukon Quest trail, in 2008. Named for an intrepid dogteam mail carrier known as the "Iron Man of the North," the Percy DeWolfe runs the Yukon River between Dawson City and Eagle, the 200 mile section of the Yukon Quest often noted as being the toughest stretch.

With so many champions and near-champions entered, and with a field of rookies which could still include a surprise 2010 champion, this year's Yukon Quest promises to be an exciting race! As Lance Mackey sagely noted after his 2008 win, "It's a dog race, and anything can happen!"

There was a media briefing the next afternoon at the Alpine Hotel, then I spent the rest of the day exploring Fairbanks with Donna and her sister, who was visiting from Outside. We had fun touring the Ice Park, where ice sculptors were working on their imaginative and delicate creations for the upcoming world championships in ice carving.

The next morning I walked among the teams getting ready and shot another hundred or so photos, then joined a friend for the annual pancake feed adjacent to the staging area. As the first mushers got ready to advance to the starting chute down on the Chena River I walked across the Cushman Street bridge and found a good vantage point from which to photograph the teams as they approached from downriver. On the opposite side I could look right down on the starting chute and I took several shots which later turned out quite nice.

Long Hard Trails and Sled Dog Tales

After all the teams were away I drove out to the Nordale bridge boat ramp and caught a few teams coming up the river, notably a great photo of Mike Ellis' all-Siberian team stretched out just coming under the bridge. I backtracked to Chena Hot Springs Road and spent an hour photographing from the top of Pleasant Hill Road, getting some wonderful photographs of the teams coming up the long straight stretch before the turn toward Pleasant Valley Store, and then I caught the last mushers from the store parking lot and a couple of teams running alongside the road.

I leapfrogged ahead and stopped at the road crossing, shooting some of my all-time favorite images of Hans Gatt and his team, and then caught the front-runners again at the Two Rivers checkpoint. By then it was long past dark, so I headed back into Fairbanks. I stopped at the Yukon Quest headquarters log cabin and when I explained what I was doing they graciously gave me a desk to work from and their wifi password. I downloaded photos and wrote articles for our Northern Light Media website and the *Alaska Dispatch* column until midnight, when the staff closed the doors and headed home.

After their traditional pancake breakfast with the fans and supporters on Saturday morning, the mushers of the 2010 Yukon Quest International Sled Dog Race filed out to their waiting teams in the dog yard, spent an hour or so posing with fans for photos and answering last-minute questions from the media, and then it was time to get down to serious business. Loads were checked and double-checked, wives and girlfriends and well-wishers were bid a final farewell, and then it was down onto the frozen Chena River in downtown Fairbanks. With a snowmachine hitched to the rear of each sled to help control the lunging huskies, and a line of handlers with strong leads attached at strategic points along the gangline out front, the mushers and their excited teams advanced slowly under the Cushman Street bridge toward the starting chute.

Promptly at 11 a.m. rookie Abbie West and her team started the race up the Chena River, hoping to survive the rigors of the trail and make it all the way to Whitehorse, 1,000 hard miles away.

Long Hard Trails and Sled Dog Tales

Quest veteran Zack Steer was second, and then a slow but steady stream of teams left the chute at three minute intervals, every team accompanied by loud cheering from the crowd gathered on the bridges above them: David Dalton, Sam Deltour, Gerry Willomitzer, Katie Davis, Terry Williams, Jocelyne LeBlanc, Cindy Barrand, Normand Casavant, Lance Mackey -- the crowd roared its approval when the four-time champion appeared -- Brent Sass, Hans Gatt, Bart De Marie, Kelley Griffin, Jennifer Raffaeli, Ken Anderson, Mike Ellis, Pierre-Antoine Heritier, and the winner of the very first Yukon Quest in 1984, Sonny Lindner. The final few teams included Joshua Cadzow, Dries Jacobs, Hugh Neff and rookie Peter Fleck. The 27th Yukon Quest International Sled Dog Race was underway!

The teams followed the winding Chena River through the birch and spruce forests east of Fairbanks, and at various places along the route groups of fans and media personnel gathered to watch and photograph the teams passing by. The first mushers reached the Pleasant Valley Store on Chena Hot Springs Road by early afternoon, where a large and appreciative crowd of fans and photographers met them. The trail paralleled the road for the next several miles, and cars pulling over to snap photos were a common sight. Near mile 26 two volunteers watched for teams and stopped traffic as they approached the first road crossing; soon afterward, the teams reached the first checkpoint at Two Rivers. Zack Steer, of Sheep Mountain, was the first musher to arrive at Two Rivers, and then just as they left the start, although in greatly shuffled order, the mushers filed into the checkpoint, some bedding down their teams for a rest, others dashing through to rest somewhere further down the trail. The night would be dark and the trail ahead was long...

My trail ahead was south, back to Wasilla, because we had a magazine to finish and send to the printer. I needed to write an editorial for the upcoming issue, as usual the last piece of the puzzle to drop into place, and as I drove south I thought about my kids and their learning and how much I'd learned from them over the years. I would stop every so often

Long Hard Trails and Sled Dog Tales

and write notes in my journal, sometimes entire paragraphs which would later be transcribed directly, and it turned out to be a pretty good piece of writing, running in our May-June, 2010 issue:

Parenting is really all about becoming a much better person, learning and growing along with your kids.

I've often claimed that I've learned much more from my kids than they ever learned from me. It makes sense mathematically: there are five of them and only one of me. It makes sense because they've grown up with some amazing tools in their lifetime, such as computers and DVD players and cellphones, which they seem to feel quite comfortable with while I can barely make them function. It makes sense because their knowledge and information sources long ago outstripped what I grew up with half a century ago. I remember getting dizzily excited about my first calculator, for gosh sakes, when calculators were still something new and special and important.

My kids have taught me how to send text messages and program my TV to tell me when a program I want to watch is coming on. But my kids have also taught me how to look at life, and living, and what's important and what's not, and how to tell the difference.

It hasn't been easy for them, because I haven't always been a willing student. I came of age in the heady sixties, in a generation which was certain it had most, if not all, of the answers. We might have nodded appreciatively when Dylan said they were 'blowin' in the wind,' but no, really, we knew the answers to life's questions. Or at least we knew how to find them.

I was probably among the worst, because I was a writer, and writers have a certain edgy need to have answers. But over time, my kids have made me see that I certainly don't have as many answers as I once thought I did, and in many cases I'm no longer even sure of the questions.

I mentioned in my opening that I've covered this ground before, so I'd like to share a little of something I wrote many years ago about what my kids have taught me:

Long Hard Trails and Sled Dog Tales

"They taught me that life makes us all learners, and that while some of us learn easily, others learn with more difficulty. They taught me that it's okay to skip knowing something. They taught me that there will never, ever be enough time to learn everything I'd like to learn, to do everything I'd like to do, and that's how it should be. My kids taught me to listen with an open heart, and to see without making judgments. They taught me patience, and perseverance, and persistence , but they also taught me to know when to quit. They taught me that love does not bring conditions with it, but just is, and they made me a much better person than I'd have ever been without them."

I think being a parent is really all about becoming a much better person, learning and growing along with your kids, developing a perspective that can only come from parenting, and finding questions and their answers along the way. I see the process continuing as I watch one of my sons learning from one of his own kids.

We are all teachers, students, tutors, pupils, leaders, learners, gurus, grasshoppers.

I followed the rest of the Yukon Quest from my computer at home, and since I couldn't be on the road with the race, I consoled myself by writing about the road in a column for *Alaska Dispatch* titled 'The Long Drive':

As team after team heads out onto the frozen Yukon River from the historic village of Circle City, the handlers driving the big dog trucks now set off in the opposite direction for a 1,000-mile drive to Dawson City, where the teams will take a mandatory 36-hour layover before setting out on the second half of the race. The mushers are now into territory only accessible by air, snowmachine, or, of course, dogsled.

The support teams have a long two-day drive ahead, over icy mountains, through blowing snow and howling winds, but also through some of the most spectacular scenery to be found anywhere. From Circle City they'll backtrack along the Steese Highway to Fairbanks, re-crossing the 3,685-foot Eagle Summit and 3,640-foot Rosebud Summit, to Fairbanks, where they'll turn south and east onto the Alaska Highway.

Long Hard Trails and Sled Dog Tales

The road passes through many small communities between Fairbanks and the Canadian border: North Pole, Salcha, Delta Junction, Dot Lake, Tok -- a major junction where the Glenn Highway heads south to Anchorage -- and then only the occasional lodge, most closed for the winter, until they reach the small border community of Beaver Creek, Yukon Territory. There's not much there... the Canadian customs office and border crossing, a couple of lodges with gas pumps out front, the town's population is only 120 or so.

Leaving Beaver Creek, the Alaska Highway heads into the remote territory north of the Wrangell, Kluane, and Nutzotin mountain ranges, an area long notorious for some of the coldest winter temperatures on record; at Snag the lowest temperature ever recorded anywhere in Canada was registered in February, 1947: -81.4 F / -63 C (the record for Alaska was set at Prospect Creek, a pipeline camp near Bettles, in 1971: -80 F / -62.8 C). It's beautiful country, crossing the glacial White and Donjek Rivers, and offering spectacular views to the south of the Icefield Ranges of the St. Elias Mountains, the highest in Canada, with seven peaks over 16,000 feet, including Canada's highest mountain, Mount Logan, at 19,545 feet.

The highway winds around the edge of the mostly frozen Kluane Lake, the largest in the Yukon Territory at over 150 square miles. The falling-in log cabins of Silver City, a 1904 trading post, roadhouse, and North West Mounted Police barracks, sits on the eastern shore of the lake. The highway crosses 3,293-foot Boutiller Summit and drops into Haines Junction under a panoramic view of the skyscraping Auriol Range, then finally turns north toward Whitehorse, 100 miles away.

Just before reaching Whitehorse, actually skirting the edge of the city limits, the Yukon Highway 2, also known as the North Klondike Highway or the Klondike Loop, heads off to the left and soon crosses the Takhini River bridge, a favorite viewing spot when the teams cross under it in a week or so. This is where the drivers once again meet the Yukon River -- it's off to the right -- and they'll more or less follow it all the way to Dawson City, 323 miles away. The highway runs alongside the 40-mile-

Long Hard Trails and Sled Dog Tales

long Lake Laberge, which Robert Service made famous in his epic poem, The Cremation of Sam McGee: "The Northern Lights have seen queer sights, but the queerest they ever did see, was that night on the marge of Lake Laberge I cremated Sam McGee."

Lake Laberge is actually just a widening of the Yukon River, but farther along the road passes Fox Lake, Little Fox Lake, and Braeburn Lake -- and then the last official checkpoint before the finish of the Yukon Quest, Braeburn Lodge. The dogtrucks roll on by for now, and pass checkpoints and dog drops along the way... Carmacks, McCabe Creek, Pelly Crossing, Stepping Stone, Scroggie Creek... and finally, the historic Klondike gold rush town of Dawson City. The trail-weary mushers will undoubtedly be happy to see them.

The race taking place hundreds of miles away kept me spellbound, as Lance, Hugh, and the Canadian Hans Gatt wrestled for the lead. I was alternately cheering for Lance, and then for Hans, whose disarming smile and quiet way with his dogs had impressed me in Fairbanks.

The three mushers arrived at the First Nations village of Carmacks, the next-to-the-last checkpoint in the race, with 177 miles to go, within 15 minutes of each other. Mackey pulled in at 5:08 am, Neff at 5:10, and Gatt close behind at 5:22. Leaving the Pelly Crossing checkpoint together, Lance and Hugh had been pacing each other for well over 100 miles, ever mindful of three-time Yukon Quest champion steadily closing the gap between them.

And then Hans Gatt's dogs were in the finish chute and the Yukon Quest's Facebook team posted: "Bib number 13, unlucky for some, but not Hans Gatt, who is the 2010 Yukon Quest Champion. He and his team have just come cruising across the finish line here in Whitehorse."

Hans set a new record for the fastest finish, at 9 days and 26 minutes, 23 hours shorter than the record set the previous year by Sebastian Schnuelle. He claimed his fourth Yukon Quest title, matching second-place finisher Lance Mackey for overall number of Quests won. Hugh Neff, who had finished second in the previous year's Quest, took third.

In an interview at the finish line, Hans said it was emotional to finish at home in Whitehorse with the crowd. "I can't even explain how this feels. I'm actually really emotional right now," he told reporters. "These nine dogs are incredible. I'm so proud of them."

Chapter Sixteen

Willow, Alaska

I posted half a dozen columns for *Alaska Dispatch* in the two weeks between the Yukon Quest and the Iditarod, with titles like *Mushing News Roundup, Magic Season for Sled Dogs,* and *Dogs, Dogs, Dogs: It seems as if Anchorage has gone to the dogs and everywhere one turns there are colorful, photogenic dogs and dog teams!*

In one column I shared an excerpt from a very thoughtful essay which appeared in *The New York Times*: "I watch the driving legs ahead of me -- 28 of them -- on dogs whose frames are small and light, nothing like the creatures I'd imagined. And as we cut through the white ash swamp, hissing across the ice, I find myself wondering, why do sled dogs run? It is not a matter of driving them. All the work is in pacing them, restraining them. When Murphy stands on the brake and sets the snow hook - a two-pronged anchor - the gangline quivers with tension. The dogs torque forward again before he can shout, 'Let's go!' All the one-word answers to my question are too simple: love, joy, duty, obedience."

Long Hard Trails and Sled Dog Tales

I also wrote a review of Lance's new book: *'The Lance Mackey Story: How My Obsession with Dog Mushing Saved My Life'* is as close as most of us will ever come to hitching a ride on Lance Mackey's sled as it crosses the vast frozen reaches of Alaska, and as such, his book doesn't disappoint. From the opening chapter, when he shares the awe and wonder of making sled dog racing history in 2007 with his unprecedented dual Yukon Quest and Iditarod wins, to the closing lines, which will be savored long after reading the book, Lance's masterful use of the written language to convey places, events, and especially emotions draws the reader into his world.

The book was edited by Joe Runyan, the 1983 Iditarod champion who broke Susan Butcher's winning streak, and author of *Winning Strategies for Distance Mushers*. He did a good job with Lance's book, but he also had some wonderful material to work with, as shown in this quote from Lance: "There is always the comfort and beauty of watching my team trotting. Muscles on their hind legs, rhythmic, trotting with so much power. Transfixed, I can stare for hours at my dogs moving across the white landscape, reminded that life itself is about moving forward -- made authentic with risk. I'm willing to take risks to keep living, and my dogs are bold, always ready to share it with me. I've learned to force myself to look around, take my eyes off the team, even ride backward on my sled and look behind, to break the trance."

It was great writing, and told a compelling story. I ended my review with another great quote from Lance:

If you've ever wondered about the personal back story of this incredible athlete, if you've ever wanted to know what it's like to be out there on the trail in the middle of nowhere depending on a team of huskies to see you safely home, if you've ever considered the demanding price he pays for his victories, Lance's book will be a satisfying read. He pulls no punches in explaining his complicated health issues, and he delights in sharing the triumphs and joys he's been rewarded with. "I was mugged, hugged, and overwhelmed. But I stole the chance, in a little moment of silence, to lean over my mother, the woman I'd put through hell for many a

Long Hard Trails and Sled Dog Tales

year and who'd stood by me for many a year. I hugged her tight and whispered, 'Dreams do come true, Mama.'"

On March third the Iditarod vet check in Wasilla saw many of the same mushers with their teams in the headquarters park lot, getting ready for the season's grand finale. The weather was too warm for the dogs at thirty-six above, but it made for a fun day of visiting with friends and photographing the dogs as the vets carefully went over team after team.

At the media meeting that afternoon I sat with my friends and took notes as the race parameters were spelled out for us. There would be 71 mushers leaving Willow this year, 16 women and 55 men, 59 from the US, eight from Canada, two from Scotland, and one each from Belgium and Jamaica. I knew the Jamaican was Newton; he'd greeted me with a big hug at the vet check and proclaimed how delighted he was that Lance was letting him take the venerable Larry as his leader to Nome!

The race statistics went on: 671 people had completed the Iditarod, twenty-eight of 2009's top thirty mushers had returned to compete again this year, and there were five past champions who had twenty wins between them: Rick Swenson with five wins; four each for Mitch Seavey, Jeff King, and Martin Buser; and Lance had three. The 2010 Iditarod was already being called the Race of Champions.

For several months I'd been working on the book we'd contracted for about the centennial running of the All Alaska Sweepstakes, and finally on March 4th it was ready to send to the printer. I was pleased with how the book turned out, as it told the story of the 2008 race with hundreds of Jan DeNapoli's beautiful full-color photos. I wrote a description of the book for our website: *'All Alaska Sweepstakes' is the story of the sixteen Alaskan mushers who entered their teams, each hoping to have their name engraved on the Sweepstakes trophy beside the great mushing legends Scotty Allan and Leonhard Seppala. And, of course, they were racing for the richest purse ever offered for a sled dog race: $100,000.00 winner-take-all!*

Long Hard Trails and Sled Dog Tales

I was glad to have the book published and the responsibility fulfilled, and I'd enjoyed the process of writing a book about something besides alternative education, which all of the previous books I'd worked on were about. I started looking through my photo files and decided I had enough good photos from the last two years at the Yukon Quest to create a photo-rich book about that great race as well. I knew from our previous publishing experience that writing books was not a short-term easy money project, but I wasn't concerned about that, I just wanted to publish the kind of books I myself would like to read. I figured the financial end of the business would take care of itself eventually.

The evening before the ceremonial start I once again found myself at Jim and Bonnie Foster's open house, mingling with friends and enjoying the sumptuous buffet. Engrossed in conversation with a couple of friends, I didn't notice that most of the guests had left until the only ones left were myself, my friend Gail Somerville, musher Sebastian Schnuelle and the 1985 Iditarod champion Libby Riddles. Gail and I were getting ready to leave when a neighbor of Jim and Bonnie's stopped by to borrow a couple of harnesses, and we waited to say our thanks for the evening.

Then the neighbor introduced a Russian friend who was a Chukchi musher and polar bear hunter, and asked if we'd like to see some slides he'd taken on a recent trip in the northern Bering Sea, off the coast of Siberia. We gathered around his computer screen and the rest of the evening was filled with incredible images of a large skin boat, called a umiak, from which they had photographed seals, walruses, polar bears and amazing landscapes showing the unmistakeable effects of global climate change. It was a spell-binding show and a wonderful ending to a delightful evening.

I spent Saturday playing hopscotch across Anchorage with the dogteams, shooting photos from the first big turn at 4th Avenue and Cordova Street, the steep Cordova Hill, the culvert under the Seward Highway, the Tudor Road overpass, and then out to Campbell airstrip.

One of my favorite shots was Lance atop his dogtruck sporting a ballcap with "The Dogfather" across the front.

At the Re-Start the next day the Willow Dog Mushers Association was selling posters, patches, t-shirts, bumper stickers, videos (including our video about Lance), and a selection of baked goods, as a fundraiser for the club. I'd been a member for a year or so, and I'd baked three dozen brownies for the sale. I arrived early and walked down to the staging area to photograph the teams. My son Jim joined me and we had an enjoyable time watching the first few teams depart, then I headed back to the community center to help with the sales table.

I was chatting with my fellow club members when a trio walked up to the table and asked if I was Helen Hegener. I nodded, and Jeff and Maureen Chandler introduced themselves and their friend from Belgium, Eric Vercammen. The four of us had communicated for some time via Facebook and email, but had never actually met, so it was great fun to finally put faces to their names.

I wrote the following introduction to my column about the Re-Start for *Alaska Dispatch*:

Under mostly beautiful blue skies and with unseasonably but crowd-pleasingly warm weather, 71 mushers, including 22 rookies, hooked up their teams and hit the trail for Nome on Sunday. Willow Musher Linwood Fiedler's team was the first to leave the chute, heading toward the broad Susitna River and then over North America's largest wall of mountains, the Alaska Range.

Behind Linwood came a veritable roll call of Alaskan mushers, some of the top names in long distance sled dog racing, including several past champions, multiple champions, near-miss champions, and hopeful future champions. But amongst that stellar collection were even more who were there simply to run a good race, to get their teams safely across Alaska and to the finish line in Nome.

Two days later I wrote this race update:

Long Hard Trails and Sled Dog Tales

The Iditarod hasn't reached the shake-out point yet, but there are no real surprises in the top 10 front running teams, except perhaps for who's not there: Lance Mackey.

The reported leaders as of Wednesday morning were John Baker, Hans Gatt, Cim Smyth, Ramey Smyth, Dallas Seavey, Martin Buser, Michelle Phillips, Jeff King, Mitch Seavey, and Sebastian Schnuelle, but there's a lot of trail ahead of the mushers, and the real shuffle and push for the lead won't happen for a couple more days.

Bruce Lee made some good observations on the Iditarod's weblog: "Looking at the current standing list will give you a feel for the speeds of the different teams relative to each other but what you can't see is how the dogs are eating and what their attitude seems to be."

Lee then shared a few observations about the front running teams at Takotna:

-- Jeff King seems to be having one of those "magic carpet ride" runs.
-- Hugh Neff is upbeat and is also posting fast run times.
-- Lance Mackey's team came into Takotna like a freight train.
-- John Baker's team looks rock solid.
-- Sebastian Schnuelle had energy and his dogs are just as upbeat.
-- Sven Haltmann's dogs ate like a bunch of alligators.

Probably the last thing musher Sam Deltour expected to find along the Iditarod trail was an unconscious fellow musher, but that's just what the Belgian rookie came across on Tuesday. Pat Moon, a rookie from Chicago, had been injured and knocked out when his sled crashed into a tree. Deltour found Moon unconscious on the trail and tended to him, and when Deltour went to check on the 33-year-old musher's team, Moon regained consciousness. Moon's 15 dogs were not hurt, but he was flown to Providence Alaska Medical Center in Anchorage, and has scratched from the race.

Five other mushers have scratched at this point: Michael Suprenant, Chugiak, scratched for medical reasons in Rainy Pass. Zoya DeNure, Paxon, who was nursing her 7-month-old daughter, Jona, until the race began, developed an infection which spread to her left arm and required antibiotics, according to her husband, John Schandelmeier. Karin Hendrickson, Chugiak, scratched because of equipment problems and damage to her sled. Kirk Barnum, of Seeley Lake, Montana, scratched at Rainy Pass, stating his dogs were tired and he scratched to protect them. Kathleen Frederick, of Willow, scratched Wednesday morning due to equipment and gear problems with 14 dogs on her team.

As the teams made their way north I posted frequent race updates to our Northern Light Media website, and remembering the conversation between the two mushers at Jim and Bonnie's open house, I spent some time doing a little research and wrote the following for *Alaska Dispatch*:

> *There are strange things done 'neath the midnight sun*
> *By the men who moil for gold.*
> *The arctic trails have their secret tales*
> *That would make your blood run cold.*
> *--Robert Service, The Cremation of Sam McGee*

There's a 1988 print by official Iditarod artist Jon Van Zyle titled "Beyond the Unknown," and it represents Van Zyle's encounter with spirits on the Yukon River. Van Zyle tells the story in Lew Freedman's book, Iditarod Classics *(1992, Epicenter Press), how he was mushing along the Yukon River between Blackburn and Kaltag around three or four in the morning, and then, "As I got closer to this area, I heard 'whisper, whisper, whisper' -- talking. A murmuring. And it got louder and louder and more distinct. That went into laughter. Nothing raucous, not 'Ho, ho, ho' -- just nice laughter. Like someone was having a good time..."*

Van Zyle explained how the laughter alternated with applause which got loud and then died off, and he continued, "Nobody was there. I wasn't dreaming, I was awake. When I came back I did a painting about it. A priest called. He said, 'I used to be on the Yukon River and I know where that spot is.'"

Van Zyle never met the priest, but he did some research and learned there was a massacre in the area, some missionaries were killed, and he wrote, "I think those are the people. They were watching a bunch of crazy dog mushers. And they gave me a little round of applause. I think it was neat. The priest told me, 'You're not the first person who's heard these people.'"

The Iditarod Trail Sled Dog Race takes the northern route this year, bypassing the ghost town of Iditarod, a notoriously spooky place. Author and musher Don Bowers, who was killed in the crash of his small plane in 2000, compiled detailed notes on the Iditarod Trail, and they're still an excellent reference for anyone interested in knowing what's out there. His entry on the section of trail from Ophir to Iditarod warns, "Even with the bustle of the checkpoint, this is still a lonely, haunted place. It's hard to believe there were 10,000 people here in 1910, and the town had electricity, telephones, newspapers, banks, and hotels. Fortunes were made and lost here, and legends about the boom days could fill entire books. All that is ancient history, and the wilderness has reclaimed almost everything. Wolves howl at night amid the old collapsed buildings, reminding you that this is their territory now. The only things that are about the same as in 1910 are the unending snow and cold, the Big Dipper swinging silently around the North Star amid the northern lights -- and your dog team."

In an article on the 2009 race, Anchorage Daily News reporter Kevin Klott told the story of a musher who saw someone messing with the wood-burning stove in the middle of the night, but in the morning learned there'd been no one there: "'I saw something, someone,' Rickert was still insisting days later..."

After leaving Iditarod there's an eerie quality to the trail between Iditarod and Shageluk. Don Bowers' Trail Notes again: "There is absolutely no human habitation for the entire route -- no cabins, no mines, nothing. The people of Shageluk rarely have any need to go over to Iditarod and Flat and vice versa, so this trail is normally only put in every other year, and then only for the Iditarod. Much of the area between Iditarod and Shageluk was burned in a forest fire years ago and some areas still have not grown back. In short, it will be pretty lonely and *maybe even a little spooky. This is a good leg to find another driver to run with, just for the company if nothing else."*

Even though they're bypassing Iditarod this year, the racers will still be crossing paths with spirits. In his log of the Iditarod Trail between Kaltag and Unalakleet, Don Bowers described the well-known landmark known as Old Woman Cabin: "The trail will swing off the sloughs and into the trees, where you'll see an old plywood cabin. This is the original Old Woman cabin, 15 miles past Tripod Flats and 32 miles from Unalakleet. It's still usable and has a good stove, although it's a bit the worse for wear and has been mildly trashed over the past few years. If you stop here, make sure you leave something (such as food) for the Old Woman when you leave. You don't want her ghost chasing you to Nome and throwing bad luck your way."

In his new book, The Lance Mackey Story, *the three-time Iditarod champion shares his own tale of the trail, which happened on the Yukon River, not far from Anvik, in last year's race: "It's common to squint your eyes when you're tired, and I've seen things on the ice like a drift log that looks like a boat, light tracers, or ice that looks like an animal. This time, I saw a woman ahead of me. She was sitting beside the trail and not really doing anything except staring at me. The closer I got, the more real she was, and when I passed, she smiled. But when I turned around to wave good-bye, she was gone. I felt I was really awake and had no doubt she was there. It was such a strange experience that it rattled me."*

The race continued across western Alaska and up the coast, with the racers jugging for position all the way. Jeff King led the Iditarod pack out of Galena an hour and a half ahead of Lance Mackey, who was down to 12 dogs to Jeff's 14. Jeff spoke glowingly of his team in Ruby: "I feel like I'm driving the Budweiser Clydesdales! All this pomp and circumstance and poise and macho studliness going down the trail is just so cool. That part is really fun!"

Lance was a little more circumspect in appraising his own team. "My team has plenty of fight in them, that's for sure. I've got 12 dogs here that would walk to the end of the earth for me. Nonstop. I'm not disappointed in their performance at all. It just happens to be a little bit slower than Mr. King."

King lost his lead at the Kaltag checkpoint, when Mackey saw King was staying and decided to get back on the trail, risking the chance he would drain his dogs' energy late in the race. The *Anchorage Daily News* article about the pass was headlined 'Deja Vu,' bringing to mind Lance's stealthy sneak out of White Mountain two years earlier while Jeff was sleeping. Lance later said it was better to make a move than second-guess yourself: "I am totally willing to gamble any time, any day. I'm not afraid to lay it on the line."

In Elim a checker had noted that Lance looked trail-weary, but focused and efficient, and his dogs appeared strong: "The sled was moving before he was on it..."

And so Lance made the play which had everyone talking and probably won the race: An unprecedented 132-mile almost nonstop run from Nulato to Unalakleet by his incredibly tough Super-Dogs.

Lance Mackey pulled under the burled arch in Nome on a cloudless blue sky afternoon, to a crowd even more excited than the crowd had been when he'd won his first Iditarod four years before, because now he was a bona fide mushing legend...

Lance had achieved what was once thought impossible, and he reveled in his victory, as described in an article for the online sports news journal, *SB Nation*: *Mackey is one of the most gregarious and personable mushers ever to run the Iditarod; he's been a fixture at the finish since the age of 2. Given the crowd size, the announcer says, this is going to be "the people's finish" of the Iditarod. Those who want to get a photo, an autograph, a hug, are almost sure to be satisfied.*

Bruce Lee, whose news reports appeared in the Iditarod's weblog *Eye on the Trail*, put it succinctly: *History was just made. For the first time ever someone has won four Iditarods in a row. On top of that Lance also won two Yukon Quests and Iditarods in the same year. We may never see a* run like this again. *Someone winning six out of eight thousand mile races in four years.*

The second musher under the burled arch was Hans Gatt, who'd won the Yukon Quest only a couple of weeks earlier. Four-time (but not consecutive) winner Jeff King was third; and then Ken Anderson, Hugh Neff, and Kotzebue musher John Baker. Jon Little, who was writing for Dr. Tim's Pet Food Company's Checkpoint blog, captured the enthusiasm felt by many fans who were following their favorite teams on their own quests to Nome:

It is no less exciting seeing the 47th place team finish the Iditarod than it was to see the first few teams. In some ways, it is more inspiring, knowing that the race for these mushers -- three days off the winning pace -- had just as much, if not more, to overcome in order to reach their goals.

Mushers such as Newton Marshall (Team Jamaica), Wattie McDonald (Team Scotland), Tamara Rose, Blake Freking (Team Siberian) and most of the others nearing Nome had steeper hills, deeper valleys and wider rivers to cross. For most of them, this was all new terrain. Not just the physical terrain, but the mental and emotional obstacles that mushers face as they press forward into nearly two weeks of hard labor, sleep deprivation, bitter cold temperatures and the smallness of being in the middle of a vast landscape very alone.

I was thrilled with Lance's history-making fourth win, and I wrote this for *Alaska Dispatch*:

It wasn't the first time a musher uttered the phrase -- in fact, it's so well-known that it's the title of a video on Sven Haltmann's rookie Iditarod run -- but when Lance Mackey said "See You in Nome" on his way out of White Mountain early Tuesday morning, it suddenly became a news-making sound bite, picked up, printed and broadcast to Iditarod fans everywhere.

Every Mackey fan who could be in Nome was there, and those who couldn't make it wished they were there under the burled arch to welcome him again.

Long Hard Trails and Sled Dog Tales

As he left White Mountain, Lance's comfortable two-hour lead assured him a record-setting fourth Iditarod championship, something no musher has ever achieved before, but longtime fans of "The Dogfather" are almost getting used to his record-breaking achievements.

First four-time Yukon Quest champion, first Idita-Quest back-to-back champion (twice!), first musher nominated for an ESPY Award (twice), first musher nominated to Sports Illustrated's Toughest Athlete competition, and now the first musher to win four consecutive Iditarod races.

His considerable mushing achievements have resulted in a video, a book, a full calendar of speaking engagements, and appearances for causes such as Lance Armstrong's LiveStrong Cancer Awareness Campaign.

Lance Mackey proved his mettle as a dogman in 2007 when he took most of the same dogs from a Yukon Quest win straight into an unprecedented Iditarod win only two weeks later.

The general consensus was that the stars had merely aligned for him; it was a fluke, he could never do it again.

He did.

Okay, said the pessimists in 2009, so he's a lucky son-of-a-gun and knows a thing or two about running dogs, but he'll never do it a third time.

Wrong again.

This year even his longtime fans were wondering if Lance could pull it off a fourth time. Hell, Lance admitted to wondering about it himself.

A second-place showing in the Yukon Quest didn't help instill confidence, but, well, the Iditarod is different. Maybe he was just saving himself and his dogs for the race his dad helped start almost 40 years ago.

Maybe.

Whatever his strategy, or no strategy -- I think he nimbly goes with the flow and relies on his hard-won trail savvy to make a lot of it up as he goes along -- Lance and his team have done it again.

Won another Iditarod, broken another record, given his fans another triumphant year's worth of bragging rights.

Long Hard Trails and Sled Dog Tales

Thanks, Lance, from all of us. We may not all see you in Nome, but we'll be seeing you in the news clips, in the record books, and in the dreams of future mushers, who will speak your name in awe.

CHAPTER SEVENTEEN

Wasilla, Alaska

As winter melted into spring I stayed busy doing some revisions on the All Alaska Sweepstakes book. When the first printed issues arrived I found a handful of errors I'd missed in the final proofing of the manuscript, so I stopped production and set to re-editing the entire book. I was also editing our magazine and two other books, writing columns for Alaska Dispatch, and contributing to a newsletter about Alaskan history.

Mark had spent the winter in Washington, and in early April he said he would not be coming back to Alaska except to visit. I was puzzled by his sudden announcement, but figured we'd sort it out the next time we got together. I didn't want to go back to Washington, but we did still own two homes and 26 acres there, and our only daughter had made it clear that Washington was home for her and her several horses.

At a Willow Dog Mushers meeting in May I proposed doing another Mushing History Conference in conjunction with their sled dog symposium in September, and my proposal was accepted. The symposium was a two-day event at the Willow Community Center, with my history conference taking place the second day. I contacted the presenters who had been at the 2009 conference, and while all were interested, not everyone was available or able to make the long trip from out of state again, so I set about finding new presenters for the upcoming event.

With four generations of our family in Alaska there were frequent birthdays, campouts, dinners, fishing trips, movies, and other events to attend, and the summer passed quickly. Dad's 81st birthday in June was a highlight, with a large family picnic on his front lawn. In July my sister and I took Dad to Elmendorf Air Force Base to see the annual airshow, and he beamed when the Blue Angels soared past, rattling the windows of my Jeep. We took long drives and talked about Mom and life, and always stopped for his favorite treat, McDonald's french fries and coffee.

My Washington granddaughters flew north to spend a month with their dad, and there were salmon fishing trips almost every weekend, with BBQ cookouts every night to share the catch. In August we took long blueberry picking expeditions into the mountains, and played along the shore of our favorite alpine lake.

One morning in late August I got a phone call from my youngest sister. She'd taken Dad to the emergency room for what seemed like a minor seizure complicated by a bad cold, but they were transferring him via ambulance to Providence Hospital in Anchorage. The world came to a stop and I spent the next two weeks holding a 24/7 vigil with my brother and sister. We'd been down this road before, as Dad had suffered a 20-year series of strokes and heart attacks which had left him paralyzed on the right side. We'd had some bad experiences over the years which left us unwilling to leave Dad alone in a hospital, no matter how competent the staff and nurses seemed to be. He was our Dad, and we weren't leaving the place until he did.

After a week we learned that Dad was fighting advanced pneumonia, but he was lucid most of the time, and late at night as I drowsed in the recliner beside his bed he would tell me stories about being a kid in Oklahoma, traveling to Arizona with his family in a Model T, their move from Arizona to California after my grandpa died, joining the Army, traveling to Korea, meeting Mom, traveling back to Arizona to get married, and on and on, adding details I'd never heard before and amazing me with his vivid recall of things which had happened 50, 60, 70 years before.

I'd always considered Dad one of the smartest men I knew, but his detailed descriptions of events like walking along the Seine River in Paris with Mom just left me breathless. He told me how the lilacs smelled, the sounds of the river lapping against the rock retaining walls, the noises of the city and the lights on the Eiffel Tower. And he told me how beautiful Mom looked in the moonlight, and that one of his greatest memories was the several years they'd spent in Europe together. This was a part of Dad I'd never seen or heard before, and it awed me, and years later I would wonder why I didn't have the presence of mind to record the stories he told me.

It slowly became apparent to us that Dad was fighting a losing battle, and we fought our own battle with hospital staff who wanted to take measures we knew Dad wouldn't want. They wanted to hook him to a respirator, saying it would make him breathe easier. A doctor who must have taken our measure as a family explained what that would mean to Dad, how uncomfortable he would be, and agreed with us when we said no. We stayed with Dad, talking to him, reading to him, listening to his increasingly feeble attempts to communicate, and one morning as my sister held his hand and cried he quietly slipped away from us.

We overheard the intensive care nurses say they'd never seen anything like it, that it was the most peaceful passing they'd ever witnessed. It just seemed to us like the way it should be.

Long Hard Trails and Sled Dog Tales

I remember walking down several long hallways and climbing stairs, not knowing or caring where I was going, until I came to an exit on the top floor of the hospital which led to an outside stairwell facing toward the distant Chugach Mountains. I sat down on the steps and cried, then called Mark and asked him to come back for Dad's funeral. He said no, and it was all I could do not to throw my cellphone as far as I could.

A few days later my brothers and sisters and I sat in the same funeral home where we'd planned Mom's burial two years earlier and listened as the director went over the same options and asked the same questions. This time things would be a little different, as Dad would be receiving a military funeral with full honors, but I was barely paying attention until my brother, Dad's namesake, asked about the make of the hearse. It was a Lincoln Continental. My brother said that just wouldn't do, because Dad had always been a Cadillac man. Well, huffed the director, we have a Lincoln. My brother said he'd do some asking around.

What happened next became a feature article in the local newspaper, written by *Frontiersman* reporter Vicki Naegele:

Billy L. Fikes always loved white Cadillacs.

The Big Lake man drove north from Arizona with his family in a 1956 white Cadillac in 1965. On Sept. 20, he took his last ride in a white Cadillac — a 1954 Superior.

But only after about 30 members of his family and few close family friends spent three grueling days making the classic car fit for service.

Grandson John Fee was at the wheel with John's brother, Chris Hegener, in the passenger seat when they pulled onto the road with their grandfather that Monday morning.

"He would have said, 'When you hit the Glenn Highway, turn left and punch it,'" Billy's son, Bill Fikes Jr. of Big Lake, said of his father.

"Dad was a traveler his whole life," added Bill's sister, Helen Hegener of Palmer.

Long Hard Trails and Sled Dog Tales

Instead of heading north, John turned the Cadillac hearse, on loan from the Museum of Alaska Transportation and Industry (MATI), south toward Fort Richardson, where 81-year-old Billy Fikes was buried with full military honors after more than 20 years of service with the U.S. Army, including serving with the occupation forces in Japan after World War II and in combat in Korea.

Billy Fikes died of heart failure on Sept. 10 after being paralyzed about 10 years ago.

When the mortuary told Bill it would be $650 to transport his father's remains to Anchorage, Bill looked at the proffered vehicle and a better plan started to form.

"We could find something better than that to take Dad in," he said.

They wanted a World War II era military vehicle, so he and nephews John and Chris, both of Meadow Lakes, headed to MATI where they found a military transport, but the back would not open. Sitting next to it was a vintage hearse. It had been parked there since 1975.

The tires were flat, the brakes were seized up, none of the wheels turned and it was nothing much to look at, but Billy's family members knew they found his ride.

"My dad had Cadillacs all his life — white Cadillacs," Bill said.

The fact it was in no shape to go on the road gave Bill little pause.

"I have extreme confidence in my nephews' abilities," Bill said. "If he (John) said he could do it, I knew we had the ride we were looking for."

With just 70,000 miles on the odometer, Billy's grandsons, who learned to work on cars from their grandpa, were confident they could get the hearse on the road.

"Other than it sitting around, it was in good shape," John said.

With the museum's permission, John and Chris brought in a flatbed truck. Chris recalled dragging the uncooperative hearse onto the trailer.

"We were digging trenches in the lawn trying to get it out," Chris said.

Back at Alaska Custom Classics, owned by Hegener-Fee family, the family got to work. They had just 72 hours before they needed to be on the road to Anchorage for the military burial.

Long Hard Trails and Sled Dog Tales

"We had to replace the entire exhaust system, all the brakes, the master and the slave cylinders," John recalled. "The first thing we did was get it running. Then we started worrying about making it pretty."

The engine was in good shape. John rebuilt the distributor, cleaned up the carburetor and flushed the cooling system. Chris rebuilt the starter. James fixed the exhaust system. The transmission was in good shape, too, and was soon up and running with some maintenance, John said. With Chris hard at work on the uncooperative master cylinder, some of the other family members took on the cosmetic work.

They took off the chrome and sanded down the paint. They cut out rust spots and replaced them. They primed and they painted.

"All the chrome and everything that would come out of the car was on my kitchen table," Helen said.

Bill meticulously hand-colored the Cadillac logos to their original hues. Helen and her sister Sue Patch made new tan brocade curtains. John's wife, Annette, reupholstered portions of the interior. Helen's son James put in new stops at either end of the casket space.

"Until this project, I never really did body work," James said, "but I learned in a hurry."

The list of Billy's family members who helped is long, but includes his son Lewis Fikes and daughter Sandy Fikes, both of Big Lake, and Sue's sons Zeb and Alex Kraft, along with Helen's son Michael Hegener, whose efforts included fabrication and bodywork. Close family friend Tom Weber pitched in, too. Even Billy's great-grandchildren were busy. Cammy Fee, 8, polished chrome and took photos of the work, while her 13-year-old sister, Ally, made pot after pot of coffee to help keep everyone going.

Perhaps no one appreciated that more than her Uncle Chris, who was awake for 54 straight hours fighting with the master cylinder.

When the day of the interment arrived, the hearse was done. Not, Annette said, as well as her perfectionist husband would have liked, but it was ready to take "the neatest man I will ever know" to his final resting place. The family scrubbed the grease and paint from their hands, retrieved Billy's body from the mortuary and started toward Anchorage.

Long Hard Trails and Sled Dog Tales

It was a cortege like few had seen, they said. Joggers stopped to gawk. Others stood respectfully. When they pulled onto the joint base, soldiers stood at attention, but not without wandering eyes at the most unusual sight of a 1954 Landaulet Cadillac hearse, Helen said.

"It was what Dad deserved," Helen said.

It was a lasting tribute to the military and family man, Bill said. "There are still 30 people living around him who love him that much."

It was tough, they admitted, but it gave them a chance to channel their grief into a tribute to Billy.

"The best part about it was bringing the whole family together to work on it," Bill said.

"Everybody had a great time," Helen added. "We laughed and we cussed."

Mostly, they cussed the master cylinder, which controls the brake system.

But they didn't give up.

"He taught us when you start a job, you finish it," Bill said.

"If you don't know how, you figure it out," added Helen.

"And if you don't have the tools, you make them," Bill continued.

"He could fix about anything with a roll of baling wire and duct tape," James said.

After the service, the Fikes family took the hearse back the museum, where it sits just outside the front door. The countless manhours of work and about $1,000 in parts were the family's donation to the museum in honor of Billy Fikes.

"Dad's legacy was the family he left," Bill explained. "A nice old Cadillac is part of it.

"It turned something terribly negative into something lastingly positive," he added.

For John and Chris, who have restored many classic cars, this was a special project not only because it honored the man who helped John restore a 1969 Chevy truck when John was 17, but because it means their work will last for decades and be enjoyed by thousands.

Long Hard Trails and Sled Dog Tales

"This one, we know is going to be around for everyone to appreciate for a long time," John said.

As for his grandfather, John is certain how he'd feel. "He'd think it was great. Grandpa would have loved it."

In late September the Mushing History Conference came together and melded with the Willow Dog Mushers Symposium very nicely, with several mushing history enthusiasts bringing a new dimension to the event.

Thomas Swan, a historical reenactor and recreational dog musher, traveled from his home in Two Rivers to give a wonderful presentation on Dog Mushing in the Northwestern Fur Trade. Linda Chamberlain and her husband came north from their homestead near Homer and Linda talked about the research she was doing for her upcoming book, *Mushing the Mail on the Iditarod Trail*.

Jennifer Raffaeli, manager of the sled dog kennels at Denali National Park, gave a slideshow about her work with the park's dog teams; and Erin McLarnon, trail boss for the Norman Vaughn Serum Run '25, shared the history of the 1925 Nome Serum Run, and described her group's preparations for the 2011 trek to Nome, with dog teams supported by snow machines retracing the trail from Nenana to Nome.

1973 Iditarod veteran Rod Perry returned with stories from his books on the history of the Iditarod, and Iditarod Director of Public Relations Chas St. George was scheduled to do another presentation of his engaging Iditarod race history, but a last-minute family emergency kept him from attending.

The keynote speaker for the weekend event was Mary Shields, the first woman to finish the Iditarod, in 1974, with the smallest team in the race, only eight dogs, and a part-Labrador lead dog named Cabbage. Mary and Cabbage also ran in the Yukon Quest and the Hope Race from Alaska to Siberia. But even more than competition, Mary enjoyed the freedom and pleasure of long trips with her dog team, exploring the wild country and meeting the people who lived in the bush communities of Alaska.

Long Hard Trails and Sled Dog Tales

"Over the winter, the country taught me many lessons. Being by myself, I had time to watch and listen. I heard the singing of my own heart, the joys, the fears, the questions, the unanswerables. A peace filled me and gave me strength I had not known before."

Mary's tales of traveling through the Alaskan backcountry with her dog team delighted and inspired her listeners, and answering questions after her presentation, she detailed the technical aspects of exploring Alaska by dog team.

Mary ended her book, *Sled Dog Trails*, with lines from a poem by Robert Service: "...the freshness, the freedom, the farness..." which were familiar to lovers of the far north.

She explained: "'The freedom' was the decision to take my time; to make the day, the seasons, the years full of meaning. Understanding the country from the back of a dog sled gave me a comfortable feeling of being at home in the wilderness."

Other highlights of the weekend included a Women Mushers Panel with veteran racers Roxy Wright, Rose Albert, Dee Dee Jonrowe, Sue Firmin, and Kari Skogen, and a surprise visit by 89-year-old Natalie Norris, who, with her husband Earl, was a legendary Alaskan sled dog racing pioneer.

Earl and Natalie Norris bred outstanding Siberian Husky sled dogs for over 50 years, literally devoting their lives to the goal of improvement in their dogs' performance. Earl helped found the Anchorage Fur Rendezvous World Championship Race, and he won it twice, and Natalie took first in the Women's World Championship in its second year.

We gathered our chairs around Natalie and listened as she told us about she and Earl homesteading the land which had become the University Center in Anchorage before they moved north to Willow, Earl ferrying supplies via dog team for climbers attempting to reach the top of Mount McKinley, and helping many mushers get their start in sled dog racing, including the four-time Iditarod champion Martin Buser.

The Mushing History Conference had been a resounding success once again, and I looked forward to making it an annual event.

Long Hard Trails and Sled Dog Tales

The relationship between Mark and I was showing distinct signs of strain. My journal for that summer was sprinkled with cryptic entries such as 'call from Mark, ended badly,' and 'argued with Mark over the phone, he doesn't want me to fly down.'

I didn't understand what was happening, why he would rail about my staying in Alaska but then say he didn't think I should join him in Washington, and he was still adamant about not wanting to come back to Alaska. I knew he was working to remodel one of the houses we owned in Washington, and I figured the strain of that combined with his many duties relating to our publishing business were just taking their toll on him. I told myself 'this too shall pass,' and looked forward to the day we could put this trying time behind us and build a home for ourselves again.

My second-oldest son and his wife took a lease on a dance and gymnastics studio in Wasilla, and helping with their remodeling and preparations for opening filled the hours when I wasn't working on the books or magazine. We had lots of fun, sharing pizzas while pulling nails and going fishing afterwards, and soon the trees turned color and the first signs of winter were whitening the tops of the mountains.

My journal for October 28 noted I dropped off my Mac computer for servicing, received confirmation that two of my articles on alternative education had been accepted for publication by mainstream magazines, and in a long phone conversation Mark made it clear that "things have changed."

I still didn't understand what that meant.

In early November I received my copy of the latest issue of our magazine and read the words I'd written as my editorial a few weeks previously:

I took my granddaughter Ally to the circus last week. I'd have taken all my grandkids, but it was a working assignment; I was photographing and videotaping the event, and Ally has proven herself a reliable assistant when I'm in the field. We got to go backstage and meet the performers, and we stayed through the entire breaking down of the circus ring, the trapeze set-up and everything. Ally went with us when I played taxicab for some of the aerialists who wanted to make a run to the local store, and she got to hear wonderful stories of their world tour and what it's like to be part of such an amazing company. Wide-eyed and taking it all in, she was learning first-hand in a way that no schoolkid could hope to learn. She was homeschooling.

Last month my father passed away, and the entire family came together in a project so exceptional and unique that it became a feature story in the local newspaper. A local museum had a 1954 Cadillac Hearse which had seen better days, and because Dad always loved those classic old Cadillacs we decided that his final journey should be in one of them.

Our sons own an automotive restoration shop which specializes in classic cars, so we had the wherewithal, but what we didn't have was time. Funeral arrangements which included a formal military burial with honors had already been scheduled, family had flown in from out of state, we had three days.

Three generations worked around the clock on Grandpa's Last Cadillac, and his youngest great-grandkids listened to many stories of his life as they helped disassemble parts, scrape paint, sand the car, polish chrome, fix meals, create memorial albums and displays, and much, much more. They were learning in ways no schoolkids would ever learn. They were homeschooling.

These are, admittedly, unique examples, but there is no reasonable excuse for separating learning from simply living from day to day. Three of my grandkids bounced into the room as I was writing this and excitedly told me they were heading out into the woods with their dads to gather firewood; they know the joys of sitting before a glowing fire on a cold winter's evening.

They also told me about seeing a moose when they were out there yesterday, describing how it nibbled the branches near them, unafraid, and how big it's feet were. What an exceptional science lesson! They were homeschooling.

Homeschooling doesn't just happen at the kitchen table with workbooks or lesson plans. It's not made up of assignments, reading directives, worksheets or other schoolish tools. Homeschooling, for my grandkids and for hundreds of thousands of other kids, takes place all the time, everywhere, whatever they're doing. It's the only path to learning that really makes sense.

In The Homeschool Reader 1984-1994 *(HEM Books, 2010), Kathleen McCurdy shares an observation from her long years as a homeschooling parent and advocate:*

"The real homeschoolers, the ones who are here to stay, are the ones who have come to understand the meaning of parenting. These parents have learned to resist the urge to 'teach' their children (as in 'teacher'). They have grown accustomed to expect that their children will learn because there is something to learn.

Whatever it is that parents do in the course of their daily living that makes them successful and fulfilled human beings is what their children will learn. These parents will help, encourage, answer questions, share in the discoveries, and maybe even learn with their children. And they wouldn't give up this privilege for anything in the world!"

Anyone who has studied the history of education knows that convincing parents to "give up this privilege" is a main component of modern schooling practices.

John Taylor Gatto has written extensively and witheringly of this in his many books and essays, such as this excerpt from The Public School Nightmare:

"Bertrand Russell once observed that American schooling was among the most radical experiments in human history, that America was deliberately denying its children the tools of critical thinking.

When you want to teach children to think, you begin by treating them seriously when they are little, giving them responsibilities, talking to them candidly, providing privacy and solitude for them, and making them readers and thinkers of significant thoughts from the beginning.

That's if you want to teach them to think.

Long Hard Trails and Sled Dog Tales

"There is no evidence that this has been a State purpose since the start of compulsion schooling. When Frederich Froebel, the inventor of kindergarten in 19th-century Germany, fashioned his idea he did not have a "garden for children" in mind, but a metaphor of teachers as gardeners and children as the vegetables. Kindergarten was created to be a way to break the influence of mothers on their children."

As homeschooling has grown and become an accepted part of American life, and life in many other countries around the globe, this concept of state schooling as a path to social control has fallen by the wayside, deemed as just another failed social experiment. But the premise of schooling in general, the idea that experts and professionals in education somehow have the inside track to learning, is still pervasive and can be paralyzing to a new homeschooling parent.

For 27 years our goal with this magazine has been to showcase the truth, that parents can and do take full responsibility for their childrens' learning, and those children can and do thrive and even excel. In many cases the parents simply help their children assume their own control over education, and again, those children show how easy and sensible it can be to determine the path of one's own learning.

One of my favorite homeschooling quotes is by an old friend and ex-columnist, Earl Gary Stevens:

"Homeschooling is an act of liberation and an act of passion. It is an occasion to walk away from institutional images of life and to embrace a vision that is filled with personal meaning and unmistakable truths for our families. The quality of awareness that comes from the heart is more dependable... Homeschooling... is about helping make it possible for children to reach maturity with healthy, curious, fully conscious minds."

© 2010, Helen Hegener

Those words I'd written seemed far removed from the reality of my days. I knew and understood the truth of them, but they didn't have any bearing on my life other than being my contribution to the publication we managed, which kept the bills paid and provided a very comfortable living. I felt something slipping away which I'd once held very dear, but it didn't alarm me. It felt somewhat like the natural progression of things.

At a Willow Dog Musher's Association meeting in November a proposal was put forward by a group of people, to sponsor a 300-mile sled dog race from Willow to Skwentna, on the Iditarod trail. There was much lively discussion, the proposal was approved, and I enjoyed learning what all went into the planning of a mid-distance sled dog race.

I joined the new race committee and volunteered to help with promotional materials and designing a race logo, and two of my sons signed on as trail sweeps, the snowmachiners who followed the last musher at a distance and made sure everyone finished safely. I strongly suspected the boys just wanted a good reason to make a long trip on their snowmachines, but I was also proud of them for volunteering their time and equipment for the race.

There were informal meetings to discuss race plans, draw up rules, approve press releases, paint trail markers, and handle all the myriad details that went into staging a race. I found it all fascinating and enjoyed the process of creating a new race worthy of being an Iditarod qualifier.

Over the course of the summer and fall I'd kept in touch with many of my long-distance friends via email, and as the 2010-2011 race season approached we began making plans to get together again when they came to Anchorage for the Iditarod. My friend Jodi Bailey, who I'd first met at the All Alaska Sweepstakes in Nome in 2008, wanted several of us to join her at the Iditarod Musher's Banquet as she made her rookie Iditarod run, so we made plans surrounding that delightful event.

Jeff and Maureen Chandler, who had introduced themselves at the 2010 Iditarod Re-Start in Willow, were avid race fans and volunteers. They lived in Anchorage and had invited two mutual friends to stay with them during the race: Eric Vercammen, from Antwerp, Belgium, who I had also met the year before; and Bob Lutz, from Hayward, California, who I'd written to but didn't think I'd met yet, although he said we had met briefly at an Iditarod event. We all bought tickets for Jodi's banquet table, including Jeff and Maureen's lovely daughter, Melissa, and a longtime friend who was traveling from Las Vegas with her, Nick Nolf.

Christmas was more subdued with both Mom and Dad gone, but it was fun to wrap presents for my kids and grandkids, to see all the differently decorated trees in the family and enjoy the holiday music, food, and events. I was delighted to learn that my daughter in Washington was expecting her first baby the following spring, and I added plans for a trip to Washington to my calendar. Besides, it was long past time to have that conversation with Mark about where our relationship was headed.

I wrote about the opening races of the season, the Sheep Mountain 150 and the Alaska Excursions 120, for *Alaska Dispatch*, then rolled out a steady march of the season's events: the Gin Gin 200, Knik 200, Copper Basin 300, Kuskokwim 300, Don Bowers 200/300, Tustumena 200, and then our Willow-Tug 300 the first weekend in February.

I drove north to Glennallen for the Copper Basin 300 again, and enjoyed the camaraderie and fun of the race organizers and volunteers. The race actually started and ended at the Paxson Lodge, some 75 miles north of Glennallen, in some of my favorite remote country. I spent two days photographing the teams and sent them to run with the column I wrote for *Alaska Dispatch*:

The 2011 Copper Basin 300 Sled Dog Race, the season's first major mid-distance race, began coalescing in earnest Friday afternoon as 51 mushers and their teams arrived in Glennallen for the musher's meeting and bib draw, held in the Glennallen High School gymnasium.

The 22nd running of this popular race has drawn an impressive field of mushers, including reigning Iditarod champion Lance Mackey, who won in 2009 and is also fielding three additional teams this year; and past Iditarod champions Rick Swenson and Mitch Seavey. Sonny Lindner, who won the inaugural Yukon Quest in 1983; Sebastian Schnuelle, the 2009 Yukon Quest champion; three-time Copper Basin winner Allen Moore,

Long Hard Trails and Sled Dog Tales

Brent Sass, Aliy Zirkle, Ken Anderson, Jake Berkowitz, Gerry Willomitzer, Colleen Robertia, Jodi Baily, Dan Kaduce, and dozens of others are running "the toughest 300 miles in Alaska."

Trailbreakers, including inaugural CB300 winner John Schandelmeier, reported a well-marked trail with a few changes in the route from past years, explaining potential trouble spots, pointing out where water and straw would be available, and answering questions about the trail and the checkpoints. A new addition to the race this year is SPOT GPS trackers to help track the progress of the teams. Temperatures were forecast to be mild through the weekend, with sunny days.

I stayed for the finish banquet at the lodge, and wrapped up the race with a surprise ending no one saw coming:

A young musher from Chugiak has won the Copper Basin 300 Sled Dog Race, pulling off a considerable upset in the mushing season's first major mid-distance race. Jake Berkowitz, 24, crossed the finish line in Paxson at 11:46 a.m. Monday with all but one of his starting dogs to complete what the Anchorage Daily News *called "a shocking victory," beating many of the marquee names in dog sled racing including "mushing maestro" and four-time Iditarod Trail Sled Dog Race winner Lance Mackey.*

The races continued: The Kusko, Don Bowers, and the Tustumena, and then it was time for our Willow-Tug 300. My daughter-in-law Annette and granddaughter Nikki volunteered to be checkers at EagleQuest Lodge, and I volunteered to create first, second, and third-place trophies for the winners. I played with several ideas but finally decided on gold pans. I purchased three 12" metal pans and painted them white, gold, and silver, then applied a black dog team cutout and appropriate lettering to each pan, with the name of the race and the finishing position. My son John sprayed the pans with the high gloss automotive sealant they used in the shop, giving them an excellent shiny finish. I was pleased with them and everyone who saw the pans thought they were very unique and beautifully done. I designed full-color certificates to present to each race finisher, volunteer, and race sponsor, with the beautiful Willow-Tug 300 logo which had been designed by my friend Linda Henning, featuring a team bounding through an enlarged number 300.

Twenty-four teams entered the inaugural race, and four-time champion Martin Buser volunteered to travel the race route and help anyone who asked for advice or assistance. The race officials, Martin, Bud Smyth, Sue Allen, and Kathie Smith, had planned from the beginning to create a race which would mentor rookie mushers while still providing a very competitive mid-distance race for the more experienced teams.

My sons Chris and Jim spent the night before the race going over their gear, food, clothes, and packing the sleds they would be towing behind their snowmachines. I purchased new arctic sleeping bags for each of them, along with matching red and gray parkas, and they looked sharp and ready to go when they arrived at the start on Willow Lake.

The day was clear and cold, the thermometer hovering at zero, almost perfect conditions for the dogs. As we watched team after team head out across Willow Lake, we realized this day was the culmination of weeks of planning and preparation by dozens of people, not only the race officials and volunteers, but the mushers, their handlers and families, the checkpoint volunteers, the lodge owners, the sponsors, and the pilots who'd flown supplies and people up the trail and would be flying the dropped dogs back. Putting on a sled dog race was really a huge community effort, and it felt very good to be part of that wonderful dance again after so many years away, especially with several of my own family members pitching in to help make it happen.

My daughter-in-law Annette and granddaughter Ally were at the start with me, and we and a few other volunteers formed a line across the lake to keep the teams on track to the opposite shore. We could see Denali rising above the Alaska Range two hundred miles to the north, changing from deep pink as the sun rose to shades of blue and purple as the sun climbed higher. Granddaughter Ally admitted to being a little cold, but she didn't want to retire to the warm community center, she preferred being on the lake, watching the teams leave. No wimps in this family.

After a bit of last-minute scrambling for one team they were all gone across the lake and we watched my sons strike out after them on their iron dogs. They'd received some final advice and instructions from Race Marshall Bud Smyth, a racing legend who'd made the very first Iditarod trek back in 1973.

Several of us retired to the small cafe at the town center gas station and ordered hamburgers and talked for two hours. We knew the teams wouldn't be reaching the first checkpoint at Yentna until that evening, but there was excitement when my son Chris called to say they'd reached the Nome sign, where the trail from Willow intersected the Iditarod Trail, and reported they'd enjoyed the ride that gorgeous day, over a beautiful trail, and he and Jim had picked up lots of lost dog booties along the way.

By 8 pm that evening the first six mushers were at the Yentna checkpoint, and an hour later we heard reports of brightly swirling northern lights over the trail. Later that night I posted this to the race's Facebook page: *Chris just called from Trail Lake, he and Jim are stopped behind the last musher, making coffee while they wait for her to take off. They'll wait half an hour after she leaves and then follow her on up the trail. He said "everything is going off without a hitch," they expect to be into Yentna around midnight. He reported "We are seeing some amazing Northern Lights, and there's no place else we'd rather be right now!"*

The next day I was delighted when Norma Delia reported that my sons were sitting at her table, listening to stories from her husband. Joe had been a checkpoint volunteer on the Iditarod since the very first race, but now, with his health failing, he and Norma were spending the last winter at their Skwentna homestead. I was glad my sons got the opportunity to spend some time with them.

As the leading race teams started back down the trail to the final checkpoint Annette and her daughter Nikki and I headed for EagleQuest Lodge, near Deshka Landing. Annette was the official checker, Nikki would be assisting her, and I was doing race updates on my laptop from the lodge. We took over the checkpoint from my friend Donna Quante around noon, and it would be early the next morning before we left, after the last musher and our two trail sweeps had passed through. The owners, Ray and Shirley Roth, were gracious and generous in giving us free rein of their beautiful lodge, even after they'd retired for the evening.

Because Chris and Jim's snowmachines were many times faster than the dog teams, they spent a couple of hours waiting at the lodge after the last musher had checked through. Annette had saved bowls of stew and slices of pie for them, not easy to do in the onslaught of hungry mushers who'd passed through, and the boys were grateful. Although they were less than twenty miles from the finish, when the last musher on the trail decided to camp for the evening, Chris and Jim stopped just short of her camp and likewise spent the night.

Robert Bundtzen, a 62-year-old musher from Anchorage, crossed the finish line at the Tug Bar in Knik on Sunday afternoon to win the race. Only eight minutes separated the first three mushers; runner-up Ray Redington crossed the finish line three minutes after Bundtzen, with Sven Haltmann five minutes after him.

The Willow-Tug 300 finish and awards banquet was held at the Tug Bar, at the end of Knik-Goose Bay Road. It was a fun event, with several members of my family there, and we all stayed late. I was happy to be a part of the race, and happy to have so much of my family involved. As a fund-raiser for the race, Annette had created a beautiful full-size quilt which was raffled off. My sons had loaded and hauled the truckload of hay which kept the dogs warm out on the trail. Several of us had helped with the drop bags, the dropped dogs, and other responsibilities, and as members of my family received recognition and applause for their contributions to the effort, I couldn't help feeling like things had finally come full circle from those first formative Iditarod meetings I'd been to back in the winter of 1972-73. I fervently wished that Mark and our daughter had been there to share the joy and the fun with us, but I was content to have the rest of my family close and working together.

CHAPTER EIGHTEEN

The Haunted Forest, Land of Oz

I need to backtrack a year or so and catch up the parallel story here. The 'long hard trail' in the title of this book. It concerned that long-running battle royale with Mimi Rothschild, who wanted to advertise her online charter schools in our magazine. The story is long and complex, and anyone who wants to just skip this chapter has my complete understanding. I'd love to have just skipped that chapter of my life.

The previous summer the publisher of a small online bookstore, Heather Idoni, published the following alert to her newsletter readers: "July 15, 2010: The following content was voluntarily removed on 3/31/2010 after receiving a legal threat from Mimi Rothschild's attorneys. At the time I thought it was prudent to do so. I am now returning to this published webpage the content that was originally printed and mailed to my readers on 8/13/2009. As it is summer again and families are considering programs for the fall, it is much more important to me that even one family be spared disappointment and financial loss by doing their own internet research on this matter."

Heather then reprinted her original notice in full:
Virtual Homeschool Fraud Warning!

Long Hard Trails and Sled Dog Tales

This is a good time of year to share this info -- hopefully it will save a few families some potential misery.

Each of the programs listed below is run by the same person -- and they are about the poorest possible choice you could make for homeschooling your children. Each "academy" is heavily advertised and well-funded due to the consistent revenue gained from the defrauding of unsuspecting homeschooling families.

Dozens of respected homeschool resource websites and several homeschooling magazines refuse to accept advertising from them, resulting in the loss of hundreds of thousands of dollars in potential revenue -- simply because they are unwilling to be associated in ANY WAY with the following organizations: Morning Star Academy, Learning by Grace, Grace Academy, Jubilee Academy, Southern Baptist Academy.

If you are considering ANY of the above programs, please feel free to email me privately and I will be glad to expound. You can also Google "Mimi Rothschild scam" or "Learning by Grace scam". -- Heather

A month later, August 12, 2010, Heather wrote to her newsletter readers again, "Little did I know that so many of you would share this information with so many others..."

She then explained a little more backstory on the situation:

At the time I first shared this information, I honestly thought it was mostly common knowledge. For years there have been complaints against Mimi Rothschild's companies. Whenever I read a forum where a newbie was asking advice about signing up for one of her "academies," someone quickly jumped in to point them to lengthy online discussions with multiple grievous complaints -- and warn them away. I honestly didn't realize how many thousands of families had no clue that anything was amiss with Mimi Rothschild and her companies. I was only really thinking about families who were just beginning to homeschool -- those who would not have been around long enough to have seen the dozens of testimonies of families who had been defrauded over the past few years. I had also been advised not to make any negative public statements regarding Mimi

Long Hard Trails and Sled Dog Tales

Rothschild (or any of her various entities), because she had intimidated so many homeschool webmasters (who have forums hosting open discussions about her fraudulent companies) into removing the content from their websites. (If they do not comply, a lawsuit is threatened.)

In addition to refusing to contract direct advertising, dozens of homeschooling related sites (who host "Ads by Google") routinely block any advertisements related to Mimi's companies from appearing on their websites.

Our business was one of those companies who actively blocked the ads from Mimi Rothschild, and we had refused thousands of dollars in advertising revenues from her. On April 14, 2008, only a week after we'd returned from the All Alaska Sweepstakes race in Nome, I'd posted this lengthy commentary at our magazine's website:

Mimi Rothschild: Taking over homeschooling?
By Helen
I've waited two days to write this post, believing it's best to err on the side of caution when the stakes are potentially very high. Having waited two days, and having considered all the harassing phone calls, all the blisteringly-written letters, all the provoking emails, all the threatened lawsuits… well… enough is enough.

Mimi Rothschild contacted our advertising manager last week "seeking to run a large ad campaign in Home Education Magazine." Knowing our lengthy history with this individual – her last contentious email and phone call were in February – our advertising manager contacted us and asked if we wanted to run her advertisements. We said no, we did not want her advertising in our magazine, for reasons which can be readily identified through our past communications with Mimi and her multiple dbas and aliases.

True to form, when we said no, Mimi called our advertising manager, Barb Lundgren, "…to try to persuade her to intercede and impress her with the Rothchild plan of spending big and overwhelming the homeschool market with K-12 options…" (Barb's phrasing). *Barb explained her concern about Mimi's plan: "She says she's just spent $28,000 with The Link, $20,000 with Homeschool Today and lots more with websites and other publications in her broad commitment to completely and effectively take over the homeschool market. She detailed this not in an egotistic way, but in a simple business strategy way."*

Well… From what we've seen, Mimi Rothschild has been working in this direction for many years. Two years ago an incomplete listing of her multitudinous websites included: thegraceacademy.org, christianhomeschoolers.info, familyhomeschooling.com, helpforhomeschooling.com, homeschoolercentral.com, homeschoolersworld.com, homeschoolinganswers.com, homeschoolingdepot.com, homeschoolingforchrist.com, homeschoolingguide.org, homeschoolinghome.com, homeschoolinginfo.org, homeschoolingkids.org, homeschoolinglinks.net, homeschoolingmadeeasy.com, homeschoolingpro.org, homeschoolingreading.com, homeschoolingzone.com, homeschoooling.com, newversion.org, radiograce.com, radiograce.net, radiograce.org, thenarniaacademy.com, thenarniaacademy.net, thenarniaacademy.org, thevictorymathacademy.com, thevictorymathacademy.org, victorymath.com, victorymath.org, victorymathacademy.com, victorymathacademy.org, cyberschoolmail.org, eschoolhouse.org, homeschoolingsports.com, interactiveeducationnetwork.com, interactiveeducationnetwork.org, jubileeacademy.net, jubileeacademy.org, kidsstarport.com, learningbygrace.org, newhopehomeschool.com, newhopehomeschool.org, readingcamp.com, satacademy.org, theimagineacademy.org, thejubileeacademy.com, thejubileeacademy.net, thejubileeacademy.org, themorningstaracademy.org, thenhca.com, thesatacademy.org, tutorbots.com, southernbaptistacademy.com, southernbaptistacademy.net, southernbaptistacademy.org, southernbaptistelementaryschool.com, southernbaptistelementaryschool.net, southernbaptistelementaryschool.org, southernbaptisthighschool.com, southernbaptisthighschool.net, southernbaptisthighschool.org, southernbaptisthomeschooler.com, southernbaptisthomeschooler.net, southernbaptisthomeschooler.org, southernbaptisthomeschooling.com, southernbaptisthomeschooling.net, southernbaptisthomeschooling.org, southernbaptistmiddleschool.com, southernbaptistmiddleschool.net, southernbaptistmiddleschool.org, southernbaptistonlineacademy.com, southernbaptistonlineacademy.net, southernbaptistonlineacademy.org, southernbaptistschool.net, southernbaptistschool.org, thesouthernbaptistacademy.com, thesouthernbaptistacademy.net, thesouthernbaptistacademy.org, thesouthernbaptistonlineacademy.com, thesouthnbaptistonlineacademy.net, thesouthernbaptistonlineacademy.org

By anyone's standards, that's a pretty serious penchant for domain names. If anyone doubts the veracity of any of the above URLs, here's where to check them out. It doesn't take long to determine that most of these sites are simply link farms to each other, creating a virus-like network of carefully inbred efforts. Link collections and "resource listings" within the sites appear impressive at first glance, but almost all of them also go back to Mimi's own sites.

A side note: Mimi's latest website is a shrill grandstanding howl about the California legal situation which has been picked up by the Reuters news agency. A much more reasoned response can be found at websites for the Homeschool Association of California and the California Homeschool Network.

Be that as it may... I can't fault anyone for making use of the Internet in creative new ways. We have quite a few domain names ourselves. But in light of her stated intention to "...completely and effectively take over the homeschool market..." her propensity for inventing websites makes me wonder if she isn't already well on her way to achieving that goal.

And here's where things start getting really interesting. Almost all of Mimi's sites include a link to her rather impressive Curriculum Vitae, which touts her as a "27 years successful veteran providing fiscal, strategic and operational leadership in education, technology and manufacturing." The site lists her as having authored seven books and

Long Hard Trails and Sled Dog Tales

over 500 articles; a CEO several times over; founder of multiple academies; Recipient of Small Business Innovation Research Award; developed the largest cyber charter school serving K-12 students in the world; a sculptor who's provided sculpting and design services to Walt Disney, Franklin Mint, Lenox China and others; developed radio programs for Christian markets around the country; and her listing of services, honors and awards is almost mind-boggling.

But with minor exceptions, the only source of information about these impressive achievements is her own vast collection of websites, which promote her as "a homeschooling visionary" and an "Activist/National Expert on Parent, Student and Children's Rights including Homeschooling and education alternatives."

What the heck's going on here?

As strange as it may seem, there are very few clues left scattered around the Internet, but years of dealing with Mimi have given me a collection of information about her which has not yet been successfully purged (brace yourself for this little tour):

American Homeschool Association's News Blog:
Is There a Lawyer in the House?

This is, in large part, an overblown reaction to a post by our old friend Daryl Cobranchi at his own blog, Cobranchi.com. There are some pretty interesting comments at that blog, well worth clicking over and reading a few. Also interesting are the email exchanges between Daryl and Mimi, which Daryl generously shares for everyone's elucidation in this post.

[An aside: As a result of the illuminating exchange between them, Mimi bought up the domain names cobranchi.net, cobranchi.info, and cobranchi.org - to what purpose is anyone's guess.]

But back to the AHA blog above, in which the conversation continued as people shared observations and comments. Here's a sampling:

"Mimi Rothschild's new company Learning By Grace is advertising something they call Partners By Grace and it looks to me like it may be a way for her to catch more unsuspecting homeschool fish with one net. My memories of her involvement with Einstein Academy are way too fresh for me to imagine that this could be legitimate."

"Just so everyone knows, Sara is probably someone from the Grace Academy. Its a long known tactic of theirs to post under many different guises as "satisfied customers"..."

"i'm always one to give the benefit of the doubt, but after hearing about the home schooling legal issues, i think it's too many accidents in her career to be a coincidence."

"Have you seen the list of lawsuits against her, her husband and their companies at http://courts.phila.gov and searching under last name Rothschild and first initial M? If you search under their company Learning By Grace you come up with even more!"

And then a comment by Mimi taking Daryl to task, followed by two gushingly supportive posts from "Shelly" and "DJ." The next post is mine, pointing out that all three posts are from the same IP address. Daryl adds that a "Lauren" at his blog has the same IP address.

I commented again: "Our office manager tells me Mimi has called trying to contact me and discern what she's done to upset me. Mimi – if you're reading this don't bother to call our office again. I'm not there and they usually don't know where I am. If you've got something to say, say it in public."

Another comment by me on the same day: "She called back and harassed our office manager, Stacy, again. Mimi asked her about our ad manager, Barb Lundgren, and our friend and ex-columnist Ann Zeise. She asked if we're Christians, called Stacy a liar, accused her of being me in disguise, claimed she's a millionaire and has a good lawyer, threatened a lawsuit... Typical Mimi stuff."

Mimi replied with another comment of her own, asking in part, "I have requested that you contact me so that I can help make right whatever it is that you think I have done to you or others. I do not believe we have ever met or spoken and I would very much appreciate the opportunity to respond to your allegations." I replied: "Mimi, I am not going to talk to you in private. If you have something to say, say it here where whoever is *interested and involved in this can read it – and many people are much more interested and involved than I am at this point. I am merely providing an interactive forum. Use it."*

There's an exchange between myself and Mie Kenedy, who is a representative of the company which made the TypePad blog, Six Apart, and a bona fide questionable post is removed at Mimi's request. I wrote, "Thank you for informing me of your decision, Mie. We are in the process of moving all our weblogs to our own server where we can control the content of situations such as this one with Mimi Roth (her real name). It's a very long, very sad story..."

The next post made me carefully consider how deep this whole thing was getting: "...this has gotten way freaky. I am sorry you have to put up with this for merely mentioning another site where the information was first mentioned. I do not understand the motivations or drive behind anyone that would persue you in this manner. At least by keeping the records public, there are multiple witnesses to the events, and not the typical 'your word against her word' scenario. Good luck Helen. This one is rather scary."

Over the next few months the comments kept coming in:

"Regardless of the smoke screen anyone may try to create, the freedom of speech, expression and opinion has always served best when done in an open, public and transparent fashion. Anyone who suggests that discussion only take place in private looks like they have something to hide."

"Our children at Einstein for just a few days. When they failed to produce the needed materials and resourses to educate our children we withdrew. To our surprise Mimi, who had been nothing but a charmer tore into us like a pitbull on bacon grease. When we tried to calmly bring the Lord into the conversation she screamed,"Don't bring God into this...". While the pressures of the moment might have been truly monumental on Mimi at the time, that one statement revealed a very troubling thought. When you are in ministry where are youi not supposed to bring God into it?"

Long Hard Trails and Sled Dog Tales

"What happened is sickening, Rothschild and Mandel (her husband) basically bilked the state out of money for a year, spent next to none of it on the students and curriculum as they were supposed to, and instead funded their own private enterprise. The fact that they appear to have gotten away with it makes me sick, and my whole experience with Einstein has made me wary of any charter schools. I would be happy to discuss this further with you, and please don't let Mimi know I wrote you, the woman is crazy and would probably level a suit at me!"

"These people have so many aliases its not even funny. Just go to http://courts.phila.gov/ and put in all versions of their names and their companies:

Mimi Rothschild
Miriam Rothschild
Miriam Roth
Howard Mandel
Howie Mandel
Tutorbots
Einstein Academy
Learning By Grace
there might be more that I don't even know of
I guarantee you will find lawsuits under each name. I would also recommend paying the twenty bucks it takes to do a public records search on Mimi. I am sure you will find it very informative."

"People do your research on what it takes to become "accredited" From the research I have done, it doesn't take much. Pretty much anyone can claim they are accredited, its almost as easy as getting something notarized. Ask Mimi who they are accredited by and then research the company that accredited them!"

"I just read all of the comments on this page... I also recently read Daryls page, http://criss-news.blogspot.com/. I've found all of it to be incredibly interesting. I have a huge story of my own with Mimi, at this time I am not sure it would be wise to share, due to incredibly similar threats I have received from her. It's amazing how I have had such a

Long Hard Trails and Sled Dog Tales

similar experience. To reveal a little bit about myself, I have known this woman for many many years, and she just recently turned on me(I had no idea about the stuff I am reading by the way about her behavior). She has made threat after threat to me over the past 7 months and I finally had to file a Protection From Abuse order against her for stalking me, my husband and his family. Then in court, she asked for a continuance twice, over 12 weeks in total, wasting my time in court, she knows how to twist any language, oh and shes not afraid to lie to the judge either. It has been a horrible experience. Like someone else said, she is simply a sad person. She feels as though she is the victim, but she doesn't realize that she needs to take control of her own actions. As one person put it, "Mimi, you will have to reap what you sew, nothing in life happens coincidentally. Events and actions lead to consiquences and reactions, you are not exempt!" It's really a sad thing and I have empathy for her, I really do. But my empathy ends when someone attacks me and my family. It's a pretty tragic story and maybe I will post it at some point. I really don't want to hurt her any more by even posting this message, but I just needed to reach out, its nice to know that I am not the only one dealing with her.(Not that I want anyone else to suffer, but there is something that helps about knowing that I am not alone, it also helps to be able to see that this is a pattern of hers, so if it comes down to it, I will be able to show the courts!) P.S. If you don't know about a Protection From Abuse order, it is not a civil charge or a criminal charge, it doesn't ask anything of the "defendant", she doesn't even have to admit any guilt. I don't want money from this woman, I don't want anything from her. All the PFA asks for is for her to stop harassing me!"

 The comments on that blog post only get worse. More condemning, more concerning, more convincing. I think there are about 60 now, and the latest one is from just a couple of weeks ago: "Learning By Grace is a joke. How can one company teach a Protestant view of Christianity and a Catholic view? While Mimi Rothschild and Howie Mandel will claim that it's up to the parents they are still misleading parents in a big way. Plus, they have thousands of students and only 20 or so teachers to "teach" them. There aren't separate teachers for each school, it's the same ones. Twenty is a lot for this time of year too. Mimi Rothschild, Miriam Rothschild, Mimi Mandel, Miriam Mandel, Miriam Rittenhouse, Miriam Roth, Mimi Roth, Howie Mandel, Howard Mandel, Duncan Rize, Learning By Grace, The MorningStar Academy, Homeschooling, Home school, homeschool, online academy, The Jubilee Academy, The Grace Academy, Diana Dahl, The K12 Free Homeschool Academy, Partners By Grace, The Southern Baptist Academy, Reverse The Ruling, The Cambridge Academy, The National Academy for the Gifted"

Moving on...

Home Education & Other Stuff

Unbelieveable!

This is the previously mentioned Daryl Cobranchi's blog, and his post is a link to a now-removed Wikipedia entry touting Mimi's "contributions" to the homeschooling movement. The 19 responses found here are interesting and enlightening, especially the prompt response from Wikipedia, which deleted Mimi's entry due to "(lack of sources / dubious notability / advertisement)."

The Wikipedia deletion log takes proper note of the event:

15:50, 3 October 2006 David.Monniaux (Talk | contribs) deleted "Mimi Rothschild" (self-promotional bio without sources)

Natalie Criss is a homeschooling mom and blogger whose Ramblings, Rants & Remedies blog is always thoughtful and well-written. Her 6/14/05 post, "Today must be my birthday!" is eye-opening, as she replies to a cease-and-desist letter from Mimi: "When dealing with a threatening person it's best to keep all this out in the open, therefore this is as direct as any response to Mimi from me will get. Just wanted to lend some perspective to anyone who might have thought I was being unfair."

HEM's own newshawk, Valerie Moon, picked up the story. Sample comments: "Yes, Tammy, there is a person named Mimi Rothschild. And the reason we care is because she has single-handedly turned the pure act of educating your own child into a circus sideshow." And "Former Learning By Grace families can only hope that someday all of their scams *will come to light and homeschooling can go back to the safe environment it started out as."*

Those comments were followed by two indignantly defensive posts from "Marilyn" and "LouAnne," which led to this comment from Valerie: "Because both LouAnne and Marilyn's comments arrived in my inbox with the same ISP number (a Kinko's in Los Angeles), and time-stamped just one half-hour apart, I looked a little more closely at their comments, and commented:"

"In any case, I didn't write anything about Learning By Grace. What I wrote about was the Wikipedia kerfluffle concerning the entry formerly known as "Mimi Rothschild." Still, the similarity in styles, and the 'coincidence' of two posts coming from the same Kinko's store within a half-hour of each other, makes me think that someone's being not quite up-front about who they are, or their interest in the discussion."

And another comment from the original discussion: "Having been to the Learning By Grace offices, I can tell you the place is a fraud. There are about 20 'teachers' for the thousands of students they educate in all of their so-called 'academies.' The materials they send out are simply public domain materials (read: over 100 years old) that have been edited into today's language. 'Teachers' simply email back cut-and-paste responses. Student work is barely graded beyond a glance. LBG is a waste of money."

So what is one supposed to make of this complex assemblage of smoke and mirrors?

Can Mimi Rothschild actually "...completely and effectively take over the homeschool market...?"

What do you think?

This entry was posted on April 14, 2008 at 2:59 am and is filed under Charter Schools. You can follow any responses to this entry through the RSS 2.0 feed. http://homeedmag.com/editorial/legal-politics/charter-schools/mimi-rothschild-taking-over-homeschooling/

The comments which followed my post were illuminating.

CHAPTER NINETEEN

Wasilla, Alaska

On August 12, 2010 Heather Idoni reported to her newsletter readers that she was being sued by Mimi Rothschild in the Philadelphia Court of Common Pleas, Philadelphia, Pennsylvania, accused of defamation and/or slander/libel: "Mimi and her husband, Howard Mandel, have demanded a jury trial because the amount of money they hope to be awarded exceeds $50,000. (Mr. Mandel is also suing me for charges of "loss of marital consortium".)"

In November we entered the fray because I had written five words in a news item for our magazine: "... *Mimi's notoriously unethical business practices...*"

The plaintiffs file this Amended Complaint pursuant to permission granted by the Court on November 2, 2010 to assert new causes of action against defendant, Heather Idoni, and to assert claims against two other defendants, Helen Hegener and Home Education Magazine.

The charges against me boiled down to reporting the news:

41. On the following day, August 13, 2010, Hegener published an article on the News & Commentary blog of the Home & Education Magazine website, titled "A Lawsuit from Mimi." See Exhibit E.

42. *In the second sentence of the article, Ms. Hegener stated as follows:*

Heather has also been the target of an ongoing campaign by Mimi Rothschild to discredit her for taking a principled stand against Mimi's notoriously unethical business practices, and now Heather is embroiled in a lawsuit brought against her by Mimi. Id. (emphasis supplied).

43. *Ms. Hegener goes on to republish Idoni's August 2010 material, by providing her readers with an excerpt followed by a link to the material. Hegener also provides a link to Idoni's initial "Homeschool Fraud Alert."*

But the tenth count was almost beyond belief:

Dated: November 12, 2010

Count X: LOSS OF CONSORTIUM – Mandel v. Hegener and Home Education Magazine

96. *Plaintiff Mandel incorporates the preceding paragraphs of this Amended Complaint by reference.*

97. *Hegener's defamatory statements have taken a particularly heavy emotional toll upon plaintiff Rothschild, who as a result of the statements has experienced severe emotional upset, frequent inability to sleep, loss of appetite, prolonged periods of depressive symptoms, recent unexplained skin rashes which required urgent medical care, and an overall loss of interest in life's pleasures.*

98. *As Rothschild's husband, Mandel had rights to the undisturbed companionship, comfort, affection, assistance and society of plaintiff Rothschild, which are collectively known as marital consortium.*

99. *By reason of Hegener's defamatory comments, and the damages sustained by Rothschild as a result of the defamatory statements, Mandel has been and may in the future be deprived of marital consortium.*

WHEREFORE, plaintiff Mandel demands judgment against defendants, jointly and severally, for compensatory damages in excess of the jurisdictional limit, for an award of [in original]

I was being sued for upsetting the plaintiff's husband.

Either these people had no shame or their greed knew no bounds. Probably both.

Unlike the well-practiced plaintiffs, I'd never been involved in a lawsuit before, so this was plowing new ground for me. I spent many long hours on the phone with Mark, discussing the situation and how to proceed, and in December of 2010 I decided an attorney might be a wise idea. Not knowing any lawyers, I started asking friends and associates for advice and recommendations, and my editor at *Alaska Dispatch* gave me the contact information for their attorney, John McKay. I recognized the name right away.

Attorney John McKay had made national news only a few weeks previously when *Alaska Dispatch* founder and editor Tony Hopfinger was detained and handcuffed by the security detail for an Alaska Senate candidate. Hopfinger had been asking pointed questions about the candidate's background and a bit of a scuffle ensued. It was quickly dismissed, but those of us who wrote for the *Dispatch* made note of the incident and I remembered McKay's name.

A quick search on the Internet brought up a 2007 article from the *Juneau Empire* titled *First Amendment champion battles on behalf of Alaskans*, and I started reading: *McKay, 56, has been guarding some of Alaskans' most cherished liberties since 1978. He believes our First Amendment freedoms of speech, assembly, petition, religion and press require constant vigilance. He likens his job to weeding a garden.*

McKay's fingerprints are all over Alaska's open meetings and open records law and its interpretation, be that testifying at hearings, arguing in court, leading open-government workshops, publishing open-government handbooks, or offering legal advice to a reporter, an elected official or just an average citizen.

He's taught communication law at the University of Alaska Anchorage since 1984. He has helped train Russian journalists. He has defended educators punished for exercising their free speech rights. And on and on.

Even when working on behalf of a big media organization such as the Anchorage Daily News, Wall Street Journal or Los Angeles Times, McKay still sees himself fighting for the little guy. That's because he considers transparent government a basic democratic right.

Though McKay is funny, friendly and fairly laid back, those disarming traits mask a driven man.

"He's been tireless and passionate about all the First Amendment values, giving unstintingly for more than 30 years," said Howard Weaver, former editor in chief of the Anchorage Daily News and now vice president for news at The McClatchy Co.

Weaver called on McKay regularly while editing the Daily News and before that in the late 1970s when Weaver ran the Alaska Advocate, a now-defunct weekly paper that happily exploited McKay's propensity for prying open public records.

McKay assisted the Advocate pro bono, a fancy term for free. To this day, much of McKay's legal advice flows freely to Alaskans.

"More than anybody I've ever known, John can honestly say, 'It's not the money, it's the principle of the thing' - and truly mean it," Weaver wrote in a recent testimonial.

McKay's dogged dedication has won him the Alaska Press Club's first-ever First Amendment Award...

He seemed almost too good to be true.

CHAPTER TWENTY

Circle, Alaska

The 2011 Yukon Quest was starting in Whitehorse, Yukon Territory, on February 5. Hans Gatt, the 2010 champion, and 2009 winner Sebastian Schnuelle were both returning, along with 23 other teams. I planned to meet the race in Circle, on the Yukon River, and follow the teams back to Fairbanks.

The drive north was relaxing until I reached the Steese Highway, which angled north and east from Fairbanks toward Central and Circle. The weather was beautiful, with what was referred to as a bluebird sky, until the last half mile of the 12-Mile Summit. A cloud was sitting on top of the mountain, and driving into the whiteness dropped my visibility from a hundred miles to ten to twelve feet, just enough to see both edges of the road and about a car-length ahead.

I slowed to a crawl and kept an eye on the shoulder until I saw the turn to the scenic view parking lot at the top, then I turned off and nosed up to a snowbank and stopped. I took a break from driving, dug into my cooler and found some lunch, and in about twenty minutes the visibility was good enough that I felt safe continuing, and within half a mile I'd driven back out into a bright sunny day.

Long Hard Trails and Sled Dog Tales

The process was repeated over Eagle Summit, with the added excitement of a snowplow kicking up a blinding wall of white just as I crossed the most scary guardrail-less section, but I just slowed to a stop and waited until I could see the edge of the road again. I figured that if I couldn't see to drive no one else could either, so there wasn't much chance of anyone running into me sitting there. I tried to imagine what it would be like to be out on that bleak mountainside with a dogteam, scrambling for the top, enveloped in that blinding, disorienting whiteness.

Just as I'd done the year before, I pulled into the turnout at the bottom of the pass and sat there staring out over the frozen landscape which disappeared somewhere out beyond the Yukon River. I thought about the thousands of miners, freighters, trappers, and other men and women who had passed this way, and considered the thought that they had worked so much harder than I had to reach this place. I was traveling in the cozy cocoon of a climate-controlled Jeep, and it gave me serious pause to wonder how long I would survive in this harsh land without it.

I also found myself wondering about my reason for being there. I could justify it by saying I was a working journalist going for a story, but that wasn't entirely true. I wasn't being paid for the writing I did for Alaska Dispatch; as I understood things the online venture wasn't turning a profit yet, but I figured the exposure for my writing and for Northern Light Media was value enough for my time, effort, and expense. The magazine paid the bills and kept me in food and gasoline, and I didn't need much more than that. I didn't mind sleeping in my Jeep alongside the road, to my gypsy heart it was better than being in bed at home, especially since I'd been there alone for so long now. Better to be where I could watch the northern lights and feel the night breeze with just a flip of the window control. I didn't mind being alone in the middle of nowhere nearly as much as I minded being alone at home.

I arrived at the Circle checkpoint a few hours ahead of the first mushers, with the temperatures bitterly cold and a fierce wind blowing off the Yukon River. I was at the Circle firehall when an ice-encrusted musher walked through the door, looking for all the world like the miner in the Robert Service poem *The Shooting of Dan McGrew*. When the frozen clothes were peeled back we saw it was Hugh Neff, and the words of the poem still fit: *"There's men that somehow just grip your eyes, and hold them hard like a spell; And such was he, and he looked to me like a man who had lived in hell..."*

I listened as Hugh answered questions from the reporters, and later that night, at the Circle school, I began writing the article which would take me two days and two hundred miles to write for our Northern Light Media website. It was later picked up and run as a feature article in the *Alaska Dispatch*.

Surprising upsets and unexpected developments were the hallmarks of the 2011 Yukon Quest. With the frontrunners in Fairbanks, and half the mushers still wending their way over the last 200 miles, there's still plenty of potential for excitement in what has been termed "the toughest Quest ever."

Hugh Neff set the pace for several hundred miles, blazing out of Whitehorse over a week ago and tearing across the Yukon Territory to Dawson City, then setting a fast pace down the Yukon River, staying well ahead of his nearest competitor and arriving in Circle City in minus 40 degree temperatures with 13 hungry dogs. He said he'd put his big "river dog," who knows instinctively where to go on the snow-blown ice, in the lead and pushed hard for the last 25 miles. Upon reaching Circle Neff said, "I'll take the cold over the wind anytime; you can dress for the cold but that wind is brutal."

As Hugh Neff left Circle on the ninth day of the race, the 2010 champion, Hans Gatt, enjoyed breakfast and then prepared to follow him down the trail, along with the 2009 champion Sebastian Schnuelle and Quest rookie Dallas Seavey. Also in Circle were Dan Kaduce and Ken Anderson, tending their dogs and taking a welcome respite from the bitter cold. Mushers still on the Yukon River were banding together to help each other through the treacherous temperatures.

Long Hard Trails and Sled Dog Tales

From Circle to Central the trail follows historic gold mining routes along Birch Creek, in an area known for overflow problems and for consistently being the coldest region on the entire 1,000-mile route.

Hugh Neff ran into overflow, which slowed him down, and Hans Gatt and Sebastian Schnuelle were gaining on him until Gatt and his team fell through overflow up to his chest.

In an update for the news media, Yukon Quest liaison Claire Festel reported what happened next, quoting Sebastian Schnuelle:

"Going through Birch Creek was like taking swimming lessons in the middle of the night."

He was running behind Gatt but he knew something was wrong when Gatt shone his light directly towards him, waved it back and forth and yelled to him for help.

When Sebastian pulled up, Hans's sled was stuck in overflow. He had separated his dogs from the sled and was pulling them back to ground. Hans was covered in ice to his chest. About halfway across what he thought was ice the whole team fell through a thin film of ice into chest-high overflow.

Sebastian helped Hans pull the dogs to Sebastian's sled. They recovered Hans' sled from the overflow and drove to a spot where they could stop to care for the dogs and Hans.

Sebastian made a fire, took off Hans' soaked boots and jerry-rigged new boots for him out of dog blankets with burlap bags over top, tied down by neck lines and tug lines. The dogs dried by rolling in the snow. After about an hour beside the fire, they continued into Central.

Gatt is taking time to consider his options. Schnuelle says he'll finish but figures his chances at second place are gone.

But Hans Gatt, four-time Yukon Quest champion and seven-time finisher, suffered second-degree frostbite on both hands and scratched in Central.

It was only the beginning of a grueling series of mishaps which would unfold over the evening and into the following day. Hugh Neff lost his lead when his dogs balked at Eagle Summit, despite help from fellow mushers

Long Hard Trails and Sled Dog Tales

Ken Anderson and Dan Kaduce. Kaduce stayed with Neff for hours as the wind howled around them, then hitchhiked back to Central for help. One of Neff's dogs, Geronimo, died, and Neff scratched from the race. A dog in Brent Sass' team, Taco, had also died of unknown causes the day before.

Sass became one of the race heroes this year after a storm blew in the trail on American Summit. Hans Gatt tried to break trail but the wind was blowing too hard and, soaked with sweat, he retreated to his sleeping bag and waited for help. When Brent Sass arrived he assessed the situation, hitched Gatt's team to his sled, and Sass's indomitable leader Silver led both teams over the summit. Later, as Sass told the story to KUAC's Emily Schwing, he stated what has become the unofficial theme of this year's Quest: "We weren't thinking about competition at all up there. It was survival."

After making it over the steep Eagle Summit and resting at the 101 checkpoint, teams made their way across Rosebud Summit and down to the final Two Rivers checkpoint. Ken Anderson led the way into Two Rivers with a 17-minute lead over Dallas Seavey and a 63-minute lead over Sebastian Schnuelle, but he was given a 30 minute penalty for not officially checking out of the 101 checkpoint, so rookie Dallas Seavey left first with a 13-minute lead. On the 75-mile run to Fairbanks Schnuelle closed the gap considerably, passing Anderson and finishing second, only 30 minutes behind the 23-year-old musher from Willow.

Dallas Seavey might be a rookie in the Yukon Quest, but he's a veteran in every other sense of the word, running the Jr. Iditarod four times and in 2005 becoming the youngest musher to ever finish the Iditarod. He finished again in 2007, and in 2009 he finished in sixth place. Last year he was again in the Iditarod Top Ten, finishing eighth in a strong field of mushers.

His father, Mitch Seavey, was the 2004 Iditarod champion and has finished in the Top Ten every year since then, and he won the $100,000 All Alaska Sweepstakes in 2008. Dallas' grandfather, Dan Seavey, finished third in the inaugural Iditarod in 1973, and Dallas' wife Jen and his brothers Danny and Tyrell are all Iditarod finishers.

Long Hard Trails and Sled Dog Tales

It wasn't a bad piece of writing, but it was disjointed and incomplete, and it rambled too much. More importantly, it didn't tell the whole story of what had happened on the trail, but that was something I wouldn't learn until a couple of years later. The mushers don't tell the reporters about everything that happens out there.

Alaska Dispatch writer Craig Medred wrote a somewhat prescient piece about the new Yukon Quest champion, noting that some mushers ....*have an affinity for dogs, an ability to go without sleep, and a comfort level in the Alaska wilderness that just comes to some people.*

Dallas showed the latter capability the first time he took a team north on the trail in 2005. It was a Seavey puppy team, and he was under orders not to race. His job was merely to get the dogs used to travel on the trail and get them to Nome. He finished 51st and seemed to love almost every minute of the journey. It was for Dallas and the team a long, pleasant, camping trip with plenty of sleep in all of the checkpoints. He took another puppy team to Nome in 2007 and had an equally good time. They finished 47st.

Then Dallas took a couple years off, finished his college education, contemplated a future as a U.S. Olympic wrestler, got married, and finally returned to Alaska to join his parents in running the family business -- Ididaride Sled Dog Tours. When he came back to Iditarod in 2009, it was as a serious contender who'd studied the game and gained an idea of what it takes to win.

The kid who grew up around sled dogs and became the youngest musher to run the Iditarod in 2005 gave warning then that he could be a serious Iditarod contender.

CHAPTER TWENTY-ONE

Nenana, Alaska

The 1925 Serum Run to Nome was a somber landmark in Alaska's history. Faced with the horrors of a fast-spreading diphtheria epidemic, Nome doctor Curtis W. Welch sent an urgent cry for help to the outside world; to stop the ravaging sickness he desperately needed one million units of diphtheria antitoxin delivered as quickly as possible.

The airplane was considered but dismissed, because it was still new to Alaska, and unproven against the harsh realities of the Arctic winter. Authors and cousins Gay and Laney Salisbury, who wrote a riveting account of the epic rescue effort, explained in their 2003 book *The Cruelest Miles*: "In 1925, the machine had not yet been built that could match the endurance, speed, and reliability of men and dogs. The airplane might be the way of the future, but for the people of Nome the dog team was the only hope for the present. If the epidemic was to be stopped, the rescue effort would have to rely on one of the oldest methods of transportation ever developed, along a network of footpaths and dog trails first blazed by the ancient peoples of the Arctic."

Dr. Curtis' frantic plea for help was answered by twenty intrepid mushers and their hardy dog teams, who relayed the antitoxin along the trail through one of the harshest winters on record, with temperatures dipping to sixty-two degrees below zero and howling blizzard conditions creating a wind chill of minus eighty-five. Leonhard Seppala, hero of the All Alaska Sweepstakes, was among the last relay racers, and his feisty big-hearted race leader, Togo, gave so much of himself during the serum run that he could never race again. Balto, the big black dog who led Gunnar Kassen's team into Nome with the antitoxin, became a hero and would be immortalized with a bronze statue in New York's Central Park dedicated to all of the dogs of the serum run.

The previous summer I'd written a review for our website about a new book titled *A Long Way To Nome: The Serum Run '25 Expedition,* by Von Martin. The author, who lived in Washington state, had run the 2009 Serum Run '25 expedition, a semi-annual trek to Nome founded by the famous explorer and adventurer Colonel Norman D. Vaughan. In 1928 the young Vaughan participated in Admiral Richard E. Byrd's first expedition to the South Pole, and Byrd named a mountain on the continent in his honor.

Vaughan drove dog teams as part of a search and rescue unit in World War II, and he raced with Leonard Seppala and Emile Stoddard in the 1932 Olympics. He ran the Iditarod 13 times, finishing four times and winning the Most Inspirational Musher Award in 1987. He participated in three Presidential Inauguration ceremonies, and in 1997 he organized the annual Norman Vaughan Serum Run '25 to commemorate the 1925 serum run to Nome.

Like the historic relay it was named for, the Serum Run '25 departed from the Athabascan village of Nenana, where the town's namesake river flowed into the larger Tanana. Frozen in the winter, the rivers were natural highways for the dog teams, and the route followed the Tanana River for 135 miles to its junction with the Yukon River, and then followed the great Yukon River for 230 miles to Kaltag. The trail crossed over the Kaltag Portage and the Kuskokwim Mountains, reaching Unalakleet on Norton Sound, then continued for 200 miles around the southern shore of the

Long Hard Trails and Sled Dog Tales

Seward Peninsula, with a 40 mile stretch across the shifting ice of the Bering Sea, for a total distance from Nenana to Nome of 674 miles.

Nenana was 60 miles south of Fairbanks, and directly in my flight path home from the Yukon Quest. It was six below when I arrived in Nenana, and the wind was blowing hard, making the flags over Coghill's store whip and snap above the mushers who were feeding and bedding down their teams for the evening. I greeted a couple of friends, took a few photographs, and then headed into the spacious Nenana Community Center which served as race central. There were chairs pulled into the center of the room for the briefing on the race, and after a few minutes talking with people I knew I took a seat near the back of the group. I later wrote this report for my *Team and Trail* column at *Alaska Dispatch,* titled *The Ghost of Wild Bill Shannon*:

It had been a long evening's presentation as the mushers, snowmachiners, support crews and others gathered in the Nenana community center listened intently. The trail boss, musher coordinator and others explained the final preparations and outlined their trip across the middle of Alaska, almost 800 miles from the small community of Nenana to the historic coastal mining town of Nome. The 2011 Norman Vaughan '25 Serum Run would be a dog team journey, with snowmachine support, to commemorate the 20 mushers and over 120 dogs who relayed crucial diphtheria antitoxin across the Territory of Alaska in the original Serum Run in 1925. More importantly, the trip would help to broaden awareness of critical health issues through the trek's unique "medical mission."

After a much-appreciated spaghetti dinner provided by the village of Nenana's senior citizens, everyone had gathered in the community center to hear the last-minute details, from a rundown of the expenses to the protocols and etiquette of traveling through the Bush country and the remote villages by dogteam and snowmachine. Fellow musher and Alaska State Trooper Terrance Shanigan had detailed the "medical mission" of this year's trip, suicide prevention, explaining that as mushers their goal was simply to make connections and introduce or open a dialogue about suicide prevention in each village they passed through. He stressed that they were not there to educate but to learn, and to open the doors for the villagers to discover more about the services and resources available for suicide prevention.

Musher Coordinator Erin McLarnon wanted to leave the group with a bit of history about the journey they were about to embark on, and with "The Cruelest Miles," the epic tale of the first Serum Run, in hand, she explained that the first musher to leave Nenana with the serum package in 1925 was "Wild Bill" Shannon, "a lanky and fair-haired jack-of-all-trades..." and "...a fearless dog driver, who was known to have the fastest team in the area." Erin then shared that she'd learned over dinner that evening that Wild Bill Shannon may have been murdered by his wife, perhaps for his philandering ways on the mail trails, and as that chilling thought sank in, the whistle of an approaching freight train sounded eerily through the night. People shuffled in their seats as comments were made about "the ghost of Wild Bill..." and then the group turned to drawing the start order and another drawing for the trail sweeps positions.

The Norman Vaughan '25 Serum Run website explains the journey and the mission in detail, and provides maps of the trail, biographical sketches of the mushers, weather details for several checkpoints, a page of Serum Run-related kids' activities, and video clips relating to the 1925 Serum Run. The 10 dog teams and their accompanying snowmachine support teams gathered on Front Street in Nenana on a blizzardy sub-zero Sunday morning, Feb. 20, to await the arrival of the serum package on the Alaska Railroad, just as it had arrived in 1925, as described in "The Cruelest Miles," by Gay and Laney Salisbury (W.W.Norton & Co., 2003):

"The distant chugging of the steam locomotive could be heard well before Shannon and the dogs saw the train. In this temperature, every sound reverberated through a tunnel formed between the warm air above and the heavier cold air below, traveling twice as far. Although Shannon could not see anything, the train sounded as if it was just around the corner.

"The crowd's excitement was infectious, and the dogs strained and leapt in their padded leather harnesses, tugging at the sled. Even before

the train came to a complete stop, conductor Frank Knight jumped onto the platform with the 20-pound package of serum and ran over to Shannon."

With the serum package secured in musher Jan Steves' leading sled, team after team started down Front Street, turned and made their way down onto the Nenana River, then ran under the big highway bridge and disappeared toward Nome. As the teams dissolved into the blowing snow one spectator commented that they looked like ghost teams...

And as the last team departed for Nome a light-colored pickup truck pulled down A Street in Nenana, toward the train depot, and its license plate read WLD BIL.

That last part was absolutely true, and it was so eerie I thought about it several times over the next couple of weeks. When I saw the pickup's license plate I thought about trying to get a photo, and my zoom lens would have caught the truck before it reached the end of the street, but I quickly discarded the idea and just sat there taking in the scene. The blowing snow, the train depot anchoring the end of town, the pale pickup with the uncannily apt license plate making its way toward the historic building.

I just smiled and turned south.

Long Hard Trails and Sled Dog Tales

CHAPTER TWENTY-TWO

Willow, Alaska

The 2011 Iditarod vet check took place under a bright clear blue sky day, the mushers chatting easily with fans while waiting their team's turn for the pre-race check-ups. Each dog would undergo a complete medical examination, with blood work and ECG recordings included in the exam process, and each dog would a have microchip implant. The goal was to be certain every dog entered would leave the starting line with a clean bill of health and a positive method of identification.

I arrived early and met several of my friends, and we chatted as we walked around taking photographs of the teams. The day was cold and windy even with the sun shining, and I was thinking about heading into the race headquarters log cabin to get a cup of coffee and warm up when I met my friend from Belgium, Eric Vercammen. It was fun to see him again and I promptly forgot about heading inside as we started talking and then set off to photograph some newly arriving mushers and their dogs.

Eric had a good eye for a nice photograph, particularly shots of the dogs, and I was delighted when he told me I could use any of his photos with my writing. Over the next few years his beautiful sharply-focussed photographs would add a measure of quality and professionalism to my work which I deeply appreciated, and we became close friends.

I was excited to see my old friend Jodi Bailey, who was making her rookie run on the Iditarod Trail. She'd finished the Yukon Quest just two weeks before, and I'd written a profile piece for my *Alaska Dispatch* column about my intrepid friend:

Jodi Bailey is attempting the rookie version of Lance Mackey's back-to-back Yukon Quest and Iditarod runs, when the now four-time dual champion made racing history and literally changed the face of distance mushing. But Jodi's no rookie when it comes to mushing, with two first place wins in the Gin Gin (2007 and 2008), seventh in the 2010 Kobuk 440, and 13th in the tough 2010 Copper Basin 300. She's proven herself a confident and capable long distance musher, placing 7th last week in what many have termed the hardest Yukon Quest in recent memory. So next week she's taking on the premier Alaskan long distance race, the Holy Grail of mushing, the Iditarod!

Married to Dan Kaduce, the 2010 Iditarod Rookie of the Year, Jodi began mushing in 1995. In their Dew Claw Kennel in Chatanika, north of Fairbanks, Jodi and Dan have around 60 Alaskan huskies from Redington, Erhart, and Brooks bloodlines; dogs they lovingly refer to as their "kids," and their combined race history has gained a large measure of respect within the mushing community. In her Iditarod musher profile Jodi says, "I've been running dogs over a decade, and as I learn more and gain more confidence I enjoy trying new challenges and trails with the kids-what we affectionately call the dogs at Dew Claw. The historic nature of the trail, or course, interests me, and I work with people who live in some of the communities along the trail."

An instructor for the Interior-Aleutians Campus of the University of Alaska Fairbanks, Jodi is a member of the Fairbanks Running Club, and she also enjoys biking and cooking. In an article for Mushing magazine titled "Jodi Who?" Jillian Rogers profiled the champion musher: "She came to Alaska in her sophomore year of college in 1989 to study

Long Hard Trails and Sled Dog Tales

Athabascan storytelling in Fairbanks for her degree in theater studies and anthropology. 'My first summer here, I really felt like Alaska was where I needed to be,' Bailey said. 'I was always a little out of place where I grew up.'"

She graduated in 1991, moved to Alaska and has been here since. "I was living in Goldstream Valley and so I was exposed to dog mushing a lot. Someone talked me into taking a dog and anyone who gets one sled dog knows what happens." But Bailey, who started skijoring after acquiring a few huskies never thought she'd be a musher. Until she met Kaduce. He also had a few dogs and was skijoring at the time and combined, they had enough for a small team. "We got a used sled and that was the beginning of the end," Bailey said.

Again from her Iditarod musher profile, Jodi says, "When you don't have bills, or work, or baggage or anything but you and them and the miles ahead of you, it is a wonderful feeling. And, over the years, I've heard so many amazing stories from the Iditarod Trail that I thought, I have to see this for myself."

Jodi wrote a wonderful long and detailed recap of her rookie Yukon Quest run for her Dew Claw Kennel website: "Picture this: Night time, full moon, above tree line, with a team of dogs you love all working smoothly together, and a 360 moonlight view of the world around you. It was amazing, so beautiful I thought my heart would explode!! At one point I stopped to snack the team, and after I fed them I was checking booties and giving everyone a little love when they broke out in a beautiful howl! Heads thrown back to the moon, beautiful howl. I just had to join in, and there we were all singing on top of the world. It is a memory I will cherish forever."

A February 2 news release quoted Jodi: "I have a sense that there are some things in life that no matter how much you prepare, study or dream about them, the only way to really know what they are like is to do them for yourself. And these 1000 mile dog sled races fall into that category."

On March 5 Jodi and her team will be at the Iditarod start chute in Anchorage, ready to see what adventures await them down that new trail.

Long Hard Trails and Sled Dog Tales

The next few days were a whirl of adventures and fun with all of my Iditarod friends. I laughed for hours with Eric and our friends Lee and Claudia and Jeff and Maureen at the Fancy Moose lounge's Iditarod trivia contest; Claudia was a veritable encyclopedia of Iditarod lore, and she'd won the contest the evening before.

My friend Gail Somerville and I spent a delightful afternoon listening to Lee and Claudia tell us about their trip several years ago to see Herbie Nayokpuk. Lee was a splendid storyteller, and his tales of the legendary Iditarod musher known as the Shishmaref Cannonball kept Gail and I fascinated for hours.

I finally met one of the most colorful personas of the race, someone I'd gotten to know online through mutual friends but hadn't met in person, the glamorous Dawson Dolly, aka Cindy Godbey. Cindy, in her Dolly get-up, was an outrageously decked out madam from the 1890's Klondike gold rush, complete with feathers in her broad bonnet, huge jewels around her neck, and painted and sequined bunny boots! She dazzled everyone with her diamond-in-the rough persona of a woman from the Gold Rush era.

Jeff and Maureen and Eric and I attended the Start Banquet again, sitting at our friend and rookie musher Jodi Bailey's table, and I accompanied Jodi as she did a couple of informal media interviews. Claudia and I had a wonderful time talking with Sebastian and his father, who was visiting from Germany and taking it all in; he would be riding in Sebastian's sled at the ceremonial start.

We sang along with balladeer Hobo Jim's classics like *'I Did, I Did, I Did the Iditarod Trail,' 'Redington's Run'* and other songs, laughed at the cutting-loose antics of our friend Newton Marshall, and I was delighted to see my friends from the All Alaska Sweepstakes, Queen Janice Doherty and Race Marshall Al Crane.

The next afternoon everyone reconvened at Jim and Bonnie's for their annual open house, and the fun and wine and friendship lasted late into the evening. My old friend Rod Perry, a veteran of the 1973 Iditarod, had brought his original 16' wooden freight sled, which he and Eric Rogers, another Iditarod finisher, would be running at the beginning of the Ceremonial Start. Rod was delighted to show us the ouija board Eric would be riding at the front of the sled while holding the long gee pole, and he pointed out an old axe handle he'd lashed into the bottom of the sled decades before when it needed repairs on the trail, a tale he'd included in his prodigious two-volume history of the great race, *Trailbreakers:Pioneering Alaska's Iditarod.*

That evening we opened a bottle of the Iditarod's special reserve wine, which got mixed reviews from those partaking. We laughed at Eric trying to photograph Sebastian's beautiful but uncooperative leader, Inuk, and shared stories and friendship until later than any of us should have been up, for the following morning was the Ceremonial Start.

In spite of the late-night fun we arrived on Fourth Avenue early enough to watch the first dog trucks arrive and pull into position, the last mushers first to ease the departure of the big trucks later. The weather was cooperative again, and while it was still cold enough to need scarves and gloves, the skies were blue and the sun was out. Walking through the crowd of mushers, handlers, staff, security, media, fans and friends was like being at a big party, everyone light-hearted and enjoying the fun, looking forward to another great race to Nome.

My friend Scott Slone, whose Alaska HDTV videos were reaching a large and appreciative audience, was filming interviews with the assistance of Payge McMahon, a statuesque blond adventurer and pro athlete from Tennessee attending her first Iditarod. It was fun to watch them work, especially when Dr. Seuss' famed Cat in the Hat strolled by and started hamming it up with Payge!

Rod Perry and Eric Rogers, with their tremendous freight sled, were in full gold rush era regalia, complete with fur hats and mitts, and they made a very unusual and impressive sight moving down Fourth Avenue. It was fun to watch the spectators gasp when they saw the historic assemblage pass by, and even more fun to see the broad grins on the faces of my old friends Rod and Eric. Always fascinated by the history of Alaska, I was thrilled that the two of them and their many hard-working friends and relatives had brought this long-lost element back to the Ceremonial Start.

    Jodi had drawn bib number 16, so she was already harnessing her team by the time we made it back to where she was parked. Lance was number 17 and parked on the other side of the same street, and it was fun to watch the two old friends banter back and forth as they put booties on their dogs and readied their Idita-riders for the 11-mile jaunt through Anchorage.

    Then it was time to head for the starting chute. I caught some wonderful photos of Jodi marching with her photogenic tricolor leaders, Jake and Elwood, known as the Blues Brothers. My friend Claudia was riding in musher Ed Stielstra's sled, with a large husky cap keeping her ears warm as she snuggled down into the sledbag. Sebastian had constructed a very unique two-seater sled, and his father and his Idita-rider cruised by with large grins for the crowd. The Cat in the Hat rode by in Hugh Neff's sled, with Hugh sporting the classic red-striped hat and a giant blue cape, much to the delight of kids of all ages!

    The Ceremonial Start ended at Campbell airstrip on the other side of Anchorage, where the mushers loaded their teams back into their dog trucks and got ready for the real race to begin the next morning in Willow, 70 miles to the north. It was another golden opportunity for great photos, and I caught some excellent ones, like my friend Bonnie astride Rod's old freight sled; my friend Janice the Queen of the All Alaska Sweepstakes with her husband, Doug, and their daughter Chrystal; Sebastian's father proudly perched on the beautiful two-seater sled behind Sebastian's very impressive dogs; and one of my favorites, Lance's stalwart leader Maple in her Golden Harness from the year before, bringing the team down the airstrip in florescent hot pink booties!

    The next morning's Re-Start on Willow Lake was another gathering of the clan, a time for laughter and camaraderie, photo ops and fun, chatting with old friends and meeting new ones. Over coffee in the community center Scott asked me about good places to photograph the teams beyond

Long Hard Trails and Sled Dog Tales

Willow Lake, and I told him about the maze of lakes the mushers would be traveling over, and that there were a number of places where the trail crossed the road and photos of the teams could be taken. I wanted to get some trail photos also, so we made plans to leave about halfway through the start countdown.

Wandering around the start area was always fun, one just had to be more cautious about taking up the mushers' time because this was their last opportunity to get things right before they left for Nome. I said a brief farewell to each of my favorite mushers, and took advantage of the photo opportunities set up by several professional media teams working the area. I took photos beside some Alaskan media heavyweights, and listened in on last-minute interviews with the mushers.

I spent some time talking with my friend Kathie Smith, Lance's mom, as we watched him getting harnesses and lines ready for the trail. She was rightfully proud of her son's historic achievements, and everyone there was aware that this reigning champion was hoping to garner his fifth consecutive win, something which had never been done before. Lance already had an enviable string of firsts, but five in a row would just be the frosting on his cake.

I made sure I was in the fenced area reserved for the media when Jodi's team headed for the chute, and I got right up close to where her sled would come to a stop. Normally I would be at the other end of the media section, to get a long shot of the whole team, but I wanted good close shots of Jodi, and when Lance, who was waiting to leave right after her, came jogging up and gave her a quick hug, I snapped what would become the best photo I took that day.

It was getting close to time for Scott and I to leave for the road crossing, and I was listening to the numbers of the bibs leaving the chute, as I wanted to be sure I was at the start line to get photos of my friends Jeff and Maureen and their daughter Melissa handling for Hugh Neff. I was in position when the time came, and as Hugh's team came around the corner of the chute and into view I couldn't believe my eyes, because Jeff was proudly perched atop Hugh Neff's sled!

Long Hard Trails and Sled Dog Tales

Eric wanted to go photograph teams on the trail with us, so we found Scott and Payge and spent the rest of the afternoon watching team after team come across one frozen lake, cross up and over the road in front of us, and disappear down the trail across the next lake. There were crowds of well-wishers gathered, snowmachines everywhere, airplanes zooming past overhead, and it all made for something of a mardi gras atmosphere, a fun way to bid the teams farewell. We laughed and shared our favorite photos and after the last team had passed we all headed to Talkeetna for dinner and the perfect ending to a perfect day.

CHAPTER TWENTY-THREE

Philadelphia, Pennsylvania

In early April my daughter in Washington had a baby boy, and on April 17th I flew from Anchorage to Seattle with my son Chris and my granddaughter Ally. Mark met us at the Sea-Tac airport and it was good to be with him again after several months apart.

Early the next morning, after a long 250 mile drive over the mountains to the eastern side of the state, we stopped at my daughter's home and I got to meet my youngest grandson. He was a beautiful baby, and it was wonderful to see my daughter so proud of her new son and happy with her life. She and her boyfriend lived on the Colville Indian Reservation, where he was tribal member, as was my new grandson. As much as I would have loved to have my only daughter in Alaska with her four brothers and I, there was no mistaking that she was right where she wanted to be, living a life filled with her new family and friends, and horses and tribal games and ancient ceremonies. She was happy, and I was happy for her.

Over the next couple of weeks Mark and I spent a lot of time talking, and it became painfully apparent that while I wanted to return to Alaska, he wanted to return to his hometown in Michigan. We managed an amicable parting, agreed to continue working together on the magazine business, and in early May my granddaughter and I flew back to Alaska, a week after my son Chris had gone home.

Less than a month after returning to Alaska I signed papers for a lease option on a two bedroom house in Willow. I'd fallen in love with the small ranch-style home the first time I saw it, sitting on five wooded acres with a lovely view across Willow Lake. My sons and grandkids helped me move in, and once I was settled into the comfort of my own home I felt a sense of peace and contentment which had been missing from my life for a long time.

I set to work on new books for Northern Light Media, and the summer swept past in a swirl of picnics and parties and fishing trips with my family. In July, with my son Jim's two girls back for the summer, we gathered everyone together for a four-day camping trip to the Kenai Peninsula, and I loved spending time exploring along the ocean beaches with my kids and grandkids. We built sand castles and watched the tide sweep them away, chased seagulls and collected interesting things the waves had washed ashore, dug holes in towering sandbanks and drove for miles along the beach just above the waterline.

We found driftwood and wave-polished rocks and beautiful shells. We watched the impressive volcanos on the far shore and feasted on campfire cooking. Late one warm evening I sat beside the flickering campfire and watched the last rays of the sun slide into the horizon, thinking it felt very close to heaven on earth, and realized I was incredibly lucky to be where I was, and I couldn't remember the last time I'd felt so much at peace, surrounded by so much love.

A month later I was back in Washington again. The lawsuit against me and our magazine had been grinding on for several months, as we researched and gathered evidence and elicited statements from friends and associates who had knowledge of the situation with Mimi Rothschild.

John McKay had proven to be every bit as principled, savvy, and tenacious as I could have hoped for, and he was doing a herculean job of handling what could only be described as a truly bizarre case. When it became apparent that we were not going to roll over and agree to paying a large settlement, the plaintiffs began an online smear campaign, posting increasingly outrageous and shockingly egregious diatribes against me, my family, my business, my associates, and anyone who was perceived to have any association whatsoever with me.

Because the lawsuit had been filed in the state of Pennsylvania we needed an attorney with boots on the ground in that state, and McKay chose a large and prestigious law firm to co-represent my case. I couldn't help wondering if his delicious sense of fun and irony had come into play in choosing the firm to work with: Fox Rothschild, LLP.

Over the course of the summer, via several hundred emails and countless hours on the phone, often in a four-way, three-state connection between my two attorneys and Mark and myself, the situation had been winding its inexorable way to what was referred to as a settlement conference. The case had been successfully transferred from the state court into federal court, where different practices and precedents would apply, and now I was en route to Philadelphia to meet my two attorneys, my co-defendant and her attorney, and my antagonists.

But first I stopped over in Washington to visit my sister Sue and her husband, and to see my daughter and grandson again. It was always fun to visit my level-headed, no-nonsense sister, and she'd been a tremendous help over the past few months as I worked with my attorneys on the lawsuit. She was familiar with the history, the players, and the details of the lawsuit, and it was good to have her considerable skills as a researcher. We made a good team, and she'd even seriously considered flying to Philadelphia with me, but in the end we decided having Mark and my two attorneys there would be enough.

The day before the settlement conference Mark decided not to attend. I wasn't particularly surprised, at that point nothing that he could have done would have surprised me, but it was hard going into what I perceived as a battle royal without the support I'd always counted on from him. I was disappointed he wouldn't be in Philadelphia, but he'd been an invaluable ally via email and the almost-daily phone conversations with the two attorneys, so I told myself to buck up and just get on with it.

I landed at Philadelphia International and found my way through the impressive Southeast Philadelphia Transportation Authority's system of light rail and busses to the downtown 30th Street Station, from which it was only two short blocks to the offices of the Philadelphia attorney. As I neared the address I'd written down, it slowly dawned on me that the towering black edifice across the street was my destination, and I stopped and looked up toward the 20th floor where I was headed. I suddenly realized what it meant to be working with a century-old national law firm with nearly 600 attorneys practicing in 19 offices across the nation, and I muttered something to the effect that I sure as hell wasn't in Kansas anymore. Onward.

I liked John McKay immediately, he was a warm-natured, laid-back Alaskan with a disarming twinkle in his eyes, and I felt comfortable with him right away. The Fox Rothschild attorney, Robert Clothier, was professional yet engaging, and I felt that between the two of them my case was in very good hands.

Heather Idoni, the Michigan homeschooling mom and bookstore owner whose alert to her customers had precipitated this lawsuit, was a kind and gentle-looking soul, but I soon learned that she had reserves of steel. Her attorney, David Gibbs, had flown in from Florida for the meeting, and he seemed professional and capable.

We talked for four hours, going over what was expected to happen. We compared notes and discussed options, determined what would be acceptable to give the plaintiff and what points we were not willing to concede. Lunch was brought in and we continued working, and at the appointed hour we headed for the courthouse in two taxicabs.

My first impression of Mimi Rothschild fit all my preconceived notions about her. I couldn't help feeling a sense of animosity at this overwrought woman who had brought us all to this situation through her crying need to be the center of attention. Her husband, who had filed a judgement against me for 'loss of consortium with his wife,' was nowhere to be seen. She explained that he wasn't feeling well enough to attend. I said a silent thank you to Mark for at least leveling with me and saying he just didn't want to be there.

What happened over the next few hours was recorded in a motion filed by my attorneys on October 4, 2011. The motion is 17 pages long and parts are boring, but other parts are absolutely riveting and beyond the pale, and only properly represented by quoting the legal document which was filed with the Philadelphia District Court:

The conference appeared to be making progress until plaintiffs, after nearly five hours, raised a demand not made before at the settlement conference and never specifically made before in this case – that defendant Hegener take down a 2008 editorial that is not even at issue in the lawsuit. Settlement discussions came to a screeching halt.

A mere two days later, on August 25, plaintiffs filed a motion for leave to file a second amended complaint that would add an additional count alleging antitrust violations and seeking removal of the 2008 editorial that is not at issue in the case. It certainly seemed that plaintiffs never had any good faith intentions to settle the case after all. Perhaps not coincidentally, plaintiffs' lawyer filed a motion to withdraw, citing "irreconcilable differences" and other, unnamed but supposedly meritorious grounds justifying his withdrawal, which he promised to share with the court if requested.

And then plaintiff Rothschild launched a relentless, mean-spirited and damaging campaign of lies and intrigue against defendant Hegener, her family and friends, and anyone Rothschild considered allied with defendant Hegener.

The motion included a page of examples of the utterly egregious behavior the plaintiff had exhibited, primarily in writing long online diatribes filled with misleading statements and outrageously abusive pronouncements against me, my family, and everyone associated with me.

The motion then continued:

It certainly seems that plaintiff Rothschild is losing touch with reality. None of her posts bear any resemblance to the truth. Her posts are a fantasy, the product of a delusional mind, and full of patently false statements about defendants Hegener and Idoni and others.

I found myself wondering if courts dealt with this kind of over-the-top nonsense on a regular basis. To me, that was what the whole thing had become, a procession of increasingly outrageous behavior from the plaintiff clearly aimed at harassing and antagonizing me into agreeing to a settlement on her terms.

I failed to see why this tripe should be cluttering up the federal district court system, and I felt somewhat embarrassed that the whole state of affairs had degenerated to this level. But it got worse, as the motion continued:

Immediately people posted comments that were highly critical of, among other things, plaintiff Rothschild's attack on defendant Hegener's family.

Plaintiff Rothschild then gratuitously attacked defendant Hegener's sister, Susan Patch, accusing her of "the same twisted sense of ethics her sister Helen has."

Not surprisingly, defendant Hegener's family members have been outraged at the onslaught of attacks impugning not just defendant Hegener but also her brother, sister, and even her mother. In anger, defendant Hegener's brother, Bill Fikes, unbeknownst to defendant Hegener, posted the following on plaintiff Rothschild's blog: "Hi there you flaming bat guano crazy deluded person. Everything I have read about you leads me to believe that you are a total fraud and Christian in name only. And if I see one more word about my mother in your pitiful excuse for journalism I might just feel the need to educate you on some of the things I have learned in over 40 years of working with computers and 10 years in the US Army working with some of the world's finest weapons and tactics."

Plaintiff Rothschild did not initially take any offense at Fikes' comment, asking him "what do you mean?" and stating "I did not say anything about your mother. I quoted verbatim a statement that Helen Hegener made about her."

Subsequently, however, plaintiff Rothschild, having instigated the dispute with her own false and defamatory posts, realized the tactical advantage of taking Fikes' comment out of context and making a mountain out of a mole hill. She phoned defendant Hegener's counsel, D. John McKay, Esquire, and accused Fikes of making "death threats" against her, calling Fikes McKay's "client" and an employee of Home Education Magazine. She also posted a comment on her blog that took Fikes' comment completely out of context.

McKay immediately wrote a letter to plaintiff Rothschild's attorney, Richard Maurer, and asked him to forward the letter to plaintiff Rothschild. The letter said that (1) Fikes is not his client, (2) Fikes is not and has never been an employee of the magazine, (3) defendant Hegener had no knowledge that Fikes had made the comment, and (4) Fikes' comment was not a death threat. Fikes himself soon confirmed to plaintiff Rothschild that he meant no threat of physical harm.

Perhaps not surprisingly, plaintiff's counsel now appears ready to use this so-called "death threat" in various filings with the Court, even though the truth is quite different than he represents and, moreover, even though what Fikes said has nothing to do with whether plaintiffs have failed to produce relevant documents. This is simply a red herring. It is also emblematic of how plaintiff Rothschild and her attorney have chosen to litigate this case.

The most outrageous and damaging situation which had transpired since the August settlement conference in Philadelphia was also explained in the motion:

...on September 5, 2011, plaintiff Rothschild posted a comment titled "Hegener scrambles to restore Home Education Magazine website: What happened?" Plaintiff Rothschild promised she would be "investigating

further into why Helen's contract to host her Home Education Magazine... was terminated without notice." Plaintiff Rothschild knew *"what happened,"* of course, because it was her threats to people who ran the server used by Home Education Magazine that led them to terminate the arrangement with Home Education Magazine. Plaintiff Rothschild boasted having done this in a subsequent blog post, where she admits to sending a copy of this lawsuit to the server host demanding that they *"stop publishing illegal material about LBG and myself and our staff."* Indeed, we now know that unbeknownst to defendant, Rothschild was causing the disruption to Home Education Magazine's internet service even as the parties were engaging in supposed good faith settlement discussions with Judge Sitarski.

Losing the magazine's website was major; because almost all of our business income came via the website. It meant all our back issue archives and articles were gone, along with our decades of work to create databases of state laws, support groups, news, resources, columns, editorials, writer's guidelines, online support... Everything was gone, and it was absolutely devastating. We had won major media awards with that website, it had broken new ground in many ways at a time when the business application of a well-built website was only beginning to be understood. This was a pointedly malicious and crippling blow to our business, which would take years to recover from.

There was more, of course. The motion outlined how Rothschild had *registered the domain names 'helenhegener.com' and 'markhegener.com' and apparently have been profiting by their deceptive use of the name of defendant and her husband. Plaintiffs have regularly employed such underhanded and improper tactics against those who criticize them...*

Repeated requests for compliance with the court-ordered presentation of documentation from the plaintiffs was typified by the request for a list of domain names the plaintiffs had registered: *Plaintiffs concede that they promised to provide a list of URLs and they have failed to honor that promise. They evasively say they 'intend' to provide the list. Plaintiffs' intentions are worthless. They admittedly have this information, and are withholding it both to prevent defendants from learning its content and to prevent them from timely using it to pursue essential investigation, further discovery, and pretrial preparation. This Court should order them to provide it now.*

The plaintiffs asserted damages and revenue losses of around $3 million, *yet they continue to refuse to produce documents on which such assertions are based, or that would enable defendants to discern the relevant facts...*

As that autumn wore on it became abundantly clear that we were up against a master of fraud and deceptive practices, and one not afraid to use them even in a court of law. We had taken the high road from the beginning, but the plaintiff's lower road was rendering everything we did ineffectual, unproductive, and unnecessarily time-consuming. We seemed to be locked in a smoke and mirrors battle of brinksmanship against an adversary who would literally stop at nothing.

The saving grace for me was the strong and solid support of my friends and associates in the business. They were legion, and their many contributions included statements of support, depositions on my behalf, taking over duties and responsibilities so I could focus on the lawsuit, and raising thousands of dollars to aid my defense. To his credit, Mark was working long hours with the attorneys, providing much-needed emotional support to me, and doing everything he could to keep the business at least functional, but the unmitigated stress was taking a huge toll on us both.

We went through a District Court hearing for a negotiated settlement and hammered out a settlement agreement, basically saying we would go our separate ways and Mimi would pay some travel expenses the attorneys had accrued, and then we spent three months haggling over the details before Mimi finally agreed to sign the paperwork.

When that was done I didn't feel any sense of having achieved anything, only a depressingly defeated relief that the damned thing was finally over. John McKay tried to cheer me up with something about having won an important First Amendment right or setting a highly significant case rule precedent, but the naked truth was the lawsuit had literally cost me everything and I was left with nothing but a thin and relatively meaningless settlement agreement.

With the magazine's website crippled I had no option but to accept an offer from Mark; he would take over and rebuild the business if I would agree to give up all of my legal rights to it. I would get nothing, but repairing the damage, which would be expensive and time-consuming, would best serve the subscribers and others who depended on the support and resources of the business. It was not an easy decision, because I'd built the heart and soul of the magazine from the very first issue while Mark handled the technical backend, but now it would all be taken over and run by someone else, and I really had no recourse but to agree. Mark did offer to keep me on his staff as an employee, but after 28 years of being the co-owner that really didn't seem like a viable option to me.

The same actions by Mimi which crippled the magazine website had also destroyed the Northern Light Media website, which was housed on the same server. The result was a similar destructive effect on that business, and with no remaining income I had to give up my home in Willow. I moved back into the apartment above my sons' shop and searched for a job, but my marketable skills were writing and editing, and available jobs in that field required degrees and certificates which I didn't have. After a few months of seeking an alternative, and with over $350,000 in legal fees accrued and no way to pay them, I had no choice but to file for Chapter 11 bankruptcy. That meant the loss of our properties in Washington, which would be sold to ameliorate the debt. Mark didn't seem concerned about that; he'd moved on with his life.

CHAPTER TWENTY-FOUR

Circle, Alaska

The unqualified support of my family, friends and former associates, who were all aware of the lawsuit and in many cases had even been involved in the proceedings, was matched by my new friends who followed the sled dog races, who had no idea what the lawsuit was about but offered support and friendship through it all. There were welcome invitations to coffee, lunch, dinner, or just to visit, and slowly the disappointment and pain of the lawsuit and all I had lost began to fade.

There had been a falling-out between the Willow Dog Mushers Association and the organizers of the Willow-Tug 300, and a new race was planned for the last week of January, called the Northern Lights 300. I'd thrown my lot in with the new race, and helping with the planning and logistics kept me busy. I built a new website for the race, designed and produced flyers and brochures, and designed trophies for the first three places with a northern lights theme. My daughter-in-law Annette donated another of her beautiful quilts for a fund-raising raffle and attended race meetings with me, and we often stayed long after the meetings were over to just visit with friends. My sons Chris and Jim would be the trail sweeps again, and Annette and her husband John would snowmachine out to the

Long Hard Trails and Sled Dog Tales

Yentna Lodge to be the checkpoint managers there. Once again our family was coming together to help with a sled dog race, and that was the best part of the whole game for me.

Over the summer and throughout the fall I'd kept in touch with my friends Jeff and Maureen Chandler, our Belgian friend Eric Vercammen, and a mutual friend, Bob Lutz from California. We were all going to join Jodi Bailey at the Iditarod Start Banquet; she was going to Nome again and this time three of us planned to be there to welcome her under the burled arch. That winter Bob, Eric, and I spent long hours exchanging emails, studying the logistics, planning our trip, making reservations, and anticipating a wonderful adventure!

The video Mark and I had produced about Lance was still selling well, and my books about the All Alaska Sweepstakes and the Yukon Quest were getting a good response from readers, so I set to work collecting many of the columns I'd written for *Alaska Dispatch* into a book about sled dog history. I figured that if I could build one publishing company from the ground up there was no reason I couldn't do it again, and since I'd always believed in the truth of following your passion in life, it made sense to try to create a way to make a living based on that passion. I knew it would take time, but that was the one thing I had in abundance now.

The columns I'd written which fit the parameters of the book included some of my favorites, such as the story of Juriro Wada, the enigmatic Japanese explorer and adventurer who'd traveled to the U.S. in 1890 and worked as a cabin boy for the Pacific Steam Whaling Company, and then at Barrow for the renowned trader Charlie Brower, where he learned to handle sled dogs.

For many years Jujiro Wada traveled widely across northern Alaska, the Yukon Territory, and beyond, leading an adventurous life and leaving his mark on the history of the north country. His exploits were the stuff of legend, as he traveled by dog team, hunting, trapping, prospecting, running marathons, and entertaining people wherever he went with his colorful stories. On one of his epic dog mushing trips he travelled from the headwaters of the Chandalar River to the Arctic Ocean, along the shore of the ocean to the Mackenzie River, and up that river and across the divide to the Porcupine River, taking more than a year, he and his dogs living on game hunted along the way.

Little-known in Alaskan history, Jujiro Wada had helped pioneer the Iditarod Trail, as noted in Yuji Tani's 1995 book, *The Samurai Dog-Musher Under the Northern Lights*. Fumi Torigai, who was documenting Wada's travels for submission to the Historic Sites and Monuments Board of Parks Canada, wrote:

In December of 1909, at the request of the town, Wada established a route from Seward to the newly discovered gold mine of Iditarod. Acting as the leader of a fleet of dogsled teams, Wada had a relatively uneventful trip to Iditarod. However, on the return trip to Seward, he and his three companions had to go through prolonged minus 60 F (minus 51 C) weather. Several dogs, including his lead-dog, became too weak to survive the extreme cold and had to be put to sleep. The hardships of Wada and his companions and the ensuing rush of prospectors into the Iditarod area were widely reported in many Alaskan papers.

The 2007 Yukon Quest honored Wada with an exhibit of his achievements in the north. The official press release read in part:

"*Mr. Wada traveled by dog team along what is now the Yukon Quest Trail over 100 years ago when it was a traditional travel route. He learned his survival skills and travel routes through the assistance of the aboriginal people in the north,*" said Lillian Nakamura Maguire, educator for the Yukon Human Rights Commission. "*He was respected for his hardiness, dog care and good character, although, as a Japanese man he experienced racism due to the strong anti-Asian sentiments in the early 1900s,*" Nakamura Maguire said.

"*The Yukon Quest is dedicated to honouring the traditions of travel by dog team in the North and the equal treatment of all dogs and people taking part in the race. Mr. Wada embodied the love and respect for his dogs that is one of the founding principles of the Yukon Quest,*" said

Long Hard Trails and Sled Dog Tales

Stephen Reynolds, Yukon Quest (Canada) Executive Director. "We are honoured to help bring Jujiro Wada's incredible story to the world."

Another favorite was the story of a dramatic face-off between the proponents of importing reindeer from northern Europe and those who felt the leggy animals threatened the work of the venerable sled dogs of Alaska. In *The Cruelest Miles: The Heroic Story of Dogs and Men in a Race Against an Epidemic,* cousins Gay Salisbury and Laney Salisbury reported a little-known aspect of Alaskan history: *In addition to trade goods, the gold rush brought some strange ideas to Alaska, and the most bizarre may have been the belief of some U.S. government officials that Alaskans would be better off living in Alaska without dogs. Ambitious entrepreneurs tried many alternative forms of transportation and communication that they hoped would be superior to dogs, including horses, goats, hot-air balloons, bicycles, ice skates, ice boats, ice trains. and passenger pigeons. But the favorite choice of several key officials was the reindeer.*

The primary proponent for reindeer was Dr. Sheldon Jackson, a Presbyterian minister and the head of Alaska's fledgling education system at the turn of the century. A staunch supporter of reindeer who argued their qualities far and wide, Jackson even testified before Congress that dogs were treacherous and unreliable beasts, and claimed that they *require considerable food for their support, while reindeer are gentle, timid and eat little, foraging on the moss and spruce of the tundra.*

Archdeacon of the Yukon Hudson Stuck challenged Jackson's assertions. He'd written compellingly in *Ten Thousand Miles With a Dogsled* that the husky dog was prized and called "the Friend of Man," and he observed *There is not a dog the less in Alaska because of the reindeer, nor ever will be...* When the Canadian government introduced reindeer into Labrador under the direction of Dr. Wilfred Grenfell, who stated his hope they would "eliminate that scourge of the country, the husky dog," the Archdeacon Stuck responded, *Instead of the reindeer eliminating the dog, there is far greater likelihood of the dog eliminating the reindeer...*

Long Hard Trails and Sled Dog Tales

With a wealth of sled dog history to draw from it was easy to put together a book, and in July, 2012 my book *Along Alaskan Trails: Adventures in Sled Dog History* was published.

It felt like a new beginning.

I traveled back to Fairbanks again for the 2012 Yukon Quest, and met a friend from Texas, Marlys Sauer, who was lots of fun and always larking about, thinking up fun photo opportunities. We traveled out to Chatanika to see Jodi and Dan's beautiful Dewclaw Kennels, and Dan took Marlys for a dogsled ride while Jodi and I enjoyed a cup of tea and caught up on mushing world gossip. Two days later, after enjoying a fun musher's meet and greet and the always-exciting Fairbanks start with Marlys, she flew home and I hit the road for Circle and Central under clear blue skies.

My friends Bonnie and Jim Foster had entered a team from their Moon Run Kennel in the 2012 Yukon Quest, capably handled by Misha Petersen, a 43 year old dog driver from Prague in the Czech Republic. I met Bonnie and her son Randy in Central, along with my Fairbanks photographer friend Carol Falcetta, who was photographing teams.

I got some photos shortly before Misha pulled her hook to get back on the trail. We followed her out the Circle Hot Springs Road, getting some wonderful photographs along the way, and when Misha and the team reached the end of the road and headed for Circle we took the opportunity to check out the old hot springs resort hotel, which had been closed for several years.

Built in 1930, much of the original material for the lodge had come down the Yukon River to Circle City, then overland by wagon for 60 miles to the hot springs. The hot springs had been used by area Athabascans long before the gold rush. William Greats was the first non-Native to discover the springs, in 1893, and in 1905 Cassius Monohan homesteaded 106 acres around the springs. Monohan sold the property to Franklin Leach in 1909, who developed the resort.

Bonnie, Randy, Carol and I were fortunate to befriend the caretaker of the old resort, who kindly let us explore and take photos of the now-closed property. As we were saying goodbye we were a little startled to see something pale in the window which we were all certain was not there earlier... Then the caretaker told us the place was rumored to have a resident female ghost.

Back at Central I took a few more photos of the teams stretched out and resting in what was known as Central Park, then joined my friend Nancy Steuer for a trip to her brother Fred's nearby business, the newly-opened Far North Mercantile and Family Rest. A bright, spacious, friendly restaurant was staffed by three women with wide friendly smiles, and it was fun to meet Nancy's brother, an old-timer in the area.

Bonnie and Randy were handling for Misha, which meant cleanup chores after the team left each checkpoint. Knowing I'd see them again in Circle, I departed Central with a huge full moon lighting up the landscape and making the drive to Circle even lovelier than it normally was. I stopped often for photos, and just past the Birch Creek bridge I met Nancy and a friend returning from a quick trip to Circle and we stopped to chat again. It was fun being back in this wild north country, and even more fun to be sharing the adventure with friends.

In Circle that evening I stood on the bank of the Yukon River and marveled over a brilliant display of northern lights with my friends from Fairbanks, Jan and Carol. The swirling, dancing bands of green were more vibrant than I'd ever seen them, and I fell asleep alongside the frozen river, more contented than I'd been in a long, long time.

The next morning I photographed Misha and the Moon Run team getting ready to depart for Eagle. After she left I joined Bonnie and Randy for lunch at the local cafe, and later wrote this article about my friends' adventures for my Northern Light Media website, and it was picked up and republished by *Alaska Dispatch*:

Moon Run Kennels in Chugiak, Alaska, is the dream of Jim and Bonnie Foster, who moved to Alaska from Florida in 2003. Jim wrote on their web site for Moon Run Kennels, "In 2001, my wife and I decided we

Long Hard Trails and Sled Dog Tales

needed to move out of Florida. Bonnie's dog obsession was in full swing by then so we included in our search places with active mushing communities. Turned out no place better to get involved with dog mushing than Alaska, and as luck would have it, this is where we found a job. On our move up to Alaska on the AlCan we stopped in at Frank Turner's kennel, MukTuk. Bonnie had been communicating with him on the internet researching Lacy's history. MukTuk was our first introduction to a big racing kennel. We were totally enthralled. I could not imagine a better life than Frank's. And so it started."

From that beginning, that love of sled dogs and the sport of mushing, Jim and Bonnie forged a kennel which they describe as a dog dude ranch and retirement center, and anyone who's been to their home knows the description is apt. The dogs are as welcome in their beautiful home as the people who often visit, and their furry friends can be found relaxing on sofas and chairs right along with their human counterparts. The vibe at Moon Run Kennels is relaxed, welcoming, and definitely dog-friendly ("We don't need no stinkin' leashes!"), and the Moon Run kennelmates, whose lineages include dogs from well-known mushers Jon Little, Zack Steer, and Frank Turner, among others, are some of the luckiest dogs in Alaska. For several years Jim and Bonnie hosted one of the most popular open house gatherings at Iditarod-time, as top-notch mushers, fans and friends all converged to fill their home with fun, laughter, memories of past races and excitement about the upcoming event!

Enter Misha Pedersen, from Prague in the Czech Republic, a 43 year old dog driver who's been mushing for over a dozen years. She spent her first two winters in Alaska with Charlie and Robin Boulding, and got hooked on mushing, moving to the state permanently in 2003. She worked for five years as a guide for Vern Halter's Dream a Dream Dog Farm in Willow, and for the 2010-2011 season she moved north to Two Rivers and worked for Judy and Devan Currier's Lara-Ke Kennel. Her first race, in 2000, was the Henry Hahn 100. In 2006 she completed the Serum Run, in 2009 – 2010 she ran and completed the Knik 200, the Tustemena 200, and the Klondike 300, finishing 6th in the K300. During the 2010-2011 season she ran and completed the Sheep Mountain 150, and the Yukon Quest 300, finishing 7th in the latter race.

And now, after traveling nearly 1,000 miles in the toughest sled dog race in the world, she's about to become a Yukon Quest finisher with a team of Alaskan Huskies from Moon Run Kennel and Yaks Lair Kennel, owned by Leslie Morrison of Eagle River. On her profile page for the race she answered the question, 'What do you love most about running sled dogs?' with the reply, 'They are like three musketeers, one for all and all for one.'

On February 1st the team hit the road for Fairbanks and the Yukon Quest: Bonnie, her son Randy, Misha, and Misha's mother, Jona, along with 15 sled dogs. Staying with friends, they made final preparations for the much longer journey ahead.

And finally it was Race Day! Bonnie's posts to her Facebook page told the story in spare but telling detail:

- February 4, 1:41 pm: Dogs looked wonderful taking off. The radio announcer said they were the most enthusiastic looking. She was around the Nordale road a bit ago
- February 4, 4:54 pm: Dogs took off looking great. At pleasant valley they looked wonderful. There will be a u tube posted and will try to get it up on fb later
- February 5, 12:54 am: In two rivers. Misha and dogs look good. All bedded down
- February 5, 8:20 am: Misha left about 5:30 AM. All the dogs look good and so does Misha....she left with 14 dogs. Next check point 101
- February 5, 2:33 pm: Misha and the dogs came in earlier than expected. All look good. She will leave about 5:30 temps are warm. I have no gloves on. She thought going over rosebud was easier than she expected.
- February 5, 2:35 pm: Clover and riot in lead over rosebud•

February 5, 8:11 pm: Misha is on top of eagle summit now. She dropped boo in 101 but boo is absolutely fine. Was told he had a wrist injury. Not. He is in the back seat of the car sleeping

Long Hard Trails and Sled Dog Tales

• *February 5, 8:13 pm: Hander's are all in circle having a cheeseburger and a beer. Misha should take about 2 1/2 hour to get here*

An 18-hour break in Bonnie's posting happens then. At the top of Eagle Summit, Misha loses a dog from the team. Bonnie's friend Sebastian Schnuelle, a Yukon Quest champion who is blogging the race for fans this year, explains what happens:

"On another table is Misha Peterson. Heartbroken, still missing one of her dogs, which has been seen up and down the trail between Mile 101 and Central. For any animal rights people crying now...., put it in perspective, house dogs turn loose to... its not a big deal and they will be reunited soon. But for Misha this means most likely to be out of the race. Another full year of training might be coming to a premature end. In this case, it's hitting very close to home for me as Bonnie and Jim, who own the team are good friends of mine. It reminds me on my 1999 Quest attempt, where things were looking bleak in Central, and led me to ultimately scratch in Circle.

Scratching is a very emotional thing. At the time I felt left out, left behing. All my friends where heading down the trail. Each checkpoint has a very distinct feel, once the mushers are gone. The high flying vibe is gone. It's very quite all for sudden. People are busy with cleanup. But no more energetic dogs lunging and screaming to go. An than.... A few minutes later. Somebody coming in the checkpoint screaming: THEY GOT THE DOG.

And not only did they get the dog, another Musher, Ed Abrahamson, a Quest 300 musher got the do. He came into the checkpoint with the dog, named Riot , in the team. BEST case scenario....., no outside assistance, no help! And Misha should be good to go and continue. Ed had quite the story to tell, with him driving a nice team of 11 big males.... And what do 11 big males do, when they see a female. They go chase..... and the chase was on, off the trail, on the trail, trying to get Riot.... All ends well in this case.... Misha just put Riot back in her team...."

And at 12:31 pm on February 6th, Misha hooks up her team and heads for Circle on the Yukon River. Bonnie continues:

- *February 7, 7:05 am: Misha getting ready to leave circle pretty soon. Will be a long run to Dawson probably pretty solitary*
- *February 7, 12:20 pm: We are leaving Circle now on our way to Dawson city, Yukon Territory, Canada for the next adventure in the Yukon Quest*
- *February 7, 8:58 pm: On our way to Tok. Saw several hundred caribou right on the road and a couple of moose. Dogs looked well rested and misha smiling as she left. Not much net on the road but will try to download some pics soon. Fulloon and warm. Two rivers was about 15 and it is 7 degrees going towards Tok past North Pole*
- *February 8, 1:41 am: So far this has been a wonderful experience. So many truly good people, great vets, friendly faces. good times, good weather, good people good dogs…life is good*
- *February 9, 10:43 pm: Presently inDawson. Neat city, fascinating people. Have been talking all night with a couple of Canadian Rangers. What a bunch of men. Have tent put up.....most of dog tent is up. Weather holding. Everything going well…*
- *February 10, 10:40 pm: Dogs came into Dawson city wagging their tails and looking happy. They ate like pigs, bedded themselves down and went to sleep. They have this part learned. Vet check is at 0800. temperature here is 27 today. Haven't worn my parka yet.*
- *February 11, 11:31 am: Dogs had their vet check at 0800 and everyone passed. Tasso will be staying back with us as she seemed to have a couple of minutes where she was unsure of what was happening. The vets thought she looked perfectly good so this is merely being very conservative. Now I have a bed dog.*

They are getting their beauty rest and lots of massages today. misha is scheduled to leave at around 0630 Sunday…from there it will be a long run. Boo and Riot are fine but they would like to rejoin their buddies. Everyone is eating well.
- *February 12, 7:19 am: Dogs left in great shape at 0630. Trotting down the Yukon River like they owned it. Temps still remain warm. Now it is a long run to Pelly*

Long Hard Trails and Sled Dog Tales

• *February 12, 6:11 pm: Dawson site cleaned up and ready to go. Each site has to be inspected before you leave. We will leave tomorrow for the next checkpoint and follow her down the highway to Whitehorse. Dawson looks like a typical northern gold town. Fascinating history Would like to come back again on the winter with a sno go. . We have met some really cool people here and the temps are amazing. It is colder in Nashville and NYC than it is here. Not good for the dogs.*

• *February 14, 10:29 am: Everything good here. Just no met for me. . Misha is doing well. So are dogs. She will be in Whitehorse probably Thursday*

• *February 14, 2:44 pm: Almost into McCabe creek. Way to go. . One dropped. Axi. The boys started to like her too much. Weather is still quit warm. 34 degrees at Carmacks.*

• *February 14, 6:58 pm: Northern Lights are out……*

• *February 15, 1:32 am: Misha just got into Carmacks….not much longer….*

• *February 15: 9:33 am: Left Carmacks……only one more checkpoint till the finish….8 hr mandatory rest there….Think everyone can use it. Vet looked at Axi again this am and thought that she looked pretty darn good. Her backside is a bit sore and she is in heat.*

• *February 15, 10:53 pm: misha is in. Team is looking good according to the quest web site. Randy and I are in Whitehorse taking care of some things here. 8 hours mandatory and then the final run. For sure, it has been a hell of a journey with highs and lows and sometimes just pure desperation and some darn good luck.*

The 'misha is in' refers to the Braeburn checkpoint, 100 miles from the finish in Whitehorse. Arriving at 10:53 pm, Misha will take an 8 hour mandatory rest and she can hit the trail for the end of the race at 6:53 am on Thursday, February 16th. Bonnie will be there to welcome her and the victorious Moon Run dogs!

CHAPTER TWENTY-FIVE

Talkeetna, Alaska

The 2012 Iditarod was a banner year for the small group who came together to cheer on my friend Jodi Bailey. Jeff and Maureen Chandler had invited us all to crash at their place in Anchorage, and it was delightful to share all the adventures from the comfort of their lovely home. The first evening we went to dinner at one of our favorite restaurants, the Moose's Tooth, with Albert Marquez, whose Planet Earth Adventures tour business would be hosting a group for the Iditarod. The week before Jeff and Albert and I had joined our friend Scott Slone and mutual friends David and Jena Taylor for a photo walk across frozen Portage Lake. I didn't make it all the way across the lake, but the photos of the glacier which the guys brought back were just amazing!

Eric and Bob arrived at Anchorage International the next day, and then it was four days of non-stop fun, with the start banquet and mushers' bib drawing, an open house at Donna's place in Willow for her friend Karen Ramstead with the "Pretty Sled Dogs" all-Siberian team, then Jim and Bonnie's popular annual open house, followed by the Ceremonial Start in Anchorage the next day. That evening we joined a gathering of friends from far and near for dinner, and the following morning we got an early start for Willow and the real beginning of the race.

After a couple of hours of visiting with friends in the starting area, several of us headed back to a good spot on the trail and photographed the teams coming out of the woods, across the road, and down the trail to the next lake. It was fun to just sit on a snowbank above the road and watch my friends excitedly shooting photos and watching for the next team, the closest ones calling out to one another when a musher was in view, and the message would echo down the line where my friends had stationed themselves. This seemed like the best part of the sport, to be out alongside the trail on a beautiful sunny day and sharing the fun with friends.

I sat there and watched the mushers coming into view one after another and wondered about their thoughts and feelings as they set out for Nome, 1,000 rugged miles away. For many this was the culmination of a dream, something they'd worked hard for and might never have the opportunity to do again. For others it was just another trip to Nome, a trip they'd made before, sometimes successfully, sometimes not, and no one trip was ever like the ones that came before or after.

All of these mushers, rookies and veterans alike, had left behind families and friends and well-wishers to venture into the back country of Alaska in a way very few people would ever experience it. I kept thinking about a passage I'd read that winter in Don Bowers' classic tale, *Back of the Pack: An Iditarod Rookie Musher's Alaska Pilgrimage to Nome*. Don has made it through the treacherous Dalzell Gorge without mishap, and now he's making his way down the South Fork of the Kuskokwim on his way to Farewell Lakes:

At one point we pass a group of long-abandoned log cabins which obviously date back to the early part of the century. This must be the old Pioneer Roadhouse I've heard about. It was one of the stops on the original Iditarod trail, just like the old roadhouses at Skwentna and Rohn. I give the dogs a brief rest while I look quickly around. One of the caved-in cabins would have been the old dog barn, another the bunkhouse where exhausted mushers rested or waited out storms.

Long Hard Trails and Sled Dog Tales

This must have been a bustling place back in the trail's heyday, from about 1910 through the 1920s. From November through March, teams would have been arriving every day carrying supplies and mail to isolated mining camps with names like Ophir, Flat, Iditarod, Poorman, Long, Council, Solomon, and of course, Nome. Some of the returning sleds would have been carrying out the season's cleanup of gold; one series of teams in 1916 brought more than a ton and a half of the precious metal back to tidewater at Knik.

It's a strange feeling to know I'm really following in the footsteps of the old mail and freight drivers who were Alaska's unsung heroes. Probably only a handful of people outside of Iditarod mushers have seen these cabins since the wilderness and hard winters began to reclaim them more than three quarters of a century ago. I get the dogs up and moving with a renewed sense of perspective; we're only the latest in a long and honored procession of teams to struggle over this trail.

A long and honored procession... I thought about those words as I watched the teams filing past, some mushers smiling gaily and waving to my friends, others steely-eyed and focusing on the trail ahead of them. In a week or so we would meet them on the other end of the trail, and some would still be smiling gaily and others would still be steely-eyed.

On Monday morning, with Jeff and Maureen off to work and Albert gone with his tour group, Bob and I accompanied Eric to the Millennium Hotel where we met with Lee and Claudia. They were flying out to their favorite checkpoint, Rainy Pass, and this year Eric was going with them. We rode in the shuttle bus with them to Lake Hood and watched as their pilot went over last minute details, then we hiked down to the plane and photographed them taking off, Eric seemingly as giddy as a school boy about getting out to a real checkpoint on the Iditarod Trail!

Bob and I went to find coffee, chatted with friends in the Millennium lobby, and when the fliers got back that afternoon we listened to stories of how our favorite mushers were doing, then we all went to dinner at another of our favorite restaurants, the Glacier Brewhouse. It was a lovely way to celebrate the end of another Iditarod for our friends Lee and Claudia, but for Eric and Bob and I the adventure was just beginning!

Because we had a few days while the teams were making their way over the trail to Nome, Albert had invited us to join his tour group in Talkeetna, so we drove north in my Jeep and went along when the group visited Vern Halter's Dream-a-Dream Kennels in Willow. Vern gave an interesting and engaging talk and demonstration for the group, and after a delightful lunch we headed out into the dog yard to watch Vern's handlers, who included our friend Misha Petersen, harnessing the teams. For the next two hours we watched the teams coming and going, played with the dogs left behind, and drove to the halfway point to meet the dog teams and take more photos; it was great fun to see the broad smiles brought on by being on the runners of a dogsled!

That evening we all enjoyed wine and s'mores around a bonfire on the banks of the Susitna River, courtesy of Darlene and Howard Hunter at the beautiful Susitna River Lodge. Over the next few years I would revisit the Susitna River Lodge many times, and Darlene and Howard would become very dear friends, and their riverside bonfires would always bring smiles and laughter, storytelling and songs, good wine and great friendships.

And in the end it was the friendships, whether found at Darlene and Howard's bonfires, in Jeff and Maureen's living room, in the Millennium Hotel lobby, at Jim and Bonnie's kitchen table, or in a race checkpoint somewhere in a wild country, the friendships forged along the trails have made all the difference in my life.

EPILOGUE

McLaren, Alaska

Writing books is not an easy way to make a living, but it is a very satisfying one, and I've been fortunate in that my books have met with a wide and appreciative audience of readers. In early 2012 my friend Bob Lutz mentioned a barn he'd seen on a trip to Alaska in the 1960s, and in trying to help him figure out whether or not that barn was still standing I became aware of the unique and untold history of the 1935 Matanuska Colony barns.

It didn't take me long to decide their story was worth a book, and when Bob and Eric arrived for the 2012 Iditarod they donated a day to accompany me around the Matanuska Valley and shoot photos. I contacted the Matanuska-Susitna Borough historian and Cultural Resources Specialist, Fran Seager-Boss, who arranged a series of opportunities to visit and photograph some of the most outstanding barns in the Valley, and Eric's beautiful photographs became the backbone of my book.

Our friend Albert Marquez took the time to contribute some very dynamic photographs of the Colony barns, and our friends Dave and

Long Hard Trails and Sled Dog Tales

Diane Rose, who owned the Rose Ridge Vacation Cabins near Hatcher Pass, donated some historic barn photos Dave had taken in the 1970s.

Another friend, Barbara Hecker, a past president of the Palmer Historical Society who grew up with one of the most beautifully preserved Colony barns, donated family photographs, accompanied me to the National Archives to research the stories of the intrepid Colonists, and wrote a heartwarming foreword for my book:

Helen brought to the fore what my mind's eye had painted as background–other Colony family stories, other Colony barns. I'd spotted most. I'd played in a few. I'd sadly watched too many consumed by harsh, bullying winds. Others were razed in favor of new barns, or, regrettably, subdivisions. Numerous Colony barns–in disrepair, unkempt, unloved–are readying to disappear forever from our Matanuska Valley landscape.

Helen's book on the Matanuska Colony barns brings education, loving awareness and essential attention to the status of our remaining Matanuska Colony barns. She provides names, story, and sense of place to each barn. Helen's work chronicles these simple, lovely, remarkable structures that symbolize, more than any other, the ambitious agricultural experiment that was the Matanuska Colony.

And still another friend, who I got to know through a winter's worth of email communications, was James Fox, grandson of two original Colonists and a preeminent Valley historian, whose own book, *The First Summer*, was considered the foremost chronicling of the 1935 Matanuska Valley Project. Jim also sent family photos and wrote a compelling and beautiful introduction for my book. After describing his grandparents' farm and the day-to-day work which centered on their Colony barn, Jim described the warm relationship between his grandmother and her barn cats and milk cows, then continued:

I loved those times of quiet communion between her and the animals. It was a natural world where each species lived in harmony, respect, and what can only be called a family. Such communion of interspecies still exists in some parts of the world today, but too many of us have lost it–or never had the opportunity to be a member of it.

Long Hard Trails and Sled Dog Tales

Helen has brought back those memories for me; and perhaps she can give those of you reading this book an idea of why these barns are so important. Today they stand as obvious symbols of the farming and dairy past of this Valley. They are also reminders of a time when people worked for themselves, when life seemed simple, was difficult, full of hard work and simple fun. It was also a time when man and animals spoke to each other and respected each other in an unsentimental natural world, full of life and of death.

My 2012 book, *The Matanuska Colony Barns: The Enduring Legacy of the 1935 Matanuska Colony Project,* received glowing reviews and brought an entirely new circle of friends into my already-full life. One of the most enthusiastic and supportive was Joanie Juster, a filmmaker from San Francisco who had co-produced the multi-award-winning 2008 documentary, *Alaska Far Away: The New Deal Pioneers of the Matanuska Colony.*

Joanie gave showings of her film at the Alaska State Fair each year at the beautifully restored Wineck barn, which was featured on the cover of my book. She invited me to join her and to present talks about the history of the Colony barns, and spending that delightful time with her has become a much-anticipated highlight event at the end of my summers.

In the spring of 2013 I completely revised my first book, *The All Alaska Sweepstakes,* adding dozens of photos and much more history of the oldest organized sled dog race in the world. The book went from a thin 100 pages to a solid 160 pages, and I felt the story was beginning to come together, although there was much more race history I wanted to include and I knew there would be future revisions.

In the summer of 2013, while on a road trip, my friend Eric and I stopped to visit my old friend Joe May and his wife Sandra, who lived in a lovely cabin near Trapper Creek. Joe was a veteran of the fourth Iditarod, run in 1976; in 1979 he came in fifth, and he had won the race in 1980. Joe had been a judge on the 2008 All Alaska Sweepstakes, and he'd spent time at the halfway checkpoint of Candle. Over coffee, Joe handed me an envelope and told me to read it later and let him know what I thought.

That evening, 200 miles away in McLaren, I opened the envelope and read aloud to Eric what my friend Joe had written for inclusion in my next revision. It was a chapter on the historic Fairhaven Hospital in Candle, the checkpoint for the 2008 race and all the runnings before that. I shared the letter earlier in this book, but it's worth sharing this last part again, as it beautifully captures the magic of this sled dog game....

Of an evening, supper done, stories told, sleeping bags unrolled–a single lantern hissed and wrestled with shadows in the far corners of the lower room. An unseen presence stirred and claimed the attic spaces for it's own–in spite of murmurs from downstairs watch-keepers. Rafters shifted, floorboards creaked, and vagrant williwaws whispered a cryptic refrain in the eaves, "time to go... time to go... time to go..." A plaintive dog wail from the river–or was it an errant echo from the hills, a hundred years lost, seemed to say, "We're ready–get your ass down here."

It was no stretch to imagine Iron Man Johnson, Scotty Allan, or Leonhard Seppala padding about an upper room in stockinged feet–careful not to wake the competition–gathering up dried harnesses, parka, and mitts in preparation for another go at the trail–always with the notion to steal a march.

Listening intently, one could easily imagine a footfall in the dark stairwell–the muted squeak of a rusty hinge as the outer door closed ever so softly–and the receding crunch of mukluks on the crisp midnight snow, hurrying away, down the hill, down the hill to the waiting dogs...

Wavery windows, crooked doors,
Papered walls and slanted floors.
Ugruk sole upon the stair,
Sepp's a-stealin'
Light as air.
   ~Joe May

Long Hard Trails and Sled Dog Tales

Additional copies of this book are available
for $19.95 plus $5.00 shipping and handling:

    Northern Light Media
    PO Box 298023
    Wasilla, Alaska 99629

    http://northernlightmedia.com
    http://northernlightmedia.wordpress.com

    email: northernlightmedia@gmail.com

Other titles available from Northern Light Media

- The Beautiful Matanuska Valley
- The Matanuska Colony Barns
- The 1935 Matanuska Colony Project
- Along Alaskan Trails: Adventures in Sled Dog History
- The All Alaska Sweepstakes: History of the Great Race
- The Yukon Quest Album
- Appetite & Attitude: A Conversation with Lance Mackey (DVD)

Long Hard Trails and Sled Dog Tales

www.ingramcontent.com/pod-product-compliance
Lightning Source LLC
Chambersburg PA
CBHW070051120426
42742CB00048B/1888